Aberdeenshire Library and Information Service
www.aberdeenshire.gov.uk/libraries
Renewals Hotline 01224 661511

WALSH, Caspar

Criminal

D0410317

Criminal

Caspar Walsh

headline
review

First published in 2008
by HEADLINE REVIEW

An imprint of HEADLINE PUBLISHING GROUP

1

Cataloguing in Publication Data is available from the British Library

Hardback ISBN 978 0 7553 1748 6
Trade paperback ISBN 978 0 7553 1763 9

Typeset in Baskerville by Avon DataSet Ltd,
Bidford-on-Avon, Warwickshire

Printed and bound in Great Britain by
Mackays of Chatham plc, Chatham, Kent

Headline's policy is to use papers that are natural, renewable and recyclable
products and made from wood grown in sustainable forests. The logging and
manufacturing processes are expected to conform to the environmental
regulations of the country of origin.

HEADLINE PUBLISHING GROUP
An Hachette Livre UK Company
338 Euston Road
London NW1 3BH

Contents

Foreword

'My dad robs banks. He robs banks and kisses lots of women. He races cars and he smokes funny fags. He's killed two people, a long time ago and I'm not supposed to tell. I think he's fibbing. He's got two big guns in the bedroom and bullets in the garage. No one at school knows. It's my secret.

'When it's dark I get scared of the monsters. Last night when I woke up there were these big black monsters – two of them. The one under my bed was the biggest. I knew he was there, I could see the shadows. Him and his friend were watching me. Big bad monster number two was in the cupboard . . . behind my toys, I could hear him breathing loud and I could see him with my torch. Special torch, for my dad's work. I could see the two monsters and hear them, but I wasn't scared 'cos I could jump off my bed and across my room before the one under my bed could grab my legs and the one in the cupboard could jump on my back. I've given them names. I call them Boris and Morris. Like the puppet spiders on the telly.'

This is the beginning of a short story I wrote in 1999. Most of it is true. There were all kinds of monsters in my house when I was a kid. Some of them were invited in by my dad and some of them forced their way through our front door with battering rams. I was an eight-year-old boy living in London in the mid seventies. Crime and violence and night-time monsters were a regular part of my life.

I'm very optimistic. It's a blessing and a curse. I was optimistic about writing this book. It brought stuff to the surface and shone a light on parts of my story that therapy didn't get to. I've had nightmares and woken in the darkness sweating, sometimes crying. I've constantly questioned why I would want to drag it all up again. But this book is about embracing what happened and acknowledging its impact on my life. It's about finding a way of turning violence, abuse and neglect into something healthy, loving and liberating.

I haven't spent much time locked up. I didn't need to. What I got was more than enough: the proverbial short, sharp shock. I was lucky enough, smart enough and scared enough to get the message before any long-term sentences were handed down to me. My dad wasn't so lucky. It was watching what his time in prison did to him over the years that made me decide to change the direction of my life.

I've been visiting prisons since I was twelve and working in them for the last eighteen years. In one way or another, I've been involved in the British prison system for twenty-seven years, both inside and out. Prison is part of who I am.

In the last ten years, my time in prisons has led me slowly but surely into my work as a teacher of personal and professional development through creative writing.

Sometimes the situations I've been involved in may shock you. They still shock me, sometimes to the bone. I have written about them with respect and care but I haven't shied away from the truth of my relationship with my dad and how crime and prison culture has shaped my life.

This book is about the decision I made to stop being a

victim of my upbringing. It is about hope in the darkest, most desperate situations. It's about the incredible changes happening in the British prison system today and the healing effect this is having on individuals, communities and the country as a whole. I intend to continue to be a part of this process. It's part of my life's work, whether I like it or not.

1

They Fuck You Up

I had just turned twelve. At 4 a.m. on a summer's morning I woke to the violent sound of another battering ram hammering our front door. I sat up in bed in the darkness, and looked up the hallway, waiting for someone to appear. I was terrified and I couldn't move.

The ramming continued like a bass drum. I felt a crackle as the hairs on the back of my neck rose. My legs were shaking. I thought I was going to piss myself. I squeezed hard and the urge to piss passed. It took a lot of courage to get out of bed.

Whoever it was had finally managed to destroy the door. There was a moment of silence then an explosion of shouted instructions, running, heavy-booted feet and the slamming and opening of doors. I made out the words, 'Stop. Don't fucking move,' from the other end of the house.

I crept cautiously up the hallway and saw a mass of uniformed and plain-clothes policemen and women running with clear, sharp intention in and out of our rooms. Most of the men were fat bastards, too big to run properly, so they lumbered from room to room. In the dawn light coming through our dirty windows I saw one of them bump into the hall wall. He called the wall a cunt.

Everyone seemed to be ignoring me. I felt invisible. Two of them eventually saw me. I tried to run in between them, going for the gap. I had a purpose. I was looking for Dad. I had no idea where he was. I wanted the big handgun to protect him. I could run with that in my hand. I wanted to shoot the fat fuckers for busting into our house in the middle of the night, when I was tucked up in bed.

I heard the crash of breaking glass on the patio. Then a high-pitched scream, like the one he made when I shot him in Morocco. It was him. It was Dad. It stopped me long enough for a policewoman to grab me by the floppy collar of my pyjamas.

'*Dad!*'

'Don't you worry, sunshine. We've got your dad safe and sound.'

I was completely distressed and shaking from top to toe. I could just about make out her face in the dark. She was wearing a uniform and she was pretty, same kind of hair as Sam.

I was struggling furiously to get away from her and I almost managed it.

'Come here, you. Everything's going to be all right.'

But it wasn't. I knew that. There were far too many of them. I wasn't going anywhere. I gave up. She took my hand gently and led me up the hallway away from the darkness of my bedroom and into the bright light of the entrance hall. The front door was wrecked. Even though I wanted to kick her shins I felt safe with her. Safer than I'd felt for a while. There were police all over the house. One of them found bullets in the big empty room we never really used. Dad was using it for firing practice. They didn't find the guns. They *did* find drugs, wads of money and the haul of antiques that clearly couldn't fit comfortably, even into our large flat.

I heard car doors shutting outside, and Dad was gone.

I was twelve years old. How had this happened?

February 1967, Chelsea, London

Mum doesn't know what time of day it is. She's always stoned or drunk, usually both and today is no exception. She's pregnant, with me, her first child of three. She's a beautiful, successful model with rich and famous men clamouring to get at her, but today she's in a bad way. She is miserable.

She's in her basement flat on the phone to her mother. Grandma is calling long distance. Florida. A few years back she struck gold with a Jewish millionaire, who took her away from London and being skint. She'd been looking for a man like him – and his money – for most of her life, running from the emotional trauma and chaos of her own upbringing since she was a child. She used to be glamorous and beautiful, too, but her beauty faded a long time ago. Her face is starting to sag from the weight of age and a lifetime of fear and venomous, misdirected anger. She still thinks she looks the business. But with that ten-year-old Florida tan she looks more like a worn-out leather suitcase than the stunning socialite she once was.

Grandma wants Mum to have her baby terminated. That's me. She wants me out of the picture before I've even drawn breath. It's up to Mum to save the day. With alcohol, pills and spliff coursing through her body she's finding it difficult to hold her own against her formidable mother. Grandma is quite a woman and her mind is as clear as glass, unlike Mum's. It's touch and go whether I'll make it into the world at all.

'Abort the baby. Do it over here in Florida. You can stay on for a few days to recover.' Grandma was going at mum like a big dog with sharp teeth. 'You're twenty-two, for God's sake. You'll be on your own with this child. That junky excuse of a man will leave you. I'll put money on it. He'll be a useless father and you know it. I don't trust him, never have.'

That man was my dad.

Mum and Dad had been together for two years. Dad asked her out every day for three weeks before she finally gave in. They had married without Grandma knowing and Grandma had good reason not to trust him. Dad was unfaithful to Mum from the moment they started seeing each other, though he told me he still loved her very much. I'm sure he did, in his own way.

'If you come out here and have it done, I'll pay for everything, it'll be painless,' Grandma grinds on.

'I want this baby, Mum.' Despite the pills and booze Mum's showing spirit, refusing to take any shit. She's got balls.

'You'll be a useless mother and you know it.' Grandma knew exactly how to put on the pressure and Mum hated her for it.

'What the hell do *you* know about having children? You're a kid yourself, for God's sake. Don't fuck up your life like I did.'

'I'm confused.' Mum has found a chink in Grandma's argument. 'Are you admitting that you fucked up *my* life or that you fucked up yours?'

Mum was upset and trying not to show it. Grandma was good at winding people up; she'd had a lifetime of practice.

'You have this baby and you won't get another penny from me. Do you hear? I'll cut you out of my life forever; that's a promise. If you go ahead with it I won't have anything to do with you ever again, understand?'

Mum took a deep breath, trying to calm herself down.

'Yes, I understand. I'm sorry, Mum, you're right. You're always right. I don't know what I was thinking.'

'Good. You're clearly not as stupid as you make out. I'll wire you the money today.' And then she put the phone down.

What a nasty, twisted cow.

Mum sat there alone, the receiver dead in her hand, crying like a child.

In a time of desperate depression after the Second World War, Grandma, a single mother, tried to smother my mum in her sleep. Mum would have been about nine years old. She woke up with a pillow over her face and just managed to fight her off. Soon after that Grandma left the gas on in the flat to try and blow her and mum up. She couldn't go through with it. She turned the gas off and went back to bed. Her mental health was in a terrible state. She was a useless mother.

No one is evil for no reason. Grandma had a tough childhood. It's not an excuse, but it does explain her behaviour. The harshness of Grandma's early life turned her into a hard, frightened young woman who would do whatever she had to do to survive and would do anything to better herself. She went from chambermaid to the theatrical stages of the West End and the inevitable affairs with high-ranking, mostly married men. Mum was the product of an affair Grandma had with a Russian soldier who was passing through London during the War. She was forced to bring Mum up in a tiny, seedy flat in west London. Mum's father refused to take responsibility for her and gave Grandma little or nothing to live on. Proper kitchen sink drama. When her body worked its way back into shape, Grandma headed, full tilt, back into her tried and tested ways of survival through seduction. Thanks to Grandma, Mum knew about sex and exactly what men wanted to do to her when she was still in school, or at least should've been. She was becoming more beautiful by the day and started to get sexual attention when she was twelve years old. Men liked the way she looked and they wanted her. They didn't care how young she was. Paedophilia seemed to be more acceptable in the fifties, or at least you could get away with it more easily. No one wanted to admit it existed.

Grandma noticed the attention that Mum was getting from wealthy men and realised she could be used as bait to hook big fish and big money. From Arab princes to English lords, there was a long line of men eager to have sex with my teenage mum. And whilst Grandma didn't necessarily expect it all to go as far as it did, she still let it happen, reasoning that two women working together, however young one of them was, were better than one. Unsurprisingly, they caused quite a stir on the social scene in the fifties and sixties. At fifteen Mum was hanging out with sophisticated grown ups in a world of ballrooms, Champagne and caviar. A kid's dream come true. She didn't know any better or any different. In those days, everyone was stoned, having a new kind of liberated sex and partying. But before the Pill was invented and made readily available, free love often led to unwanted pregnancy. My parents enjoyed making me, but it hadn't been deliberate.

Mum's best mate Laura let herself in and walked through the coolness of the damp basement and out into the spring sunshine. Mum was in the garden, lying on a sun lounger. She stood over Mum, casting her gorgeous long-limbed shadow.

'Will you get out of the sun, for fuck's sake?' Mum liked having a go at Laura, it made her feel bigger. 'Where have you been for the last three months?' She had missed her.

Laura didn't answer. She was looking at Mum's body, at the slightly rounded belly beneath her relaxed hands. 'Are you putting on weight?'

Mum took a sip of her Pimm's. 'I'm pregnant.'

'For fuck's sake! You told your mum you were having an abortion! You are in serious trouble, girl.'

Mum turned on her side. 'Mum's abortion money'll come in handy. She's helping me out, just not in the way she wants.'

'You lied to her. She'll kill you.'

Mum knew very well what Grandma was capable of.

Dad loved me from the moment he saw me. He'd been there, in the delivery room, at my birth. He wouldn't have missed me being born for all the world. He told me that later, and I believed him. He was happy that day and he was singing, his way of celebrating. Throughout my childhood, his singing would always calm me down. He'd talked and sung to me through Mum's belly for nine months. By the time I was born I was already used to his voice.

But Mum and Dad's relationship started to break down before I was born. They were still speaking and having sex but Mum was getting sick of Dad constantly being out of it, stealing anything he could get his hands on and always on the prowl for new women. One night, after too much California Sunshine LSD, Mum found him cowering in the corner of their kitchen.

He started to whimper like a frightened child. 'Promise you won't, please, please promise.'

'Promise you what, for God's sake?'

Dad's oversized red eyes peered at Mum through his skinny, trembling fingers. 'Promise you won't peel me.'

Mum realised she'd had enough. Shortly after, she threw him out. I was a year old. At first they agreed that I should live with her. She couldn't trust Dad not to do acid when I was around. He said it would be a good growth experience for a son to see his father shift dimensions. Mum wasn't having any of it. Spliff and booze were OK with her but acid was too dangerous and out of the question. And this, in the middle of the summer of love, was the kind of fucked up family I was born into.

Dad loved me, but he also loved breaking the law for a living, getting stoned and screwing the best-looking women he could find. He was constantly distracted by the colourful fireworks displays of psychedelic love and drugs on offer just about everywhere in sixties London. He made an easy living hustling, dealing and thieving. It was all fair game. It was easy to survive well in the sixties.

Mum was sharp and beautiful and streetwise but she easily spun out on drugs and booze. She changed her mind like the wind, a kid in a grown up's body. One minute she wanted me, the next minute she wanted her freedom. More often than not she was led by her desire to get stoned and be on the King's Road with all the other beautiful, messed up swingers in their colourful clothes and cool cars.

Mum and Dad were the same in a lot of ways. That was the attraction. They did it all together: meditated, read Ginsberg, Jung, had sex, partied, fought and thieved. Parenting was a new and mostly unwanted concept. They argued about who should have me. I moved back and forth between them a lot in the first five years of my life. Just as I got used to being with Mum she'd pass me over to Dad. I'd love being with Dad and then he'd hand me back to Mum. I didn't know if I was coming or going. Each transaction felt like a rejection, and it marked me with an insecurity that would stay with me for a very long time.

By the winter of 1972 I was five years old. I remember a woman walking me down Tite Street in Chelsea, my hand held way too tight in hers, hurting me. It was cold and soft, icy rain covered my face. I wanted to be inside, in the warm. My blue coat was damp and heavy with the rain. I had no hat, no gloves. I couldn't feel my fingers. It was the middle of the day and it was already getting dark. I was upset and tired. I wanted to cry but I was too scared. I didn't know what was going on but it felt like I'd done something wrong.

I didn't like this woman any more. Emily used to be nice to me and would cuddle me, when she wasn't kissing Dad. But now she was crushing my hand, holding on in case I ran away. She didn't talk to me or look at me, just walked. Too fast. Down the steps to where Mum lived, in the basement.

'Stand there. Don't move. Do you hear me? Don't move. Just stay right there.' Barked instructions. Why was she shouting at me? She rang the bell and walked back up to the street. Why was she leaving me? I didn't want to be on my own. I was scared.

Eventually I heard soft footsteps padding up to the other side of the door. It was unlocked and swung slowly open. Mum was standing there.

'Where's Emily?' she said. 'She could've bloody waited. Useless cunt of a woman.'

She reached out her hand to me and I took it. It was warm and completely swallowed mine. She took me into the flat. The whole place smelled of bolognaise, a damp mustiness that came off the walls, perfume, sweet tobacco smoke, wine, chocolate and the stuff Mum washed the sheets and blankets with. It made me feel safe, soft and warm. I wanted to be there, always.

Mum put the telly on. I lay down on the sofa, still in my wet jacket. She leaned down, kissed me on the head. I started to warm up. The sofa was huge and I snuggled in. Mum got me a multicoloured woolly blanket and put it over me, gently, tucking it in around me. My eyes closed and I started to dream.

I woke up crying. There was a man in the room. He was shouting at Mum and waving his arms about, cigarette in one hand, a glass in the other. Ash and wine flying all over the place. It was Jack. Jack was Mum's boyfriend. He hated me. He was jealous of my relationship with Mum. Jealous of a kid. He smelled of tobacco, alcohol and anger.

Mum was shouting back. She was always up for a fight. I heard my name and realised they were fighting about me. I wanted to shout at them to shut up, but I couldn't get the words out. I couldn't stop crying. I couldn't see a thing. My eyes were full of tears. All I could hear was my own crying. I was finding it hard to breathe.

Mum was pacing up and down in front of me, pulling at her hair, trying to tear it out. Jack started to shout louder. 'I can't fucking stand this. Will he ever shut up?'

'If you keep turning up pissed and angry with me of course he's going to be upset. He was asleep, for God's sake.'

'I don't want two children,' Jack ranted. 'I want one. I want the one in your belly.' He jabbed a finger towards her tummy to make his point. 'That's mine and that's all I want. I don't want this little fucking nightmare. Christ! I can't hear myself think.'

I pissed myself a little. Sweat ran down my back and neck. As I cranked up the crying, Jack got even angrier. 'He never stops bloody crying. Jesus! Why does he never stop crying, for fuck's sake?'

'He doesn't cry so much when you're not around, Jack.'

'So it's *my* fault. *Your* hysterical, nightmare of a son is *my* fucking fault.'

'You're drunk. I'll make us some coffee.'

'I'm not having it. Either he goes or I go.'

Mum stopped in her tracks, halfway to the kitchen. 'What?'

'You heard me. Either Caspar goes back to Frank tonight, or I go for good.'

'You bastard. He's my son.'

'Well, you've got another one on the way. You clearly find it hard enough with this one, so two would properly fuck you up. Make your mind up. I'll call you later.'

Jack walked out of the room, up the hallway and slammed the front door behind him. I stopped crying. My body was numb, my legs were trembling. Mum sat down next to me and, with shaking hands, lit a cigarette. She didn't look at me, though I could feel she wanted to. After a long time, the two of us just sitting without saying anything, she picked up the phone and started to dial.

It wasn't long before Dad arrived. He always smelled clean and looked smart. He took enormous pride in his appearance. He was wearing a dark blue suit and pink tie. He stood in the middle of the room, silently smoking a cigarette. He looked like James Cagney, but with longer hair and without the hat. Mum, still upset, stood facing him. He was angry, but he was holding it in. He looked at me and his face softened. He smiled briefly, then looked back at Mum. His face tightened again.

'We had an agreement.'

'I know. I'm sorry, Frank. It's got seriously fucked up. I didn't expect this, really.'

Mum sat down at the table and lit a cigarette.

'I'm sorry, Frank. Really, I . . .'

'Bollocks to *sorry*. If I take him now, if he comes with me, no more fucking around. This is it. You won't ever have him back. I mean it.'

Mum didn't say anything. She put her head in her hands.

'Do you understand?' He was glaring at her. He looked powerful, like he meant business.

After a long silence she looked up at him. 'Yes. I get it.'

I got it, too. She wanted Jack more than she wanted me.

'Will I see him?'

''Course. But he'll never come back to live with you again. I'm sick of this shit. Caspar needs a break. No wonder he's crying all the fucking time.'

Dad came over to me, leant down and picked me up off the sofa. I didn't want to leave Mum but I definitely wanted to be with Dad. I felt safe in his arms. He smelled like summer. His grey jumper was soft like skin. He knew what he was doing: at least one of my parents was in control and able to make a decision. I buried my face into his cashmere chest.

Mum came over and kissed me. She squeezed me tight: tight enough to say that however confused she was, she still loved me. The whole flat had felt like a place where I had wanted to be. Now, as we headed for the front door, it became cold and alien. This wasn't my home any more.

Dad carried me out of the front door, up the stairs and into the light of the street. I looked over his shoulder and saw Mum looking up at me. She was crying and trying to hide it by putting her hand over her mouth. She gave me a half wave. Tired. Weak. Defeated. I gave her a full wave back.

The dying sun came out from behind grey, black clouds and gently lit up the wet pavement. I was with Dad for good now. Till death us do part.

2

The Family Business

We wander up and down the King's Road after our massive meal at the Casserole Restaurant, our favourite. Dad wanted to cheer me up. I think he wanted to cheer both of us up. Now he is worrying about where to go and what to do next.

I'm enjoying the sunshine, running ahead, chasing invisible gangsters and goblins. We stop for a while in Sloane Square and I paddle in the big fountain and chuck dirt at the pigeons. Stupid birds keep coming back for more. A policeman has seen me and is coming across the road towards us. Dad pretends not to know me, lights a fag and walks away. I can run much faster than the fat copper and hide behind some parked cars. Sweaty and puffing he gives up on the chase and leaves me alone.

On the third walk up the length of the King's Road, towards The World's End, just when my legs are tiring, Dad bumps into an old mate called Theo near the Roebuck pub. They have too many drinks. I'm bored. But the man offers Dad his house while he goes on a three-month trip to find enlightenment in Marrakesh.

CRIMINAL

Autumn 1973, London

Theo came back from Marrakesh. He'd been gone a lot longer than three months and he'd definitely found some enlightenment. His skin was darker and his hair was longer, dirtier and had beads in it. Theo and Dad had a bad argument about the state of the house, particularly the fire that had broken out when Dad had fallen asleep with a candle alight. A table had a hole burned right through it. Most of the bedroom had been burned as well, and everything in it. I'd been asleep on the sofa. I'd woken up to find three huge firemen standing over me. They'd picked me up and carried me downstairs, out on to the pavement. One of them brought my duvet down to me and wrapped it around me.

Now Theo was pacing back and forth, tugging anxiously on his new beard. He was smoking a big joint but he was still very angry. The more he smoked, the angrier he got. He wouldn't stop going on and on about the table and all the stuff that had been burned.

'Look, Theo, man, I fell asleep. I should've put the candle out but I didn't. It was an accident. Caspar and I are lucky to be alive. I'll pay for it.' Dad wasn't going to pay for the mess, no chance.

'Look, man, this is a bad scene. I just got back from this amazingly peaceful vibe in the mountains and I don't like the vibes movin' between us. It is fucking with all my root chakra work. I've done a lot of healing on my repressed childhood and I don't need this shit fucking with my energy direction right now. You have seriously trodden on my kind heart and that is not the kind of karma you want to be fucking around with, believe me.'

Dad gave him a look for a few seconds then hit him hard, twice, in the side of the face. That shut him up. He held his jaw like he was contemplating the meaning of it. We packed, slowly, and left in silence.

Winter 1974, Wimbledon Common, London

Dad had stolen a World War Two ambulance from some 'old geezer in the country'. We were now living in Dad's favourite place in the whole world: Wimbledon Common. Surrounded by trees and bushes, he loved getting stoned in nature.

It was night time. I had been woken up by the cold winter wind and the roar of the bike engine in my ears and a rumbling vibration under my bum, legs and feet. The stars flickered on and off between the leaves of the trees, and the half moon above my head followed us wherever we went. I was lucky to have a dad with a chopper motorbike as well as a van that had saved people's lives in the last war. I felt lucky to have a dad who was always looking for an adventure, day or night.

I loved being with Dad. There were no rules. He wasn't interested in making me like other kids. I went to bed when he did, got up when I wanted, ate all the sweets I liked and I wasn't at school. I didn't need to be. I was learning everything I needed to learn from him. He walked me around the common for hours and told me about the trees and the wildlife, the stars and the wizards and witches, druids and warlords. We were together day and night. We visited Mum once a month. He said it was important that I see her. 'Regular enough to remember what she looks like. Every kid needs a mum, even if she is a bit fucked up.'

But apart from Mum, there was no one Dad could leave me with so I went everywhere with him: pubs, parks, friends' houses, shops, girlfriends' places. The few times he did drop me off at a stranger's house for a few hours I'd kick off so much he realised it was more trouble than it was worth. Pissing in the corner of someone's living room or setting fire to other kids' toys was usually the best way to get me back to Dad. I was his sidekick.

'What are we doing, Dad?'

'Wimbledon Common is the best place to do acid, kid.'

I could just about hear him above the rush of wind. 'What's acid? Does it burn?'

'If you're on a bad one, sure. You had some last year, but that was an accident. Ask me in ten years. Maybe we'll do some together.'

'What accident?' He pulled the bike up to the big pond.

'That arsehole, Theo, left a bag of pills on the table before he went to Marrakesh, remember? You must've thought they were Smarties or something. You ate three tabs. He kept going on an on about how he'd messed your mind up. I told him to relax. You sat in the corner of a room and drew these incredible pictures for three days solid. I was proud of you, kid. My little Picasso. You were cool though. Whacking him on the chin was partly for being so fucking irresponsible with his drugs.'

He kicked the bike back into action and we continued riding around the common in the half moon light. After a while I fell asleep, strapped to the high back of the motorbike. The vibration of the engine was soothing.

The van was parked in a small car park near the big pond. It still worked and when we had enough petrol we'd drive it down the King's Road with Miles Davis blasting out of the open windows. Everyone would stare. It smelled of patchouli and old leather and wood. Dad told me it had been used to rescue people from burning buildings. It had been driven by heroes. It was seriously cosy, with blankets on the inside walls and lots of cushions scattered around and more blankets on the floor. There were candles and a torchlight for reading bedtime stories. There was an eight track tape deck in the front. We listened to Miles Davis and Charlie Parker, Billie Holiday, Van Morrison, Crosby, Stills, Nash and Young. We didn't have any money so Dad would steal our food: baked beans, carrots, sesame seeds and Mars bars for pudding. For a six-year-old, it was like living inside heaven.

Each night I could hear owls and other animals like foxes and mice crawling about outside the van. Sometimes they got under the van to sleep but Dad would whack the floor and they scuttled off into the dark. It was the best of both worlds, like living in the country but with the cool parts of London just down the road.

Sometimes at night I'd hear Dad leaving, but it didn't scare me, even when I heard him roll the chopper across the gravel and start it up a long way off so as not to wake me. I wasn't scared because he always came back.

I liked listening to the night noises. He usually went for a spin on the chopper to help him sleep. He often brought stuff back, and the longer he was gone the more stuff he'd bring. Little antiques, silver cutlery, cash, purses, wallets, clothes and, very occasionally, small, sparkling stones. When I asked him where he'd got them he'd tell me that a good magician had been helping him out. I almost believed him.

A woman came to see us. Jane. She was pretty and smelled of roses. We had dinner together on the grass outside the van. Chicken and salad and juice. The ground was lit up with candles. After she'd left, Dad told me what was going to happen next. He had a plan.

'She's got lots of money, kid, and wants us to go and live with her in her big flat in Kensington. I could do with my own room for a bit and we could both do with some regular meals. Do us the world of good.'

After six months in the van, I liked the idea of living in a house again. Maybe I would get my own bedroom, too. I was happy that we were moving but I would miss the countryside with all the trees and sunshine, the wind, rain, animals, light and stars. The country calmed me down and made me happy and would prove to be a rare constant in my life, a comfort I could always rely on.

We moved in with the pretty woman who smelled of roses. It was a lot of fun for a while, but after a couple of months she and Dad started arguing. She wanted more commitment from him and he wouldn't give it.

She got Dad a big Cadillac. We drove everywhere in it, especially on custom car night down the King's Road, the last Saturday of the month. One morning, when we got into the car to go to the park, there were three big dents in the windscreen, with a spider's web of cracks spreading out from the centre of each. Dad and Jane weren't speaking. He had three small scratches across his cheek.

'What happened to the windscreen, Dad?'

He looked at Jane, then back at me. There was a prolonged, uncomfortable silence. Finally he answered.

'Some stones flew up from the road, last night, when I went to get the Chinese.'

I knew he was lying. He couldn't lie to me properly. Later, when we were alone, I got the truth.

'Jane and I had a ruck last night. A bad one. We were a bit pissed.' Dad wasn't good with alcohol.

'Did she scratch you?'

'Certainly did. She's got some arsehole that one. Looks sweet as anything, but give her a couple of vodkas and she turns into a lunatic.'

'Did you hurt her?'

'I had to stop her jumping on me, so I held her back.' I thought that that's what I'd do if someone was trying to hurt me, I'd hold them back.

He pointed at the windscreen. 'She did that, too. She came out of nowhere with a fucking brick in her hand and started trying to smash the windscreen. She hit it three times before I got it off her. She needs locking up, kid.'

The brick scared me. It was an act of violence towards Dad and it felt like an act of violence towards me. This woman was clearly a bit nuts, especially on the booze.

'She's gonna have to go, kid. Can't be having this kind of thing going on around you now, can we?'

'No, Dad.' I was looking forward to having him back to myself.

We moved out of Jane's big house and back to Wimbledon Common.

Dad decided to introduce me to the 'good magician' he'd talked about. This meant taking me to work with him. Dad's magic was based on deception. He made money in an array of ways, little, if any, involving an honest day's work. Nicking from shops for food, books and clothes was his most regular activity. Thieving from people, cars and houses we either visited together or he burgled alone was a good, second favourite. 'Kiting' – paying for goods with stolen cheques – was a third way to get whatever we needed. At that point, selling narcotics, including hash, grass, LSD, speed, uppers, downers and occasionally cocaine and heroin was a less regular form of income, but he did it as often as he could. Buying and selling 'goods' was what he liked best because it meant negotiation, hustling and being a good enough liar to rip off the hardest, smartest businessman. Hustling meant conning people out of money, making them think they were getting a good deal when they were really getting fleeced. Dad could act and his early learning life on the streets meant he'd perfected the art of ripping people off. Buying and selling stolen antiques was an excellent source of higher income. He would steal from a small shop, or barter the guy right down, then head for the bigger places on the New King's Road. There he would whack the price right up. If the piece was stolen, it was all profit. He often took me with him on his work days. My cute face softened up both buyers and sellers and worked as a good distraction when he was thieving. Dad also used me as a trust barometer. I would recoil from people who I sensed were dodgy, the people who were trying to rip Dad off. This instinct would prove useful in the future.

King's Road, Chelsea, London

Every once in a while Dad would strike lucky and meet a woman who would stop him dead in his tracks. Mum did it in 1965 and Sam did it in the Spring of 1975.

Sam had grown up in a big country house with a lot of land. She was now working as a model and living in a townhouse in Kensington. Her rich dad had bought it for her. Sam was upper class. Posh. For Dad, the higher the class, the better. He was excited by Sam's breeding.

I met Sam for the first time in my favourite hamburger restaurant on the King's Road, The Great American Disaster. I was supposed to be on my best behaviour, which always wore me out. I didn't really understand what it meant. Dad had never taught me manners. He didn't see the point. We liked to eat with our hands, not with forks, and I liked being the wild kid who everyone had to keep an eye on in case I nicked something or pissed on their best carpet. I liked how it shocked people. Sam would have other ideas about this kind of behaviour.

Sam was yet another beautiful woman in Dad's life, but she stood out. She buzzed with something soft and magnetic and, just like Dad, I fell in love with her the moment I saw her. She was tall, thin and ethereal, with a big, innocent country smile and diamonds in her eyes. There was a shyness about her but it concealed an unexpected power.

A few weeks later, Dad and I moved into Sam's house in Kensington. It was perfect. We were living rent free in one of his favourite spots and he had a wealthy, sexy, smart woman on his arm. I had a new super-posh area to run riot in and, best of all, I had a new mum.

I liked being in Sam's house at first. She bought me toys. I had my own room. I got a hamster and a goldfish. She had a dog, Bella. She was great most of the time but she was also neurotic and vicious and she would bite me. I deserved it. I used to wind her up, poking her, jumping out at her and tickling her when she clearly didn't want to be tickled. Her skin-piercing teeth were her way of telling me to fuck off.

Sam cooked me fantastic meals. She'd learnt to cook at a finishing school in Paris. She made sure I was in bed before nine, which was a first. Dad couldn't believe it. I did as I was told but always read under the covers with the 'special torch' my dad used for his work. He could fit the small torch into his back pocket or his mouth when he was working on locked doors or climbing through windows. If someone was trying to protect whatever Dad was after, he would use force, sometimes violence. He didn't like violence but it was part of the job. His time in the street gang when he was a teenager taught him how to finish a fight in two punches or less, sometimes a cosh round the side of the head. Knives and guns were to be avoided wherever possible. Someone could get killed and the jail sentence would be much longer. If he was caught.

He preferred the empty quiet of sleeping buildings and the booty they held. He loved the buzz of 'creeping' about a house in the half dark. If someone was sleeping in the house then the buzz was all the better.

He had a lot of different tools. A slither of Perspex was always his tool of choice for entry. Longer and more flexible than a credit card, he would slide it into the space between the door frame and the lock in order to open the door. Failsafe, as long as it wasn't double locked. He always kept a small sheet of it in his inside pocket, just in case.

Some of his tools looked like spy gadgets to me. Some looked as though he'd stolen them from his dentist: mirrors of two different sizes with telescopic arms attached to them were a real favourite of mine. The smaller of the two was designed to slip through big gaps, the bigger one to go through letterboxes. Both were used to see the best way into buildings from the inside or to spot guards or residents. You could see a key in the lock with them or determine from the outside whether something bigger was needed, like a crowbar into the door hinges. If there were keys in the lock he had another tool that was designed specifically to take keys out of locks and back through the letterbox. It had a flexible metal stem with a feisty four-pronged claw on the end. At the opposite end of the arm was a trigger you pushed to make the tiny claws grab the keys on the other side. I never figured how he managed it, holding the mirror arm steady in one hand while manoeuvring the wobbly claw up towards the key in the lock with the other. That took some co-ordination. I played 'spies and double agents' for hours with those tools.

He also had a series of high-tech 'listening in' gadgets. He was particularly proud of these. Short-wave radios, bugs, devices you point at people half a mile away to hear what they were saying. Dad told me they were for listening into the competition and staying ahead of the game. Listening and recording the back-biting gangsters and spivs to prove their two-faced lies and double dealings at a later date. For the most part he just loved the equipment and he let me play with it. Proper James Bond.

He was a robber, too, which meant using force. It was part of the deal. He was generous with his goodies when he got them: he fancied himself as Robin Hood. But robbery always came a poor second to the kick of entering a property by night to burgle it. Robbery was rougher, scarier and lacked the class of turning over a posh property in Chelsea for its goods. If he knew someone had something on them that was worth the trouble, he would follow them, pick their pocket or create a diversion with a mate to nick a briefcase or wallet. Dad was imposing when he got angry. If someone resisted him in the middle of his work a verbal threat was usually enough to scare them into submission.

For me the distinction between burglary and robbery was whether you took from a building (burglary) or direct from a person (robbery). Dad was well qualified to do both. It was a skill he had been working hard on since he was at primary school with his mate and number one partner in crime, George.

Dad was a bank robber way before I was born. He used to drive the getaway cars. He'd keep the cars running, ready to make a quick exit. His mates, masked and loaded with money, would jump into the vehicle and Dad would whack his foot down, cover the road in rubber and tear off through the backstreets of London. He knew London like a cabbie. He might have been a cab driver, like his dad. I once asked him why he hadn't done what his dad did.

'The money's shit and it would have bored me rigid,' he said, scarcely able to imagine how dull life would be. 'I preferred getting chased by the young coppers in police cars. They never caught me. They had a good time trying, though and they loved it '

As a dad in his late twenties, he said he had had to slow it down a bit. Most of his work was on foot and most of it happened at night. He wore dark clothes. Not all in black, that would be too obvious. Dark clothes under a light-coloured jacket did the job until it was time to clock on, then the jacket would come off and, if he had to, the balaclava would slide over his face. He rarely got caught. He was quick off the mark, if he needed to be. He was small and thin, light on his feet, fit and very agile. His physique made him good at fighting, good at getting through small spaces and jumping from ledges and across rooftop gaps.

Now that we were officially out of the van and had somewhere permanent to live and Dad seemed to be in a stable relationship, he could focus on trying to make as much money as he could as quickly as he could.

'No long ways around a simple solution; always take the shortcuts to get the cash.' Dad's words of wisdom.

Any money made through thieving was usually invested in something potentially more lucrative. By the time I was seven, Dad's idea of becoming a successful antique dealer – funded, of course, by theft – had evolved into the more realistic business plan of becoming a dealer of class A drugs. Dad wasn't a career criminal. He was basically lazy and wanted it easy and, where possible, exciting. Crime was simply how he made a good living in the shortest possible time frame.

By the time I was eight years old I'd started my own small-scale thieving from bags and wallets. A lot of people came to visit us. If they weren't stoned when they arrived they soon would be. It was only a matter of waiting for the smack gouch or a spliff nod – they always fell asleep – and I was good at waiting. I'd either rifle through their belongings there and then or sneak the bag into the loo for a proper look. I'd steal from Dad and Sam, too. Creeping into their bedroom was the best buzz. Dad was a surprisingly easy touch. I tried Sam's purse once. I was two feet from her sleeping face. I unzipped her purse, spidered my fingers in for the fiver. The next thing I knew she had my wrist locked in her alarmingly tight grip. I almost pissed myself with fright.

'Put it back and get back to bed,' she growled at me.

I did as I was told.

I'd been caught for the first time. The buzz of stealing had just got better. I now knew a little bit more about the risks. I enjoyed the fear of getting caught more than the handfuls of cash I more often than not got away with. I could see why Dad liked creeping around houses, not knowing who or what was around the next corner. I was watching him closely and listened carefully to his stories. If I was going to be like him I needed to pay attention. He was happy for me to watch him at work but, in his eyes, that was all for now. He had no idea I'd already starting nicking. He thought I needed to be a lot older before I could start work.

Within a couple of months of them meeting, Dad asked Sam to marry him and she said yes. They got married in Chelsea registry office on the King's Road. I wore a white jacket we got from Orange Hand in Sloane Square. I looked the business. Dad wore a cool blue suit and Sam wore a Zandra Rhodes dress specially made for her. At the party I was given the job of serving the Champagne. I drank a lot of it and after an hour or so as the kid in charge of the bar I tripped over and dropped the tray and the glasses and the bottle all over the floor. I was drunk as a skunk and very happy. Sam knew Dad was a bad boy but didn't realise how bad until after they got married. He had kept that part of himself mostly hidden while he was making an impression.

I liked the attention Sam gave me. We lived with her for nearly a year without any real trouble. This was a record by Dad's four-week relationship standards. But then she and I started fighting for our respective pieces of turf. I decided to push the 'family' boundaries she was trying to establish. But she wasn't someone to fuck around with. She pushed back harder. I would get sent to my room if I gave her lip, no dinner if I didn't do my chores, no telly if I got back later than I should have. Dad would never intervene.

'You need to know when to give the right impression, kid. When to be polite, when to nod your head intelligently when what you really want to do is rip someone's head off, when to pretend you wouldn't hurt a fly or steal a penny from a Hooray's purse.'

Under Sam's influence I'd moved from being as good as feral, living in a van on Wimbledon Common with no electricity, no heating, eating food with my hands, shitting in the woods and washing my arse in a pond to dressing like Little Lord Fauntleroy and saying 'Yes, please' and 'No, thank you' to every question I was asked.

Sam and me, we had an invisible key game we carried on for two years. It was a simple way of rewarding good behaviour and getting positive attention. 'Look, I've got an idea,' said Sam. 'You let me put this key in your back . . .'

'What key?' I was confused.

'This invisible, wind up clockwork key.'

I liked the sound of where this was going.

'Whenever good manners are called for, I put this key in the slot in your back and wind it up eight times.'

Eight was my lucky number.

'As long as it's ticking round you sit up straight at the table, elbows down, mouth closed and no talking when you're eating. No one will know except you and me.' By the time I was ten years old our game would have run out of steam but the manners were now in my system and on automatic. Dad was right, courtesy helped me through previously closed doors and safely out of a lot of tricky, sometimes dangerous situations, even if at times I did want to rip someone's head off for not giving me what I wanted.

One weekend evening, Dad had gone out and Sam wanted me in bed. I refused to go. I was watching a

Frankenstein movie and I wanted to see the end of it. It was frightening the life out of me. It was way past my newly defined bedtime. Sam made the deal clear.

'You can watch ten more minutes and that's it. If you give me any hassle I will carry you up to bed.'

I drank a quarter of a bottle of Mexican tequila in less than five minutes. The alcohol was so strong it burned my stomach. The room started to revolve. By the time Sam came back I was rocking back and forth in agony. Without hesitation she went to the kitchen and got a bucket, she lifted me up and carried me to my room. Dad didn't come back that night. Even though she knew my alcoholic agony was self inflicted, that I'd done it deliberately to piss her off, she sat with me for the rest of the night. She patiently and lovingly let me puke the spirit out of my system.

When Dad was home, I resented how much time Sam spent with him and they always seemed to be having sex. I drew pictures in my mind of what I thought must be going on. It was all about the sounds that I could hear on the other side of the wall, or sometimes even the other side of the room. The sound of the covers as they began to respond to movements underneath. The smack and click of kissing. The long exhalation of relieved breath. Skin gliding on skin. Movement and breath of pleasure speeding up and slowing down. Everything stopping long enough for me to think it was over, then the gut-wrenching realisation that it was only a fag break. There was love under the covers, no doubt about it. Passion, heat, lust and affection. It was all around me and often too close. I didn't ask for it but I got it and part of me, after a while, started to like it.

There were always men's magazines around the house. *Playboy. Men Only. Lui. Penthouse.* Dad mocked himself by telling his mates he preferred *Playboy* because it had, he said with a wry smile, 'good articles in it'. There were always slapstick sex cartoons in these mags, a little light relief to ease the intensity and fantasy of the photographed flesh. In my search for the funnies I found images I knew were connected to the sounds I listened to. Like everything else, Dad was casual about it. 'The more lessons for life the better, kid.'

Sex was all around me. Beautiful women in Barbara Hulanicki dresses from *Biba*, Gavin Hodge haircuts, high platformed heels and musky perfume getting them more attention than was good for them. It was in the air; the tension and possibility of sex was everywhere and I was infected by it. Part of it scared me, part of it confused me and part of it lit a bright hormonal spark in me that I couldn't put out.

I was eight. It wasn't long before I started taking those magazines into my room and imagining what it would be like to have one of the women from the glossy pages between my sheets.

3

A Criminal Education

Dad says not everyone is bad but that most people are and you have to be very careful what you say and who you trust. So he's teaching me everything I'll need to know in life just the way he likes it himself and just the way he does it: how to have the most money and the most freedom; how to find my own way in the big, nasty world; how to be happy just for me not just for someone else; how to get one over on whoever is trying to get one over on me.

Each day he teaches me something new and it's a lot more fun than anything you get taught in school. Dad says life is for living and that you can have whatever you want, as long as you know who's got the keys and which doors to unlock.

'Kid, you'll get everything you need to know about life from reading books, watching movies and, best of all, watching people.'

'How do I watch people?'

'You watch what they do and what they say and see if it matches up in your head and in your tummy. You ask yourself, "Do I have a safe feeling around this person or does something about them scare me or make me angry?"'

I give him a blank look.

'It's all in there, kid.' He points to my tummy. 'All you need to

*do is feel what it's like in there. Go by that and you won't go
wrong. It's called instinct and it'll never let you down. No real
rules, kid, except the ones you make for yourself. Just let the fuckers
think you're doing what they want you to do.'*

*I put my hand on my tummy to see if I can feel anything. I
can't.*

Dad's ideas about education were so left field they were
bordering on fundamentalist. He believed in complete
freedom of choice to do whatever you wanted. He was –
though he wouldn't admit it because it was 'another
fashionable label' – an anarchist, more to the point he was
amoral.

'Most teachers are very misguided, kid. They could all do
with a month in the desert on peyote and the works of
Castaneda to really get where a kid's head is at. All the stuff
they learn and try to download into our heads lacks any real
humanity or emotion and has fuck all to do with real life and
dealing with real people.'

I liked where this attitude had got him and how he dealt
with people, especially the tricky ones. And he looked to me
as though he was having a pretty good time – he seemed to
enjoy life. He was happy a lot of the time. I decided to do as
he told me.

Summer 1976, Suffolk

If it wasn't for the school inspectors banging on our front
door at seven in the morning, Dad would happily have let
me carry on learning about life, the universe and everything
by watching him and his stoned friends, reading the books
he gave me and watching the movies he'd said I would find
the secret to life in. I was a month away from my ninth
birthday and I hadn't been to school for as long as I could

remember. Sam was getting increasingly pissed off that I wasn't in school and was hassling Dad to sort one out for me. She believed in mainstream education. She had had a proper education herself. It had been private and expensive.

I was learning that the way to earn money as a grown up was not from a good education in a proper school and acquiring lots of qualifications. Fast money was got by taking it nice and slowly, watching for the thousands of opportunities that pop up every day. Dad didn't have to work hard. He knew how to take shortcuts, no matter that pretty much all of them were completely illegal. He let other people do the legwork for him and this included me. He liked, more than anything, to relax, lie in the sun and get stoned. This took time and money. Time and money he very successfully stole from other people.

Sam and Dad argued about what kind of school to send me to. They reached a stalemate. I thought, at the time, that she just wanted me out from under her feet so she could have less of me and more of Dad. I found out in my teens that Sam had put a lot of her own money into getting me a good education. They came to a compromise: Summerhill School in Suffolk. Sam knew about it because it was a few miles from where she grew up. Dad knew about it because he'd read a lot of writing by the headmaster, A. S. Neill, who thought that playing games and knocking about with your mates was as important as going to lessons. It was the only school of its kind in England at the time and the selling point was that if you didn't want to go to lessons, you didn't have to. Dad was bang up for this kind of choice. So was I. I had no problem with going to Summerhill, but it meant that I had to be away from Dad.

Summerhill was heaven on earth. No rules. Not normal ones, anyway. If I was hungry I'd go to cookery and make cakes. If I was bored I'd go to woodwork and make a sword or a gun. I was more into playing in the woods and creating new worlds in my head than sitting in a classroom. What kid wouldn't be? The difference was that if I wanted to, I could do it.

Even so, I continued to push my luck at Summerhill. I wanted to see how much trouble I could get into before someone finally said 'Stop'. I wanted to see who could contain me and control me. I was looking through the hand-me-down lens of Dad's view of the world. And when I think about Dad sticking two fingers up at the world it's the Harrods incident that comes to mind.

We were in the toy department one Christmas when the alarms went off. It was a bomb scare. We were told to get out, an order that alerted Dad to an obvious opportunity. The place was full of posh people. Everyone headed for the exits in a quiet, polite manner; everyone except me and Dad. After a few minutes we were alone. I wasn't sure what was going on. His face was lit up like a Christmas tree.

'Wait here, kid. I'll be back in a second.'

There was no guarantee that there was actually a bomb but as far as my imagination was concerned there was a big one, and it was ticking. The seconds ticked by into minutes and I became anxious. Dad finally emerged from a different department. He had things in his hands that he was pushing into his pockets.

'What are you doing, Dad?'

'Getting some Christmas presents.'

He never missed an opportunity, especially one created by the IRA. The evacuation turned out to be a false alarm.

I was starting to see the difference between my life and the lives of other kids whose houses I went to. Their parents didn't do drugs, nor did their parents' friends. Not in front of us, anyway. They ate cakes, oversized Victoria sponges, not rose-flavoured Turkish delight fresh from Morocco. The dads worked nine till five. The mums stayed at home. Everything was spotless in other people's houses. Everything in my life was loose and relaxed and I loved the lack of normal boundaries. Life was dangerous and exciting. I liked not knowing what was going to happen next.

I also hated it. The price for the absence of the kind of boundaries that define a Victoria sponge childhood was that I felt very unsafe most of the time. Sam had drawn a line of respect around herself that I knew I wasn't to cross. This meant I could trust her. She was a grown up and behaved like one. Dad was a grown up but, most of the time he behaved like a kid in a sweet shop. His sweets were drugs, money and sex. Even so, I wanted to be like him when I grew up and the sooner that was, the better.

Dad started showing me more and more of the tricks of his trade. It was mainly about me watching and I never really knew that class was in session until it was over.

We were in a newsagent in Chelsea one freezing January afternoon. I loved my comics. Dad loved his magazines. He liked the ones that had photos of the life he wanted: the slickly designed lines of newly built houses, the sexiest women, the fastest cars, the exotic beaches of unknown countries. Magazines were a mainline to his fantasies and he needed a weekly hit of the most expensive and glossy ones they had on the rack.

This newsagent was a hundred yards from Chelsea police station. There was a police constable standing at the till talking to the shopkeeper. Dad started sliding the latest editions of *Vogue*, *Omni*, *Playboy* and *What Car?* into his long coat, tucking them snugly under his arm. I started tugging at his sleeve, trying not to be seen.

'Dad, Dad! There's a copper in here!' I whispered in barely disguised panic.

He looked down at me and smiled. 'Best time, kid.'

I had no idea what he meant and was too panic-stricken to ask. The PC finished his chat and walked past us. Dad smiled at him. He then went to the till, paid for a copy of *Country Life*, a *Beano* and a bag of Lucky Dip and we left. When we were safely out of earshot I asked him what he had meant by 'best time'.

'The best time to nick from a shop is when there's a copper in it. The newsagent is off his guard and the copper thinks no one would dare.'

It made sense.

Until Sam came along there was no yearning to stay up late, to bunk off school or whine constantly for what I didn't have. I was already getting what I wanted. There was very little for me to rebel against. But I did have a thing for killing insects; taking their legs off one by one, then breaking their bodies up, ripping or plucking their antennae off and finally their heads. They didn't seem to be in any pain. They didn't make any noise or protest, apart from the pointless rotation of their legs looking for purchase in the air. I was fascinated by the process of taking them apart, bit by bit. The crazy scientist figuring out how they ticked.

I soon got bored of entomology. I knew what I wanted to do next even if I wasn't clear why. I had a strong desire. Consequence wasn't a concept I had any grasp of. I lived in the moment and did what I wanted, when I wanted. I wanted to feel what it would be like to kill something bigger.

One half term a friend and I bought a mouse from his local pet shop. It cost ten pence. I rushed back to his house with it hidden in my coat pocket. I could feel it sniffing around in there, checking out its new home. Something older, bigger and darker inside me was calling the shots. We rushed upstairs to the bathroom and I took the mouse out of my pocket. We both stared at it for a few minutes, then I turned the tap on. I held its head under the rushing stream of cold water. It made a high-pitched noise broken by the tiny mouthfuls of water it was swallowing and choking on. Its clawed feet scratched at my hand, trying to get away. It swung its head back and forth, trying to avoid what was coming. The short hair on its body stuck fast to its skin and it shined. The squeaking made what I was doing more real and more alarming. I began to ask myself why. Before I had the chance to answer, the mouse had stopped moving. Death hadn't taken as long as I thought.

I had hoped I would get some kind of relief, satisfaction from the killing, some kind of peace of mind. I was left with a sense of twisted power, gut-wrenching guilt and a feeling of complete pointlessness. The kid next to me was dumbstruck. I gently wrapped the mouse in a pink flannel and put it into a plastic bag, which then went into my jacket pocket. I felt ashamed and strangely alive.

The following Monday, Dad sat me down in our front room and got me to look him in the eye.

'Jake's mother told me you killed a mouse.'

'I didn't.'

'Don't lie to me, Cas. I know when you're lying. I always know.'

'I didn't mean to.'

'Jake said you bought the mouse, took it home and drowned it in the sink.'

'I was playing. I didn't mean to.'

Dad didn't believe me.

'There are a lot of things you and I can do and get away with, Cas. No problem. And there a lot more things I can do than you. Killing for the sake of it is not on, Cas. Not on at all.'

'Have you ever killed anything, Dad?'

'Lots of things. I know what I'm talking about.'

35

'Have you ever killed a person?'

'Come on, Sam's got dinner ready. Early to bed. You've got school tomorrow.'

He was avoiding the question.

The following day I took the dead mouse to Hyde Park. I had a small hammer and some nails in my pocket. I looked for just the right kind of bark. I wanted it to be gnarled and old. I found an ancient tree standing on its own. I gently unfolded the pink flannel and looked at the small, dead animal. I knew exactly what I wanted to do but, again, I wasn't sure why. I put the mouse back in the bag, held the bag between my teeth and took a nail and the hammer out of my pocket. I held the bag up against the tree and looked at it for a minute. It felt respectful. Then I hammered the small, brown nail through the clear plastic bag. It went easily through the mouse and into the bark of the tree. The mouse bled a little into the bag. This was my idea of a natural burial, some kind of homage to the murdered creature. It was also a statement that I was in charge.

I stood there and watched the bottom of the bag collect a small pool of mouse blood. Then I hoisted myself up on one of the massive, low-hanging branches and started to climb the crooked old tree. It took me a long time, scraping my body through thickets of leaves and an infinite thickness of branches. When I was halfway up I looked down and could just make out the mouse in its plastic coffin.

Hot, scratched and out of breath I finally reached the top. I was on the summit of the newly leafed crown of what must have been a four-hundred-year-old oak. I sat up there in the natural silence and felt peaceful. The only noises were the creak of the tree as it responded to the hiss of the wind. It was like sitting in the crow's nest of a massive pirate ship. The motion created by the wind was the motion of the ocean. This was the kind of place I felt most myself, most at home. I sat and looked across the park for hours. Nobody knew I was up there. I watched the people below me. I stayed there till dusk, till I got hungry.

After half term Dad and Sam drove me back to Summerhill. I hated going back. The sky was clear blue and it was hot in the orange BMW. Dad loved his flash, unusual cars and he loved people staring at him. The leather inside smelled like the old World War Two van. I was on the back seat looking out of the window at the road as it rushed out behind us. We drove out of the city and into the country, slowly, savouring the unfolding scenery. A green blur of trees and fields stretched past the windows. It reminded me of being on the back of Dad's chopper on Wimbledon Common. I fell asleep.

I woke up as we passed through the gates of the school and began heading down the long drive. Dad pulled up outside my boarding house. I didn't want to get out of the car because I knew I wouldn't be able to get back in. I cried. Dad opened my door.

'Come on, kid, you know I hate this bit as much as you do. You love it once you get back into it.' He took me by the hand and led me inside. I was angry and wound up. Sam brought in a massive brown teddy bear she'd hidden in the trunk of the car and put him on my bed.

'He's going to keep you company and keep the monsters away. He's got teeth, big ones.' I didn't let her see that it made me feel better. 'You can cuddle him if you're finding it hard to sleep. Look at the size of him. He's almost as big as you.'

Dad was looking a bit choked. 'Take it easy, kid. We'll be back to see you in a couple of weeks. Don't set fire to anything, for fuck's sake.'

I loved watching things burn. I knew it was dangerous. This made it all the more exciting starting small fires and stamping them out just before they got out of hand. My last incineration was a red and blue, wooden drummer boy. His arms had looked good on fire.

Before I knew it, it was bedtime and lights out. With no city street lights outside it was pitch dark. I felt very alone, even with the bear. I started to cry and couldn't stop. I was ignored by the other kids but I wanted them to hear me. They started talking about girlfriends and boyfriends and who fancied who. I wanted to be with Sarah, a pretty girl who I knew liked me, in her bed. I cried a bit louder. The other kids in the dorm started to get angry.

Sarah leant down from her bunk, and peered at me. 'Leave him alone.' Her voice immediately calmed me. I was getting the attention I wanted.

'I want to get into your bunk bed, Sarah. I want a cuddle. I miss my dad. I want to go home.'

I wanted more than a cuddle. Sarah thought about it for a minute.

'I don't think I want to cuddle you, Caspar.' Her voice was soft and warm in the darkness of the cold dormitory.

The thought of being in Sarah's bed made my heart thump hard. 'Oh, let him, Sarah. Maybe he'll stop crying.' Another voice in the darkness.

Sarah sighed. 'Come on then, you can lie next to me for a little bit.'

I climbed up to her bunk. I got into her bed and I felt like a grown up. It was confusing and exciting. She let me get on top of her and cuddle her and she let me kiss her, just once, goodnight. She smelled like Mum's blankets and sheets. I had seen how Dad had been with his girlfriends and with Sam. They seemed to like it. It was comforting. I stopped crying.

The freedom in Summerhill was incredible. But I was easily bored and I often found myself wandering around the school with my mate Boris, looking for something to do. It was nearly bedtime. I had my brown bear with me.

'Do you want to see what this stupid bear looks like with his head on fire?'

'Sure,' said Boris. 'Sounds good.'

'Go downstairs and wait at the bottom of my bedroom window by the hall windows.' He gave me a military salute and ran off. 'And stay out of the lights!' I shouted after him.

I headed for my bedroom and leaned out of the window with the bear in my hand. I could see Boris looking up at me from the shadows. I got out my secret stash of matches, lit one and held it to the bear's ear. The bear caught fire immediately. It must have been made out of nylon. Toys usually took longer to get going. I'd found cotton was much slower to burn. I held the bear out of the window with his flaming head pointing down to the ground. The angle made the flames lick higher.

Boris was jumping up and down in excitement, all boredom gone. 'Drop him, drop him, drop him!' he shouted.

I held the bear by the legs for as long as I could, but the flames were now ferocious. I dropped it and watched it fall through the darkness, lighting it up in roaring orange and yellows. I could see Boris's gleeful face illuminated by the flames as the bear landed with a dull thud on the ground next to him. He danced round the flaming bear, chanting. I ran downstairs and outside. We stood and watched the bear's head rage in flames up into the blue-black sky.

A teacher leaned out of the window. 'What the bloody hell is going on down there? Caspar, is that you, you little toerag?'

I stamped on the bear's head to put him out.

There were few rules at Summerhill but the bear fire was definitely against them. I was in trouble and it felt good. The whole episode pissed the school off. But what I did next got me into more trouble than I bargained for.

CRIMINAL

An older kid and I decided to rob the football clubhouse that stood in a field next to the school. We wanted the sweets we'd seen through the dirty window at the back. It was the older kid's idea. He wanted me, the donkey, to chuck a big rock through the window for him. That night we climbed through the hedge, into the field and headed for the back of the hut.

The rock was as heavy as I had expected. I only just got it high enough to chuck it. The older kid did nothing to help. I lunged at the pane and watched it glide through the window followed by an explosion of glass.

'Go on, Caspar, get in there and get the sweets, like we said. Pass them over to me!'

'There's broken glass sticking up all over the bloody thing. It'll cut me.'

'You scaredy cat.'

No one called me a scaredy cat. He gave me a bunk up and I crawled in. I cut my hands on the shattered, splintered glass. I passed him the bloodstained chocolate and fizzy drinks and we ran back to the school, sharing out the football club booty with our friends. I felt incredible. Was this how Dad felt after a job? My heart was beating so hard I thought it was going to break out of my chest. I was a bad boy Robin Hood and everybody liked me. Just like Dad.

Within half an hour, the headmaster's wife was in my room.

'That's it, Caspar. I've had enough of this. You've pushed me over my limit this time. You're on the first train back to London tomorrow afternoon, right after you've spoken to the police. You had your chance. Enough of this nonsense. Pack your bags.'

I had thought it was impossible to get chucked out of Summerhill. That's what Dad had told me.

I woke up the following morning thinking that maybe

I'd had a bad dream. But my hands were covered in bandages and when I sat up I saw my suitcase at the bottom of the bed. My heart hit my feet. I went down for breakfast. Everyone stared at me. I didn't like this kind of attention so much.

Later that morning me and the older kid were shown into a small room, deep in the main school building. A plain-clothes policeman was sitting at a desk, holding a smart pen over a sheet of white paper. He looked up.

'Sit down there, the pair of you.'

He was wearing an old, crumpled suit and smelled of pipe tobacco. He didn't say anything else for ages. He took his time on purpose.

'Now, we know you robbed the football clubhouse. There are about twenty kids with chocolate all over their faces who will back that up, and neither of you seem to be denying it.' He looked at my hands. 'That will explain the blood all over the window and on the inside of the club-house tuck shop. Right bloody mess. But what I'm more interested in is if either of you know anything about a cash robbery at a coal yard just outside Aldeburgh on Monday?'

We shook our heads. I was a kid, for God's sake, not a bank robber. We left the money in the football clubhouse till because we wanted the sweets. It was a shortcut. If we'd taken the money it would only have ended up in the sweet shop till down the road. We were saving time. It seemed sensible.

The policeman finished his long list of questions about the coal robbery. We weren't guilty but we didn't feel very innocent, either.

'I think being thrown out of school is enough of a punishment for you two. Besides, you're too young to lock up. No doubt you'll be seeing more policemen in the future, the pair of you.' He pointed at me with his pipe. 'Especially you. Unless of course you can learn your lesson from this.

Believe me, you don't want to end up in prison, they can be very nasty places indeed.'

What little I knew of prison was mostly from the TV; from the American black-and-white gangster movies that Dad loved to watch. The policeman was trying to frighten me. I wasn't scared. At least, I didn't show it. He shuffled his papers, got up and left without saying goodbye. I didn't speak to the older boy. He'd grassed on me. Dad had told me never have anything to do with anyone who grasses. I strode past him and pushed him up against the wall. I gave him one of my mad stares, eyeball to eyeball, something I'd been practising. The boy was bigger than me but he didn't push back.

I went to my room to get my bags.

As the train pulled into London, I leaned out of the window as far as I could and saw Dad standing on the platform, waiting. He was wearing a poncho, cowboy boots, jeans and a scarf around his neck. He looked like Clint Eastwood. I was so excited to see him I nearly jumped out of the train door there and then. He was happy to see me and he was angry, he couldn't hide that.

'What am I going to do with you, kid?' The anger disappeared and he gave me a long cuddle.

I never liked being away from him, no matter how much fun I was having. Being with Dad outstripped the fun I could have anywhere on the planet.

4

Watch and Learn, Kid

Summer 1977, Chelsea, London

I'm in a new school now. Made some cool new friends. It's daytimes only and a twenty-minute walk from my house or a two-minute motorbike ride or a five-minute car trip, depending on how Dad's feeling. Summerhill was fun but it's more fun being close to Dad and back at Sam's. London is a much bigger playground. There are more things to climb and smash up and set fire to.

It's Saturday morning. I'm sitting in my pyjamas in our kitchen with an empty cereal bowl in front of me. I've just finished my third helping of Sugar Puffs. I didn't see a single mouthful as I shovelled it in. My short-sighted eyes are glued to our twelve-inch Sony Trinitron TV. Noel Edmonds is on the phone to some kid who wants to swap his inflatable dinosaur for a bike. It doesn't sound like a very good deal. I'm only interested in the cartoons coming back on. I'm fed up waiting for them so I take a risk and turn over. Tiswas is on ITV. It's in full swing with grown ups chucking custard pies and buckets of water at each other. It looks great fun but I'm nervous, waiting for one of the adults to get angry or violent. Some of the kids in the studio start to get involved in the pie chucking and all hell breaks loose. Now everyone is covered in custard, water and green slime, even the cameraman and the camera. I would love to be there.

Saturday morning TV is my weekly religion. I get out of bed for it and I'm loyal to the two main channels throughout the morning, only breaking to eat or go for a pee. I'm on my own. I like it. I like silence when I'm watching. I can only really concentrate on one thing at a time. I don't know where Dad is. He's gone out somewhere. He's not usually up this early on a Saturday. He'll be back, though. He always comes back.

Footsteps came up the stairs from the street to the front door. I recognised Dad's as one of them. There were two others. Keys rattled into the front door lock. I heard voices. Men. Dad laughing. It was the half real, half fake laugh, which said, 'I think you're funny, sure, I get the humour, but I'm in charge, know your place, mate.'

That laugh always pissed me off.

They headed downstairs to the basement. I turned the TV up. Dad came in first, ruffled my hair and gave me a kiss. He was wearing a brown three-piece suit with flared trousers, black shoes and a blue tie. His hair was long and blond and he had a tan. He always had a tan, usually from a bottle. He looked the business.

'What's up, kid? Bit loud, isn't it? And you're sitting way too close. We need to get you some glasses before you blind yourself. This is Tony. You know George.'

'Hi, Tony. Hi, George. I don't want glasses.'

I squinted at George. Tony stood quietly at the other side of the room. George was big, like a boxer, with curly hair and sideburns. His open-necked shirt revealed a massive gold sovereign hanging on a thick chain, nestling inside his hairy chest. He'd told me he was really a pirate and it was one of a thousand doubloons he'd nicked. He was all right, George. I felt safe around him. He was always there if we needed him – for anything. There weren't many friends of Dad's like George. They had been to school together just ten minutes from where we now lived. They'd known each other for thirty years. The expression 'thick as thieves' fitted them well. Dad said George was very good to have around if a fight kicked off. They would often pretend to be undercover police officers and bust the houses of other criminals, confiscating whatever was worth snorting, selling or keeping. George and Dad worked together a lot.

I wasn't sure about Tony. I didn't like the look of him. He was skinny and trying to hide it inside a long black leather coat. He thought he was hard and cool but he looked well out of his depth in Dad and George's presence.

Dad got some of his favourite German lagers out of the fridge, handed George and Tony a bottle each, cracked the top of his and took a long swig. It made me thirsty to watch. He put his bottle on the table, came over to me and pulled my chair away from the telly.

'Me, Tony and George have put a bet on the gee-gees. A big bet and we're going to win. We need to watch the racing.'

Ignoring my protests, he rolled the dial to change channels. The pie fighting turned to a hiss of silver static and then a green racetrack and a sea of horses and riders slogging it out. The horses were being whipped. They looked terrified. George and Tony sat down and lit cigarettes. Dad stood behind me, hands on my shoulders.

I wanted to go to my room and lose myself in a game of toy soldiers but I didn't want to break contact with Dad. The horses raced round the track. I was so bored I let my focus go. They slipped into a blur of brown on green. The commentator was ridiculously excited about such a dull sport. Dad, George and Tony watched with no emotion, which I thought was weird. After all, there was money at stake.

Halfway through the race, Dad got up and turned the telly off. In silence, George and Tony stood up too and the three of them headed for the stairs.

'What are you doing, the race hasn't finished!' I needlessly pointed out to them.

'Seen enough, kid. It's a winner. Back later. Don't get too close to the screen. Glasses next week.'

I switched the telly back on, relieved to get back to the last of my cartoons.

That evening Dad and George came back. I was still watching telly. Sam was making dinner. Dad put a briefcase on the table and opened it up. It was full of cash. Twenties stacked and bound together, sitting in neat rows.

'Wow! Where'd you get that?' My eyes were on stalks.

'Watch and learn, kid. Watch and learn. Check the form and you'll pick a winner . . . every time.'

'You won *that* on the horses! There must be a million pounds in there!' I couldn't believe it. 'How much, how much is in there, how much?'

Dad ran a hand across the money. 'About five hundred grand.'

'Half a million pounds! There's half a million pounds in that case!'

'Something like that. George will count it; he's methodical and enjoys that kind of thing. Don't you, George?'

George winked at me. They were seriously pleased with themselves. I could feel the excitement in the room and it was infectious. I started taking money out of the case and looking at it. Sam was watching quietly, the country girl on an adventure with her bit of London rough.

'Get dressed, kid, we're going out to celebrate.'

Two weeks later, Dad told me that he hadn't won the money on the races after all. My gut had already told me that. When anyone asked me what my dad did for a living, I'd tell them he was an antiques dealer. I was always asking him what he'd done at work that day, or night. He would usually shush me and tell me not to ask so many questions. This time, though, he was pissed and wanted to talk about it.

'We didn't win a bet, kid, we robbed a ff . . . ffucking safe. Bastard to open but we cracked the fucker.' He was slurring. 'One of the biggest I've ever seen . . . a beauty. Nearly didn't make it, though. Fucking arsehole, that Tony.' Dad moved from his empty glass to the bottle of Stolichnaya and drank it like I drank Tab.

The robbery that Saturday morning had been on a wages office on the other side of London. They'd been armed but there was no one there to put up a fight. Even so, within a few seconds of arriving Tony had spooked like a horse and run from the building. He had nearly got them all caught. He was no longer in the circle.

'Why did you tell me you won it on the horses?'

'Needed an alibi. Not for the police . . .' He knew he'd covered his tracks well enough not to get nicked. 'For the people I know. There's always some useless cunt who gets too stoned or pissed to keep their mouth shut or is just plain jealous and wants your old man out of the way.' He was waving the bottle around now. 'Tony says a word, I'll do the bastard's kneecaps,' he told me, smiling proudly.

I got him another bottle of vodka to make sure he didn't dry up. The details unfolded over the next drunken hour and I paid very close attention. George and Dad were left on their own in the wages office. As it was Saturday, no one was there. Not even the security guard. The money was in a safe and the safe was built into a wall. George spent two hours hacking it out of the wall while Dad stuck his feet up and watched the street. It was his job – he'd set it up – so that was his prerogative. When the safe was finally free, they'd hauled it on to the window ledge and dropped it three storeys down into a backstreet. It embedded itself six inches into concrete. They stuck it on a blanket, dragged it to the car and drove it to a scrapyard in Fulham. Dad got a garage mechanic mate to melt the hinges off with an oxyacetylene torch. There was much more money inside than they had thought there would be.

The following day, after he'd sobered up, he came to me and told me he needed to speak to me alone. I loved the intrigue. We went for a walk.

'Now, the golden rule here, kid, is that you keep this to yourself. It was probably about time that I told you about some of the heavier stuff I get up to. I trust you. Not a word to anyone. Not a soul. At school or at home. If you say anything to anyone I might end up in prison and I don't want to be away from you. Ever.'

This was the kind of deal I could make. And I kept my promise. I never told anyone at school, at home, anywhere, not a soul. It was crystal clear that this was family business. There would be a lot of trouble if I said anything to anyone and they weren't able to keep their mouths shut. I felt grown up and privileged to be told. I was proud of my dad.

Dad had expensive taste in just about everything: food, drugs, women and clothes. To stay looking sharp and up to date he nicked a new suit from Stanley Adams menswear on the King's Road every month. I used to go in with him to watch him work and act as decoy. In the changing rooms there was a big bench seat, big enough to get in and play in, which I did. One day, an idea popped into my head. Dad would usually walk into a shop with a bag or case to slip the goods inside. This was his routine in Stanley Adams. I suggested that he save some time and take in a bigger bag and get more suits in one go: fill the bag with newspaper and make it look like he was carrying something heavy, take a couple of suits at a time into the changing room, without the assistant knowing exactly how many, put the newspaper in the bench seat and fill the bag up with suits. When he left, the bag would look the same as it had when he'd arrived, only this time it would be genuinely heavy with suits. He smiled at my idea. The following weekend he tried it out and returned home from the men's outfitter with £500 worth of Yves St Laurent. His best haul yet. My dad was proud of me.

The wages robbery had made one of Dad's dreams come true. We now had enough money to go travelling. I took six months off school. Apart from having to take some work with me, I was the luckiest kid in the world. Dad bought a massive, brown Mercedes van and gutted it. He had aeroplane seats put in, a shower, a kitchen, a loo, an eight-track tape system, a single bed for me and a double bed for him and Sam. And we were off.

Autumn 1977, Southern France

We'd been driving for three weeks. It was fantastic seeing all the sleepy French towns and villages shimmering quietly in the baking September heat. We stopped for a break in the Dordogne and rented an apartment by the water. We were in our kitchen one lunchtime eating cheese and hot French bread. The sun was intense and bright. I could hear the crickets and the blackbird that came in the afternoons. The postman came to the door just as I was tucking into a yoghurt; he had a telegram for Dad.

Dad looked at it for a while, as though he knew there was something bad inside. He opened it and read the single sheet of paper for a long time. Sam walked over to him and put her hand on his shoulder. Dad didn't look at her. He spoke in a mumble.

'It's from Grainne. The old fucker's dead.'

'You mean John?'

Grainne was Dad's sister. John was my granddad. Lung cancer had killed him two days earlier. We'd visited him in hospital before we left. I didn't think he was going to die that quickly. He and Dad didn't get on at all, in fact they seemed to hate each other so much they weren't speaking. Not even in the hospital. Dad had just sat there reading a magazine while Sam had made all the conversation. She was good at talking to people but that was taking the piss.

Granddad was a black marketeer in the Second World War. He came over from Ireland at the turn of the twentieth century. He was working class, smart and knew how to make money on the streets of London. Dad learnt a lot from him. Grandma was also an aspiring socialite, a working-class social chameleon. Dad loved her deeply.

Our heavenly time in the Dordogne was about to end.

Dad took a bottle of vodka out of the fridge and went and sat outside in the shade of an old poplar tree in the garden. He stayed there all afternoon, drinking and clearly not enjoying it. In the absence of stronger narcotics, alcohol was a means to an end.

I finally got the courage to go out to see if he was OK.

'You all right, Dad?'

'Leave me alone, kid. I'm all right, I'll be fine. I'm just feeling upset. Bit confused. I'll be fine.'

He didn't look like he was going to be fine. He looked angry.

Three days later and Dad was still drinking. He went out for hours at a time. Where to, we didn't know. He drove drunk. Each time he went out I got scared he was going to kill himself by crashing the car, a Cadillac he'd borrowed from some strange Frenchman. I couldn't sleep. I wanted to be with him, to keep an eye on him. He started shouting at Sam. I'd never heard him lose it like that before. I could see it wasn't really about her. It was about Granddad. I didn't like this part of Dad. On the fourth night he was determined to fulfil a promise to take me out with him in the Cadillac. He was drunk again. I was scared, but I wanted to be with him. It didn't really matter how out of it he was or how weird he was being. It was way beyond my bedtime, but Sam was asleep so we snuck out.

As the headlights cut into the darkness, the winding French country roads appeared, bend by bend, before our sleepy eyes. It was beautiful. The road started to twist and turn more sharply. My stomach lurched. I didn't think Dad could keep it together. He was a good driver but not when he was drunk. Despite my fear, I couldn't resist the tiredness. In the end I gave in to it and nodded off.

I woke up to the crunching violence of car metal on rock. The car was on its roof and we were sliding down a dark mountain slope. The car was screaming. Dad was swearing. The car rolled several times and I was slung around the inside of it like a rag doll. I was convinced we were going to die. We hit something big and solid and the car whacked to an abrupt halt. Dad was panicking. He rarely panicked about anything. He seemed to have sobered right up.

'Jesus fucking Christ. You all right, kid?'

'I think my back's broken,' I said, easing myself out of the car.

'Your back's not broken, kid, you're walking. Don't say that. You scared the shit out of me.'

The car was wedged up against a huge tree. Beyond it was a steeper descent into darkness.

'It hurts. I thought we were going to die. What happened?' I whined.

'You'll be fine. I fell asleep. Stupid bastard!' He cursed himself. 'Killing myself would be OK but killing you would be unforgivable.'

'Is the car OK?'

Dad hobbled around it. 'Look at that! Yank cars. Built like fucking tanks!'

We got back in and it started first time. Dad found a dirt track to take us back to the main road. Fully sobered up he drove slowly and carefully back home.

Sam completely lost it with us when we got back. She was sitting in the front room with a drink in her hand. She didn't usually drink, not that late at night. Dad told me not to say a word but she knew something had happened. My back was hurting and I couldn't hide the limp. She was so upset by it all I thought at that point she might leave. I really didn't want her to go. I loved her and she was beginning to feel like the only sane adult in my life.

Dad swore to us both that he wouldn't drink or do anything stupid again but he was drunk again the following afternoon. He wanted to go out. I didn't want him to die. I thought that if I went with him I could keep him awake, but I didn't want to be with him in case I couldn't even keep myself awake and we ended up in another valley.

Sam and I decided to bury the car keys in a flowerpot. The plan went wrong. Dad was very wound up. His eyes were wide and he looked crazy, like I'd never seen before. He moved right up close to Sam's face.

'Give me the keys. I'm just going out for a drive. I need to clear my head.'

Sam kept calm. 'Frank, no, not tonight. You've been drinking again. You said you wouldn't. Please.'

'Give me the keys.'

'Dad, please don't go out again. You promised.'

'Give me the fucking keys!'

Sam took my hand and led me into the sitting room. Dad came after us.

'Sit down there, Cas, and wait. Here, read your comic. I need to talk to your dad.'

The door clicked gently shut behind her. It was quiet. I could hear the night crickets. The air in the room was warm. I ate a banana from the fruit bowl and started to read my comic. Then I heard Sam scream, followed by what sounded like chairs and tables being dragged and scraped on the stone floor. Sam sounded beside herself with terror. Dad was still shouting at her about the keys. I flung open the door and saw her in the corner of the dining room with the tables and chairs pushed up against her, trapping her. She was stock still and white as ice.

'If I can't go out or move about freely, then no fucker can,' he was shouting.

I went to the flowerpot and got the keys. He took them from my outstretched palm, headed straight out to the car, skidded on the gravel drive and was gone. It was quiet again and I was grateful for it. I helped Sam out of the confusion of tables and chairs and we sat down together. She hugged me. I wasn't sure if Dad was going to come back alive.

When I woke up the next morning the car was outside and Dad was asleep in the sitting room, slumped in the massive armchair. He was going to have a nasty hangover and for the very first time in my life I didn't want to be anywhere near him.

5

Stoned

Tangier, Winter 1977

We've travelled from Southern France, through to the bottom of Spain into Cadiz and are now on a beat-up old car ferry going to North Africa.

I'm running around on deck, back and forth, like a nutter. Every time I ask Dad for another 7-Up he gives me more money. I'm buzzing from all the sugar. The sea is green and blue and the sun is shining and sparkling all over it, like diamonds. It's hot and my neck is burning pink. It hurts so much I can't touch it.

Sam is sunbathing on an upper deck, Dad is down on the car deck, in the van. I head down the steel stairs, jumping three at a time, down three decks to see Dad. I run up to him, out of breath and beaming. He puts his book down and starts crumbling something black on to a mound of tobacco. I think he wants me to see what he's doing. More lessons.

'What's that?'

'Opium.'

'What's opium?'

'Calms the mind, makes you feel warm inside. It's a bit like liquorice.'

'It smells sweet.'

He's being gentle with it like it's a precious jewel. He finishes rolling the joint and lights it up.

'Why are you smoking it?' I want some.

'Because I like it.'

'Aren't you supposed to eat liquorice? Can I have some?'

'No, it's for grown ups,' he replies smugly and hands me some more money so that I can get my buzz elsewhere.

I run off, back upstairs and on to the main deck again. I down another 7-Up. There's sweat all over my back and I'm starting to feel jittery. I head back to Dad. I stand in front of him breathing heavily for a long time, trying to catch my breath.

'You all right, kid?'

'My chest hurts. I can't breathe properly.'

It doesn't hurt much but I'm getting his attention. He looks at me for a moment, scanning my face to see if I'm lying. I'm a good liar. He breaks off a small piece of opium from the big chunk on the dashboard.

'Special circumstances. This is not to smoke. Chew it. It'll help you breathe better. Medicine for your chest.'

I take it, look at it, smell it then put it in my mouth and chew slowly. It's bitter. Nothing like liquorice. I run off to invent another game.

About half an hour later I'm floating. I'm smiling and feeling happy; warm on the outside and cool on the inside. I like this feeling. I can see why Dad likes it. I slowly get up off the sunbed and try to stand up. I lean on the deck rail. I look at the sun's rays still sparkling on the sea and see loads of small fishing boats. It's like a picture. I like opium and I want some more.

As we arrived in Tangier I started to feel less dizzy from the opium. My legs felt more solid, less wobbly. The swirling, wavy sensation that had been running through my body levelled out and my reactions got back to normal. It was dark on the car deck and smelled of engine oil and ancient sea salt. I could hear the boat bumping and scraping along the harbour wall. A high-pitched whining started and I put my hands over my ears. The car ferry doors opened with a mechanical screech of chains. Hot afternoon sunshine blasted into the darkest corners of the deck. There were loads of black Moroccan men standing on the harbour wall in kaftans, fixed grins, poised to sell us stuff. Dad bought us all kaftans. His was brown, mine was blue and Sam's was pink. We looked like we were trying a bit too hard.

We drove to the Walled City. Dad was on a mission to get some dope. We all wanted something: Sam some new shoes, me, one of the lethal-looking toy guns I'd seen in a shop window. Dad found the right Moroccan man in the right café down the right narrow alleyway. Constantly nodding, he led us through a maze of streets into a complex of connected buildings. We moved inside through an iron-studded mahogany doorway, into a candlelit courtyard with a small fountain at its centre. It looked promising at first, but we ended up at the very back of the house, in a small room with no windows. It smelled of sweat, leather sandals, camping gas, hot mint tea and dope. The cushions rose so high from the dirty, black floor that I could disappear inside them; which I did.

Dad, Sam and me sat in silence, waiting for business to begin. As usual, I was keeping an eye out for Dad. He'd told me I had 'pukka instincts'. He said I should start trusting them. I was slowly beginning to get a better idea of what he was on about. I called it *pirate radar*.

The Moroccan man started to roll a joint. Dad always smoked some before he bought it. He took out five Rizla papers from an orange packet. He licked the thin, white papers and stuck them together into the shape of a letter 'T'. He laid them gently down on a small wooden table. He put a little tobacco in and took out a lump of black hash the size of an apple from a blue velvet bag. It was the biggest lump of dope I'd ever seen, even Dad looked impressed. He burned a corner of it on the candle flame until it started to smoulder. His smile vanished. He was concentrating. The dope smelled strong and sweet and made me feel sick.

'What are you doing, Mister?'

The man looked up at me then at Dad, as though he was waiting for him to answer.

'Why are you burning that black stuff, Mister?'

I knew exactly why he was doing it. But pretending not to know about drugs was very much part of the game. Dad went along with it and finally answered me.

'He's rolling a joint, kid. We're buying some dope for our holiday and to celebrate winning all that cash on the gee-gees.'

The Moroccan nodded at me again and smiled. He finished rolling the joint. I didn't completely trust him. Something in the radar felt wrong. I pulled Dad's shirt three times. This was our signal. Dad looked at me, nodded and winked.

I had liked the opium. Now I wanted to find out more about dope.

'Can I have some?'

Before Dad had a chance to open his mouth, Sam interrupted. 'No, you can't, Caspar, and you bloody well know it. You're way too young for this. Maybe in about ten years' time, when you've left school. Bloody hell, Frank, he shouldn't even be here with us.'

I knew I could talk Dad into things that Sam didn't want me to do, especially if I put on the face. I was surprised how often it worked.

'Please, Dad.'

Dad looked at Sam for a moment, then back to the Moroccan.

'This is as good a time as any to put you off. Don't want you growing up like your old man now, do we?'

The joint was lit and passed to Dad, who took a long drag on it. He looked at the joint as though it was something alien, then nodded twice and smiled. He liked it. The dope smelled even sweeter now that it was burning in the Rizlas. The thin white smoke hung in the air, then drifted into the darker corners of the room.

Sam was no longer merely uncomfortable, she was fully pissed off and glaring at Dad, who pretended not to notice. He passed the joint very slowly over to me. He was making a point. This was a special moment.

'Here you go, kid. Just the one toke, mind. Put your lips over the end and suck it in, like you're taking a breath before going under water.'

I followed his instructions carefully. I put the joint to my lips. The fiery orange glow of the tip lit up the darkness around me. The moment the smoke got into my throat I started to cough. A little of it got into my lungs. Most of it went up my nose and into my eyes. Tears started running down my face. I couldn't stop coughing. Sam started to pat me on the back. It didn't help. Dad passed me his beer.

I took big, quick gulps. I coughed a few times into the can and the beer splashed back, all over my trousers. As the coughing started to ease I felt a soft rush of something warm in the middle of my head. This wasn't like the opium at all. It felt good for a second. Then it switched to bad. I started to dry heave, the beer rose back up into my throat, followed by the lamb meatballs I'd had for dinner. Within a few seconds the cushions around me were covered in warm vomit. I started to cry.

CRIMINAL

*

After a lot of hassling – no whining, he hated that – Dad
bought me the toy gun I wanted. I think he felt bad about me
throwing up. The gun fired big caps that flared up in a white
and blue flash followed by a plume of thin smoke, almost
like the real thing. It was better than anything you could get
back in England. He also bought Sam the shoes she wanted.
She was very pissed off about me being sick. Dad was trying
to make peace. The shoes just about did it. And any anger I
was feeling about throwing up was lost in the excitement of
my latest weapon.

Three days later I found myself running around the
backstreets of Casablanca. It was a dangerous area and I had
been told not to go there. But I was hunting pirates, monsters
and police. I liked to mix up my fantasies. The streets were
great for hiding in: narrow alleyways with lots of corners and
doorways and shadows to duck into. I was, very specifically,
on the hunt for the Chief of the Moroccan Police for
smuggling opium from Cadiz to Tangier. If I caught up with
him I'd probably have to shoot him in the shins to stop him
from running – he always ran, despite being a fat fucker. *He*
was supposed to be catching the baddies, but he was the
biggest baddie of all, a big, sweaty bastard who liked best to
hang out with the Moroccan drug dealers.

'Stop! Don't move! I need to search your bags, lady.'

The old Moroccan woman stopped in her tracks and gave
me a scowl. She waved her walking stick at my face as though
she wanted me to fuck off. I waved my gun back at her. For
all I knew she could have been the Chief of Police in disguise.

'Stand against the wall. One false move and I'll shoot
your kneecaps clean off. Try me.'

She cocked her head back, then brought it back down
and laughed in my face. She looked at me for a long second
and spat something nasty and black on to the ground at my

feet. The Chief of Police was always a hard man to catch. Then she continued walking slowly up the street with her shopping – were the drugs in those bags? I fired a few warning shots in the air. She didn't turn around. She disappeared quietly into the shadows of a whitewashed alley.

I was out of caps. I needed more for the big chase so I headed back to the van. Getting the caps was going to be trickier than hunting down monsters and fat Moroccan cops. I had to get into the van without Dad and Sam hearing. They were usually having sex at that time of day.

I snuck in through the passenger door and took out a strip of caps from the glove compartment. I saw Sam's purse. I opened it up and took out some dinar: notes and a bit of change. As long as I was smart and didn't get too greedy, I wouldn't get caught. I snuck back out and reloaded.

Suddenly the back door of the van flew open.

'Who the fuck is that?'

It was Dad. He was naked, stoned and covered in sweat; he looked crazy. This was really embarrassing. I desperately hoped nobody would see him. I had to get him back in the van before anybody did. I ran and dived across the ground and sprung up in front of him, both my hands on the cocked gun.

'Don't move, punk, you're surrounded. Get back in the truck and nobody gets hurt.'

Dad put his hands up. 'OK, kid. I don't want any trouble. Go easy on that trigger and I'll do as you say.'

He was enjoying playing cops and robbers even if he was stoned and naked. I was about to make an arrest and I was excited. My hands were trembling. My sweaty finger slipped on the trigger and the gun went off. There was a puff of black smoke and a big flash of blue and white flame; like a firework. Something had gone wrong. It wasn't my fault, it was an accident. I heard a high-pitched screeching, followed by a long howl. Dad's hands were over his face and he stumbled out of the back of the van, landing on his side on the dry, hard ground. Sam jutted her head out in a panic. She looked at my writhing dad, then at me, then at the gun.

'What the hell's going on, Cas?'

'I shot Dad. I'm sorry, I didn't mean to. It just went off in my hand.'

Dad was rolling around on the ground, making a lot of frightening noises. His hands were still over his eyes. I'd never hurt him before. I would never hurt him. After what seemed like an age he clambered to his feet. There were a few people around by now, wanting to see what was going on. I was crying. Dad had a large black, scratchy mark on the side of his face and flecks of blood on his chin.

'I'm sorry, Dad. I didn't mean . . .'

Before I could finish my apology I felt a sharp, hard sting across my face. I had been slapped.

'Never say you're sorry, kid. Not unless you mean it.'

I did mean it but I was too scared to say anything else.

He climbed back into the van. Everyone saw his skinny arse. Sam looked down and gave me a half smile. She wasn't angry.

'He'll be all right, Cas. He didn't mean it. Go get something to eat. It'll be OK.'

She gave me some dinar and closed the back door of the van and locked it this time. I now had double the dinar. I spent the money on cakes, 7-Up and chocolate. The sugar rush gave me a buzz strong enough to quieten my fear and anxiety about Dad's anger.

It took four days for things between us to cool off, and four days for his lurking anger around Granddad's death to resurface, though it wasn't directed at me. I was grateful for that.

We were sitting in a café in a big square in the middle of

medieval Casablanca. It was early evening and the sun had almost gone. Lights were coming on in the cafés and lots of Moroccans were out for a stroll. They looked busy but moved more slowly than people in England. Most of them took a moment to check us out. There were hardly any tourists, hardly any white people. The three of us stuck out like zoo animals.

Sam was sipping mint tea and reading *Vogue*. Dad was stirring a tiny spoon inside a tiny cup of thick, black coffee. He was smoking a fat cigar. I was having yet another 7-Up. Dad took a loud sip of the coffee. 'Christ, that's strong. That's like a line of coke!' Even I knew he meant the powder not the drink.

Sam smiled at him. He spat on the ground then took another sip of the coffee; he spat again. A Moroccan walked up to our table and spoke to Dad.

'*La terre ici est sacrée et c'est un sacrilège d'y cracher. Excusez-vous.*'

Dad gave him the look he used when he wasn't sure about someone, when he was sizing them up for a fight. He was making sure the other guy wasn't going to fight back harder. He leaned slowly across to Sam. 'What's he saying, babe?'

'He says this is sacred ground and it is sacrilege to spit on it. He wants you to apologise.'

'Does he now? How do you say "Go fuck yourself" in French?'

'I don't think that would be a good idea, do you?'

Dad looked the man up and down, finished his coffee, put the cup gently back down on the saucer, looked at me, smiled, then spat on the ground again. Everything around us went stiffly silent. People were staring, waiting to see what was going to happen next. I could feel violence in the air. I was scared again. I nervously sucked some 7-Up through the straw. The Moroccan looked really angry with Dad and stared him out for what seemed like forever, then walked off.

Dad narrowed his eyes as he watched the man go, still sizing him up. 'Cheeky little cunt. Who the fuck does he think he is?' I'm bringing good money into this shit hole. He should show *me* some respect.'

I always knew when Sam was really pissed off. She didn't have to say a word. Dad knew it, too. She carried on reading her magazine and, without looking at him, said, 'It's not exactly *good* money, is it?'

He ignored her and carried on ranting. 'You don't get many tourists round here and you shouldn't go pissing them off.'

'Frank, it's a cultural thing and you know it. *You're* the one who should be showing some respect.'

He got like this, even when he was in the wrong. I was the same. Someone was telling him what to do and he wouldn't have it. He ordered another coffee. The people at the other tables started talking again and I felt a little easier. But after a while it suddenly fell silent again. I looked up and saw the Moroccan man coming back to our table. He had another man with him. Reinforcements. They looked pissed off and they were both big fuckers. I felt my stomach shrink and tighten.

'The man . . . he's coming back and he's got a mate with him,' I whispered.

Dad didn't look up. I knew what he was doing. He was getting ready. I'd seen this before. 'Babe, pick up your tea. You too, kid. Get your 7-Up and head inside with Sam.'

Sam shook her head and tutted. She'd seen this before, as well. But she did as she was told. She picked up her tea. I looked back as we walked inside. The two Moroccan men were just a few feet away from Dad's table; they slowed right down. Everyone had stopped what they were doing. I took up my position inside the café and watched through the grimy window. Before the two men could get any nearer Dad picked up the table and hoisted it above his head. He let out a roar, and the Moroccans completely bottled it. They turned around and ran, fast, down through the square. Dad followed, wielding the table. I could hear one of them shouting at Dad, without looking back at him, as he ran.

'*Nous allons vous bombarder de pierres.*'

'What did he say?' I asked Sam excitedly.

'He said he wants to stone him to death. But I'm sure he doesn't mean it.'

'Go on, Dad, get the bastards!' I shouted. Sam pulled me away from the window and stood behind me, her arms wrapped around me. We watched all three men get smaller as Dad carried on his raging pursuit. I carried on cheering him.

'Be quiet, for God's sake, Caspar. You're worse than your father sometimes.'

He was still running, still holding the cast iron table high above his head. He made it looked easy, the iron in his hands as light as a feather. Everyone in the café was standing up and watching. My dad, a white man in a sea of black faces, chasing two scared Moroccans down a dark alleyway.

After about half an hour he finally came back. The only mark on him was my gunshot scar. He was out of breath and displayed a triumphant, psychotic smile.

'Did they chuck any stones at you, Dad?'

'Didn't get a chance. Fucking cowards. Took the rock out of his shaking hand and threatened to cave the fucker's head in. I'll put money on him shitting himself just before he ran off. I'll spit when and where I like.' He started singing. He was happy. 'Another 7-Up, kid?'

*

We were in Morocco for four months. We saw everything I'd wanted to see. Eventually, the clear blue skies had become boring. Almost every day I had lain on my back, on a beach, on a roof, in a field, and looked up at that bright, sharp sky. I'd wait hours for some elusive clouds to pass by so that I'd have something to look at; something to make stories out of.

I had asked Dad for more opium to ease the boredom. He'd said no. But I'd found his stash and nicked some anyway. Not much, just enough to make the white clouds on blue turn into something interesting.

Dad had been less angry but it was still inside him. He was a like a sleeping wolf, waiting for one good reason to wake up one morning and rip someone's head off. The robbery money was running low and that was making him nervous. Sam was our cash flow back up. Dad always had a back up.

We slowly made our way from Cadiz, through Spain. We spent most of our days driving in the van for the first week. It was hot and bright and the roads were shit. The German suspension did little to stop us being flung out of our seats as we navigated our way through the mountain roads and country lanes. I couldn't read my comics when we were driving. It made me feel sick. Wanking was the best way to pass the time. I did it while watching the desert and mountains and scrub rush by the open window. Neil Young and Santana blasted out of the eight-track and disguised my irregular breathing.

We made slow progress. Dad kept meeting ageing, leather-skinned hippies and stopping off to 'hang' in the small fishing towns on the coast roads. The opium had run dry. He'd started drinking heavily again. He was ignoring me a lot. I would usually get some time with him on his own in the mornings, when he was dealing with his hangovers but come the afternoon he would be off into the town or village to get stoned or pissed. He was in no hurry to get home. Then one morning, Dad woke up and looked different. He was pale, frightened. Not something I'd seen before. He'd been AWOL the previous day. He'd got into an argument with two local Arab men. That night we were in a taverna having a late plate of paella when Dad announced we were going to split up for the last leg of the journey home. I was going home with Sam. He said something about being in trouble but didn't go into any details. I was devastated at the prospect of having to separate from him. I cried all night, hoping it would change his mind. It didn't. The following morning Sam and I left in the van. Dad had left in the night. I wasn't sure if I was going to see him again.

I asked Sam over and over what had happened. At first she wouldn't say anything, other than that Dad had been in a fight. But I wore her down over the next five days of travelling with my relentless questions. One evening at dinner, after she'd had a couple of glasses of wine, she finally leaked enough information for my imagination to work with.

Dad had got drunk and had started pissing off the locals again. Two young Arab men who were well connected to a big criminal gang that ran a lot of the area took objection to the way he was flirting with the waitress at their boss's taverna. This time the locals weren't running. Dad had no weapons. Instead, he got into the car a hippy had lent him and tried to drive off. The two locals chased him and he quickly got lost in the narrow streets of the old town and stuck down a dead end alley. The Arab men were standing at the top of the alley, completely blocking his exit. He had run over them as he was trying to get out of the alley.

'It's OK,' she tried to reassure me. 'They weren't badly hurt.'

Dad needed to travel back to England alone to avoid getting arrested.

That's what he told her. It was an accident. Sam was starting to look worn out with the drama of living with Dad. She was twenty-seven years old.

Neither of the Arab gang members were OK, he told me, shortly after he got back to England. He thought he had killed at least one of them.

'I meant to scare them, but the fuckers wouldn't move out of the way. I kept reversing and revving and they just stood there, baseball bats in their hands, waiting to crack my skull open.'

I listened, rapt, half in terror, half in forbidden excitement.

'I carried on reversing and they didn't move, so I went right over them. The car bumped up so hard I whacked my head on the roof and nearly knocked myself out.'

'Were they dead?' I asked, mouth dry.

'One of them didn't get up. I saw the other one lurch up off the ground, covered in dust and blood. He staggered down the main street. Had so much blood on him I couldn't see his face.'

Why was he telling me this? It felt like he was offloading on to me to help him deal with the guilt. But he then swore me to a silence that really messed with my head.

'It's our secret, kid.'

I began to have a nasty feeling that my childhood was vanishing right in front of my eyes. I was caught between wanting to cling on to my innocence and wanting to launch myself, way too young, into what was going to be a dark, adrenaline-fuelled adulthood.

6

Back to School

Alex and I are in Clapham, hanging out, looking for something to do. We haven't got any money but I have got a tan. I look the business.

'What's that on your shoulder?' Alex is prodding me.

'That's a sunburn blister. Stop fucking poking it.' He'll like this. 'Wanna see some Moroccan sea water?'

'Go on, then.'

I take out my penknife, open the hoof pick and press it into the blister until it bulges. It swells up on one side. I give it one final push and it bursts its warm, salty liquid down my back.

Alex is impressed.

'When's the next train due?' I ask him.

'Couple of minutes. We gonna show our arses, or what?'

' 'Course we are. I've been away too long. I've got some serious catching up to do.'

We sit down in front of the railings and wait. I spot a massive rock. After a few minutes we hear the electricity running along the railway lines. The train is going to be packed with people going home from work. And I've got something extra for them.

We stand up, unzip our trousers, wait for the engine to start rolling by, then drop them. We turn around and shake our pale white arses at the passengers as they whizz past. We bend our heads down between our legs and scream.

It's a long train. Alex is still shouting when I stand and pull my trousers up.

'What are you doing, man?' he yells at me, head still between his legs. 'There's at least another five carriages to flash! You lost your bottle on your hols, or what?' He carries on screaming.

I bend down and pick up the big white rock.

'What are you doing, Cas?' Alex is worried. I know what's going to happen next and he's unsure.

Alex stands up, his trousers still around his ankles, his mouth hanging open like a soppy fish. 'What are you… ?'

The question hangs in the air as I stretch my arm right back and scream at the top of my lungs. I hurl the rock straight at the train; the last but two carriages are moving past. It smacks into the glass of the final carriage and makes a massive web of cracks and a deep dent in the centre. But it doesn't shatter. Safety glass.

'You. Fucking. Nutter! What are you doing?' Alex shouts at me.

He starts to run away from the railings, trousers half pulled up, he stumbles over some brambles, disappears for a second then springs back up, checking to see if anyone had seen his part in my mindless vandalism.

'Come on, man,' he urges me. 'We've got to get outta here, you crazy freak!'

Trousers now fully up, he sprints off across the common.

As the train slams to an emergency stop I stare with pride at the mess I've made. Smiling, I turn quickly around and run after Alex.

February 1978, London

When I got back to school, no one believed where I'd been or what I'd seen. They didn't know the half of it. I couldn't be bothered trying to convince them about the drugs and the sex and the fighting. We returned to wrecking the building site where the tramps lived. We used the dead fluorescent light strips we found as light sabres. They were everywhere. We'd added the vooming sound effects as we role-played Luke Skywalker and Darth Vadar, kicking the shit out of each other. When the time was right, one of us would proclaim the impending death of the other and the glass weapons would make contact, shatter and explode into a million silver shards. Very effective. Dead TVs made good toys, too. If you hit them hard enough with a brick, the glass would splinter, crack, implode for a silent second, then the screens would explode like mortar fire.

We wandered up and down the length of the King's Road on Saturday afternoons, squeezing the tits and arses of the best-looking women we could find. We were so young most of them just laughed at us in disbelief as we sprinted off down a side street.

With Sam in our lives and Dad's robberies and daily cons and hustles proving more and more successful, we had more money than we'd ever had. I was always getting new toys and clothes and being given bits of extra cash, but it was never enough. So I'd steal. A tenner from Sam. Forty quid out of the jacket pocket of Dad's lazy, drunken builder. The man was convinced I was the thief but he had no evidence. I hid the money in the back of one of Dad's beaten up JVC speakers and left it there till the focus was off me. I eventually dug the stolen money out and took it to the local newsagent. I got the man to change the two twenties into forty crisp, green one-pound notes; it made it feel like I had more. I went to the local arcade and won a heap of change on a fruit machine with half-naked women painted all over it. I was now loaded in notes *and* silver. I stashed the cash in my brand-new cowboy boots.

I got to school, in my own sweet time, and arranged for my mates to meet me in the playground at lunchtime. Out of sight of the windows, I got them to gather around me. I held the silence for a powerful second then slid my boot off, raised it above my head and shouted at the top of my lungs. 'Scramble!'

I scattered the notes and change across the playground, as though I was sowing seeds, and watched the kids dive down to the tarmac, scrabbling and fighting for the money. It was worth losing most of what I'd stolen for the attention.

To celebrate being back, Dad had a party, selected invites only. Kaftans were out. Flares, Cuban heels and big hair were back. It felt good, familiar, safe. For the first time in six months I knew where I was. I got to stay up till two in the morning, which is about the time I got bored of the stoners talking about what they were going to do with their lives when they 'got the money'. Most of them were on the dole and hustling for the shortfall.

Dad put on our Super 8mm film from our holiday. When that finished, he put on a porn film where a man pretended to be a chauffeur. He was picking up these pretty women and having sex with them on the back seat of his boss's Rolls Royce. It was like watching *The Benny Hill Show*, except the stars in this were fully naked. I couldn't believe it was meant to be serious. I thought he'd never be able to have that much sex with that many pretty women, not in real life. Not with that stupid moustache and a pot belly. I couldn't understand why Dad and everyone else wanted to watch it so much. I'd seen it at least three times which meant they'd seen it loads. I would hear it at night, when I was in bed. I often got confused between the sounds of sex coming from the TV and the sound of sex coming from the bedroom. Dad and his mates were always laughing and taking the piss out of the porn film, but there was something they liked about it, too. Sometimes they'd go quiet and I could see them concentrating hard on certain bits. Watching it sometimes gave me a sensation like the one I'd had when I was lying on top of Sarah at Summerhill. It felt exciting but wrong.

As Dad had threatened, I had been given some tortoiseshell National Health glasses with plastic frames. The glass was thick and I looked like a geek.

'Do you promise you'll wear them?' Sam asked me.

'Yes, I promise.'

This was now a problem because I stuck to my promises with Sam. I had grown to love her. She cared about me and looked after me. Sam kept it together like a grown up, even when she was stoned. For her sake, it was time to put my glasses on. But I was nervous I'd be laughed at.

My first lesson of the afternoon was history with the teacher who taught me most often. He was a gay man – he'd been inappropriately open with us – with a violent temper. It would flare up at the slightest trigger. Worse, if he could get away with it, he'd touch up the boys in class. When we had been on a week-long school trip he had got into the showers with us and had just stood there, right in front of us, washing himself with a half-mast hard-on, pretending that nothing was happening. I should have had him nicked. If I'd told Dad he would have done something bad to him. So maybe it was best I kept that to myself.

That afternoon he touched up one of my classmates. He told the kid he was doing a good job on the class art project. He wasn't. The kid was shit at art. He'd drawn a picture of an old circus from 1800s London.

'You are *so* clever, deary!' the teacher cooed. 'That's a lovely picture.'

The picture was dreadful, even for a ten year old. Then he slipped his hand on to the kid's inner thigh and said, 'Well done, dear, top of the class.'

I was a better artist. I wanted to be told I was being good

73

and doing well, but not if it meant I had to be touched up. The kid winced at him, trying hard to make his face smile. He was too scared to say anything about the roving hand. I could see it, gently kneading. I knew the bastard didn't like me because I was always giving him a hard time. He knew I didn't want him anywhere near me. I put out the right kind of vibes, which told him to stay well away from me. Dad told me I had to be careful about putting those kinds of vibes out. I could change a room's atmosphere in a heartbeat.

I was enjoying the lesson, but I couldn't see the board properly. I got the courage up to put on my glasses for the first time. I could definitely see better, but the teacher was in the way. I was getting frustrated. He was rubbing out what he had just written in order to chalk more on, without asking if we were ready.

'Sir, I can't see what you're writing on the board. You're in the way,' I protested.

The class went completely silent. I could feel the teacher's hackles rise but he ignored me.

'Sir, I . . .'

'Shut up and listen, Caspar. Follow what I'm saying and keep up, for God's sake.'

I often felt left behind at school and struggled with most subjects. I was worried I was going to be left even further behind in a subject I actually enjoyed. 'What's he writing?' I whispered to Alex.

The teacher spoke without turning around. 'No talking, Caspar. You've been warned.'

And he carried on writing, as though he was enjoying being an arsehole. I whispered again to Alex, who was clearly nervous about being in the firing line, and hesitant to reply. But before I could finish my whispered sentence, the teacher turned on his heel away from the blackboard, and in one motion, with his full body weight, slapped me hard across the side of the face. My glasses flew off and landed on the other side of the classroom. My cheek and the side of my head began to sting.

'I warned you,' he hissed. 'Now get out. Go and sit outside the headmaster's office.'

He was trying to act as though he was still in charge but he had lost it. He'd hit me and was panicking with the realisation of what he'd done. It gave me strength. I calmly picked up my glasses and looked at them. One lens was cracked. I walked out of the room. I carried on walking out of the school, into the playground, out on to the street. I headed for a phone box and called Dad.

'That poof bastard just slapped me across the face for no fucking reason and broke my glasses.'

Dad's voice was calm. If he hadn't been my own father it would have scared me. 'Go back and wait outside the classroom. Don't do anything, just wait. Don't speak to any of the teachers. Just sit and wait. I'll be there at 3.30.'

Holding back the tears, I returned to school and sat outside the head's office and waited. Alex was sent out of the class to speak to me.

'He wants you to come back in.'

'No. I'm not coming back in. I'm staying here. He can go fuck himself.'

Impressed, Alex gave me a high five and headed back into the classroom with my defiant message.

At the end of the school day Dad arrived on one of his bigger motorbikes, wearing full leathers. He didn't take his helmet off. He went into my classroom, my cue to move from the headmaster's office and find somewhere to watch events unfold. My mates and I huddled around a small window just outside the room, peering in with excitement. Something good was about to happen.

Dad got hold of the teacher by the shirt and slapped him

eight times across the face, in time with his words. 'Don't. Ever. Hit. My. Son. Again. Understand, you nasty little cunt?'

My teacher understood.

I earned mythical status from that incident. So did Dad.

Dad started to use Sam's place more and more as an office, somewhere convenient from which to expand his criminal network. He wanted to make as much money as possible as quickly as possible. Having a smart address in Kensington opened up lots of previously closed doors. Banks were happier to lend money. Hire purchase deals were set up and defaulted on with greater ease. He used a number of different names to get the goods and cash he was after, all from Sam's address. She seemed calm on the surface but regularly complained to him and asked him to slow down. She didn't scream or shout or chuck things around the house or at him. She confronted him in the way she was brought up, with reserve and intelligence. I would often see her talking to him in a corner somewhere or hear them in the bedroom. Dad *was* listening. She was laying down new ground rules and reminding him of ones he had forgotten about. It didn't change what he was up to but most of the time he let her speak without interruption.

Sometimes he would tone things down for a while to make her happy. But whether underground or above ground it was always business as usual with George and the various other punters and colleagues he surrounded himself with. Sam loved Dad completely and put up with a lot of shit. She was relentlessly loyal to him and gave him everything she had. But in Spain I'd noticed cracks appearing in her resolve to stand by him. By the time we returned to London she had pulled herself back into 'keeping it all together' mode, a lot of which was definitely for my benefit. But she upped her drug intake to help deal with Dad's increasingly crazy career trajectory.

One evening I was watching a Bond movie in the tiny basement TV room at the back of the house. Dr No was giving Sean Connery a hard time. During the ad break I heard a lot of footsteps outside in our cul de sac. This was unusual. I crept out of the TV room, across into the kitchen at the front of the house, and looked through the window up to the street. I saw lots of pairs of shoes passing by at eye level. All of them were black and polished and most had Blakey's, tick-tacking busily along the pavement. They stopped at the bottom of the steps that led to our front door. I scuttled back into the TV room. I heard Dad shout something at Sam, something else at George, then a loud knocking on the front door.

'Frank Walsh, we have a warrant for your arrest. And a search warrant for this address. Open the door.'

I turned up the telly and moved closer to the screen. The knocking increased in volume. I could hear Dad and George running backwards and forwards upstairs. The cistern was flushed. The window above the TV room snapped open and I stuck my head out to see what was happening. Dad's skinny arm shot out and hurled several white packets and plastic bags across the darkening sky. They flew over the back wall and into the shopping precinct our house adjoined. The knocking turned from banging to hammering. I could hear several different male voices shouting for us to open up.

The grown ups were feverishly evacuating anything that was incriminating. The thumping footsteps of Dad and George were panicked and fast. The hammering and shouting outside sped up, too, in line with the frenetic activity going on above my head. The police were now hitting the front door with something heavier than boots and fists. I looked out of the TV room window again and watched more objects flying out: drugs, small hand-held weapons including Moroccan daggers and coshes, a bundle of money. The only thing Dad couldn't chuck was his crossbow, but the arrows made it. For me, it was as though the Bond film had jumped out of the telly and was in my house. But we were the bad guys. I was scared. And I was loving every second of it.

No one was paying any attention to me so I ran from the basement to the upstairs bedroom and looked out of it on to the drama unfolding below. It was a spectacular view. There were about twelve policemen in uniform and a couple in plain-clothes. Two of them were holding a small, well-worn, silver battering ram and were whacking it into the centre of our wooden front door. They were having a lot of difficulty making headway. Dad had reinforced the door with steel plates and the frame with bolt locks just after we'd got back from Morocco. He'd known this was coming. The police kept running at the door and bashing it and the ram kept bouncing back off. Most of the time they were out of sync and ended up in a heap against the door. I was seriously enjoying myself. Finally a big fucker from the back shouted at his colleagues to move out of the way. He lifted a big sledgehammer above his head, took a few paces back and ran at the door. He hit the solid wooden frame above the door. The sledge reeled back and tipped him over on to his mates behind. Five of them rolled back down the stairs and landed in the street.

'Are you the Sweeny?' I shouted down at them, laughing.

The house was clear, so Dad opened the door. He smiled at the mess of police in the street. 'Good evening, gentlemen,' he said in a mock posh voice. 'I trust one of you bright fuckers really does have a warrant?'

They piled into the house, turned it upside down. They even searched my swimming flippers. Sam was sitting alone on her sofa struggling to stay calm while they turned her smart townhouse into something that resembled a south London squat. This was my first bust, too. Apart from the state they left my room in, and the toys they smashed in their desperation to find something incriminating, I'd enjoyed it. Dad and George were used to it. Without any objection, they sat down and watched the police go about their work. They didn't find a thing in the house. The money from the safe robbery had already been spent. Everything else was lying in a roof recess above the sleeping shopping precinct. Dad would get it all back later.

St Christopher's School

I left my primary school when I was ten. I passed my 11+, just. I was surprised. I turned eleven in the summer holidays and when the new school year came around started at my second boarding school, St Christopher's in Hertfordshire. It was a vegetarian Quaker school with forward-thinking teachers and a few wild kids. I counted myself among them.

On my first night I was homesick to the stomach. I was in a dorm with five other kids, sharing a bunk with a boy called Leon. He'd been at the school for a while and knew the ropes. He could hear me crying. From his top bunk he leaned down and handed me a bag of sweets. The sugar eased the sadness and we talked into the night, the first of many. We ended up sharing a double room and it was there, at night, that I started to tell him about the darker stuff going on at home. I was crossing a family line of secrecy and it felt good. It was a big relief to be talking about it to someone outside of the family circle. I was getting older and my need to talk about my confused feelings was getting stronger.

School life at St Chris's was good and got better by the day. I was in the lush countryside at term time and in London during the holidays. Two different kinds of playgrounds with equal scope for wrecking, stealing and exploring. A pick 'n' mix of concrete and green. I made more friends and got my first girlfriend. I was starting to enjoy learning. I was told I had a good imagination. I could write stories. Finally, I felt I had found something I was good at.

Home life, on the other hand, was deteriorating rapidly. Since the raid, Dad was playing it safe and money was running out and becoming harder to find. Sam and Dad's arguing was becoming more regular and more frightening. Dad's streak of bad boy good luck was coming to an end. As he became more skint he became more desperate. As he became more desperate he also became more creative about finding ways to rob, burgle and hustle. He started to dress up in convincing disguises, using beards, hats, glasses and limps to 'kite' shops with stolen chequebooks for clothes and food and jewellery. He 'purchased' a fleet of American limousines in a crazy attempt to start up England's first ever US-style limo hire. His inspiration was twenty-five years too early and he was too stoned to be bothered with the details necessary to make it work. The business collapsed within a matter of months. He had burgled the stately home of a girl he was having an affair with. The massive haul of antiques was worth a fortune but he was unable to find any buyers.

It was a catalogue of disasters but despite it all he still had the look of success about him. He was always well-groomed, clean shaven with freshly washed hair, smart suits, Italian shoes and always a small amount of eighteen-carat gold jewellery, usually antique. And despite the lack of cash, we'd moved into a bigger house near Earl's Court. It was four times the size of Sam's place. The wooden-floored hallways were so long I could skateboard up and down them with ease and speed. This posh mansion-block flat was way too expensive for Dad and Sam's combined budget. They struggled to keep up the payments from the moment we moved in.

Our new house had a monster lurking in the basement. He was patiently waiting for an opportunity to meet me.

7

Breaking and Entering

Summer 1979, Kensington, London

'Why have you got two big guns in the bedroom, Dad?'

'Some arseholes think I've done them out of their share of the robbery I did last month. Wankers. I hardly got fuck all. They're for protection, for all of us.'

His answer makes my stomach flip and my balls retract. Dad's had weapons before, but I've never seen guns this big. 'Are they loaded?' I gawp at the massive handgun and the pump action shotgun.

'Sure. Always keep them loaded, always keep the safety on.'

He shows them to me like they're rare antiques. They're anything but. They gleam and sparkle and fill me with nervous excitement. 'You can look, but no touching. Understand?'

I nod without taking my eyes off them. The handgun has a chrome barrel and a brown handle. It fits into his hand perfectly. He likes looking at it. He turns it over and looks at each side. The sun through the window bounces off it and hits my eyes. The shotgun has a jet black barrel and a dark brown stock. It looks way too heavy to run around with.

'Have you got extra bullets?' I ask.

'In the garage. You're not to touch them.'

I'm gonna touch them as soon as Dad is out.

'Are you going to use them, Dad?'

'Not if I can help it. Fire off a round into something solid then hold it to their forehead and tell 'em to run off and hide. Usually does the trick.'

If they fucked me around, I'd shoot their kneecaps off, I think.

He stands in front of the mirror and draws the handgun from its holster like a movie gangster. I don't know if he's being funny or serious. I'm excited about the guns. They make me feel safe.

As soon as Dad and Sam were out I snuck into their room and checked the guns out properly. The big handgun was sitting on the shelf. It was amazing to see close up and for real what I'd only previously seen in the movies. I touched it and held it out in front of me, like Dad had. I clasped it with both hands, just like in Morocco with the cap gun, just like Dad in the mirror. I tried out several different styles of holding, ducking down, leaning tight against the door frame, kneeling, and using the big double bed as cover. I ran my finger across the silver barrel. The safety catch was on. I wanted to fire it. But I put it back, like it was a precious stone.

I could hardly lift the shotgun. Its weight scared me. My heart started to beat faster. If I couldn't lift it properly it would properly fuck me up if I fired it, I thought. I'd seen in *The Good, the Bad and the Ugly* that there's a kick to the bigger guns, and that they could chuck you across the other side of the room if you weren't big enough to stand your ground. I wasn't. Not yet.

I heard keys in the front door and nearly dropped the gun in fright. I put it gently back against the cupboard door, exactly where I'd found it, took my shoes off and ran silently down to my bedroom. My heart was beating madly from the feeling of power I'd got from holding Dad's weapons. I wanted to touch them again.

Dad was clearly in trouble. I could see it was starting to wear him down. He had gone to the nastier side of west London in his search for work. He was dealing with heavy, dangerous people. He always said everything would be OK, that he could 'manage any fucker' with his intelligent, dishonest charm. But I was no longer sure. He had a positive attitude towards danger. He thrived on it. These people, however, didn't care too much for charm, and even less for smart mid-level, well-dressed crooks like my dad.

They had set the job up for him. It was, as ever, meant to be a straightforward robbery of a house thought to hold a lot of cash. Dad went alone. There wasn't anywhere near the amount of money he was told would be there. His employers didn't believe Dad when he told them. They wanted their cut from a stash that didn't exist.

Up to this point he believed he was invincible. He had got away with crimes for most of his adult life, by a sharpness of intelligence and the skin of his teeth. I'd grown up seeing him take whatever he wanted from whoever, and whenever he wanted it. No one stopped him. But there was now a clear feeling in the house that the monsters of law and disorder were closing in. He was trying to be upbeat but I could see he was scared. He looked like someone being hunted. And he was. We both were. His ten-year crime spree, doing whatever he liked, forever evading arrest, was soon to be over.

I had just turned twelve. At 4 a.m. on a summer's morning I woke to the shocking sound of another battering ram hammering our front door. I sat up in bed in the darkness, and looked up the hallway, waiting for someone to appear. I was terrified and I couldn't move.

The ramming continued like a bass drum. I felt a crackle as the hairs on the back of my neck rose. My legs were shaking. I thought I was going to piss myself. I squeezed hard and the urge to piss passed. It took a lot of courage to get out of bed.

Whoever it was had finally managed to destroy the door. There was a moment of silence then an explosion of shouted instructions, running, heavy-booted feet and the slamming and opening of doors. I made out the words, 'Stop. Don't fucking move,' from the other end of the house.

I crept cautiously up the hallway and saw a mass of uniformed and plain-clothes policemen and women running with clear, sharp intention in and out of our rooms. Most of the men were fat bastards, too big to run properly, so they lumbered from room to room. In the dawn light coming through our dirty windows I saw one of them bump into the hall wall. He called the wall a cunt.

Everyone seemed to be ignoring me. I felt invisible. Two of them eventually saw me. I tried to run in between them, going for the gap. I had a purpose. I was looking for Dad. I had no idea where he was. I wanted the big handgun to protect him. I could run with that in my hand. I wanted to shoot the bastards for busting into our house in the middle of the night, when I was tucked up in bed.

I heard the crash of breaking glass on the patio. Then a high-pitched scream, like the one he made when I shot him in Morocco. It was him. It was Dad. It stopped me long enough for a policewoman to grab me by the floppy collar of my pyjamas.

'*Dad!*'

'Don't you worry, sunshine. We've got your dad safe and sound.'

I was completely distressed and shaking from top to toe. I could just about make out her face in the dark. She was wearing a uniform and she was pretty, same kind of hair as Sam.

I was struggling furiously to get away from her and I almost managed it.

'Come here, you. Everything's going to be all right.'

But it wasn't. I knew that. There were far too many of them. I wasn't going anywhere. I gave up. She took my hand gently and led me up the hallway away from the darkness of my bedroom and into the bright light of the entrance hall. The front door was wrecked. Even though I wanted to kick her shins I felt safe with her. Safer than I'd felt for a while. There were police all over the house. One of them found bullets in the big empty room we never really used. Dad was using it for firing practice. They didn't find the guns. They *did* find drugs, wads of money and the haul of antiques that clearly couldn't fit comfortably, even into our large flat.

I heard car doors shutting outside, and Dad was gone.

He managed to get released on bail. The one condition being that he sign on at the local police station until his court appearance. This was bad news for him, humiliating even. Buying the bail privilege of staying at home had cost him the last of our money. Sam was more and more in charge of what was going on at our poorly furbished mansion flat. I could feel she wanted to get out of the relationship with Dad but her loyalty to him was still there, and she was well into the role of mother to me. She wasn't going anywhere.

Dad had to sign on twice a day. Once in the morning, once in the evening. I went with him as often as I could. He liked the company and I liked seeing the inside of Kensington police station. It was exciting. The lights were always too bright and part of the unnerving effect. I never saw what went on out back, only the reception desk. That was where the cells were, where they held Dad for two days and nights before he went for his court hearing.

Sometimes I heard crazy drunks or hookers pleading to get out, promising to be good if they could just have one fag. The policemen on the other side of the desk got to know me. I was a bit scared and wary, but I liked them. Though for Dad's sake, I agreed with him that they were arseholes. He would spend most of our return walks slagging them off, or anyone he thought had power over him. They all did.

Much to Sam's objection, Dad decided he would rather we all leave England than deal with the situation head on. He was still refusing to speak to the West End gangsters who thought he owed them money and there was no way he was going to let himself get locked up for a few small bags of smack and a haul of antiques.

Dad had always had a dream of living on a white-sand beach with palm trees for shade. And at last it was confirmed: we were heading for paradise. A new life in Mauritius. I'd never even heard of the place. It took me ages to find it in my atlas. I was going to be away from my mates, from London, probably forever. I didn't like the sound of it one bit, no matter how good the pictures looked or how much Dad bigged it up.

Being on bail meant we wouldn't be able to get through customs. We needed new identities. It wasn't safe to buy passports. We had to find new names for ourselves. Dad's use of disguises was about to come in handy. Like he told me, he got some of his best ideas from the movies. In *The Day of the Jackal*, Edward Fox's character assumed new identities by finding names on tombstones of boys who died around the time he was born. He would get the birth certificates from the registry office. With the certificate he got a new passport. This was Dad's plan and it worked. We walked through Brompton Cemetery for the best part of a week and we each found the grave and headstone of three very young children.

'Right, kid. You've got to learn his name, name of his father, where he was born. It has to be second nature. No umming and ahhing if anyone asks you.'

The dead kid's name was Edward. I wasn't even a teenager and was getting ready to leave England under a new identity. Part of me felt like some kind of James Bond character and part of me was scared and didn't want to leave. The whole thing felt bad.

Dad was going ahead of us to set up a place for us to live. It was better that we travelled separately. He would be breaking bail and it was likely that within a few hours of him not turning up at the police station, the police would bust our house again. They would be looking for a family of three. Airports would be the obvious place to start.

Dad's new name was Nigel. He made himself look like a geek – bad hair and stupid glasses. That night, he came to my bedroom to tuck me in and say goodbye. I wasn't going to see him for at least three months. I cried myself to sleep.

I got up the next morning and he was gone. I got into bed with Sam and cried some more. She hugged me. She didn't say anything for ages. Something was wrong.

'Cas.' She was building up to telling me something I didn't want to hear. 'Dad's gone.' She paused, struggling to get the words out. 'He didn't get on the plane.'

I felt a rush of heat go up my back. I thought I was going to throw up.

'He's been arrested. They came early this morning.' She rubbed her forehead. 'Someone knew we were going.' She lit a cigarette, working out what to say. 'I'm kind of relieved. I'm really, really sorry about this, Cas. You shouldn't have to go through any of this at your age.'

I was relieved as well. Not about Dad being nicked, but that we were staying in England. Running away to Mauritius sounded exotic and exciting, but I wanted to stay in London.

Dad was still in the same country and it would be a lot less than three months before I saw him again. That had to be a good thing.

The police had been tipped off that we were leaving. God knows how anyone found out to grass us, but they did. At least I knew it was no fault of mine. The Met had come round in the middle of the night to arrest him for intent to break bail. They found the aeroplane tickets and the new passports. He heard them coming up the stairs at three in the morning and before they could ring the bell or destroy the newly fixed front door he let them in. He didn't want to put me through the trauma of another battering ram.

For my sake, he went quietly.

8

The Basement

Me and Sam have taken the bus all the way from Kensington. We haven't got a car any more. I've been awake since seven. Way too early for me. The adrenaline of seeing Dad got me out of bed. But we're late. At last, the heavy wooden door is opening for us. It's like the door to a castle. Just like the one in Porridge.

We go through and stand in front a thick reception window. It's scratched and a bit fucked. Sam hands in our visiting order to a guard. It's like having one of Willy Wonker's golden tickets. He checks her ID, looks at me for too long, then shouts 'Next!' He sounds bored.

There are other kids here and we check each other out. Not in a friendly way. One of them looks tough and dangerous. He's younger than me but he's got crazy eyes. I reckon he could have me easily. Everyone is smoking. All the mums look stressed. Sam is nervous, but she's doing a good job hiding it.

We go through the first air-powered door. A group of us huddle in the small holding space. The door hisses and slides shut behind us. A second door slides open. We walk through into a room with no windows. It smells: old fags, body odour and disinfectant. The chemicals can't hide the stench and it makes me feel sick.

They search Sam's bags and move us on. Most of the prison officers are pretty fucking rude. We head through two more rooms and then into an open courtyard. The cold air feels good in my lungs. There are big puddles in the uneven tarmac and I kick them as we go, splashing water everywhere. I can just see the white and blue sky boxed in by the massive walls. We carry on towards the visiting hall. There are screws with us all the way. My heart beats faster. We're at the front, but the mums and other kids catch up with us at each door before it gets unlocked. The wild kid is right behind me. He sticks something in my back.

'Stick 'em up,' he snarls.

I'm scared. I should raise my hands to avoid getting into a fight and they're almost in the air when I turn around and grab the little bastard by the throat and press my thumbs into his Adam's apple. His legs buckle and his face quickly goes purple. His eyes bulge and the craziness vanishes from them. They're now pleading with me to stop.

'Caspar! Hurry up, for God's sake. Stop spacing out. We don't want to be any later than we already are.'

Sam is just ahead of me and the kid is staring at me. My hands haven't moved.

Early Summer, 1980

The visiting hall was huge. There were iron bars painted white on all the windows and a tuck shop at the far end, with a tired woman at the counter. The room smelled the same as all the others in the prison. Most people lit up fags. It helped. The place was worn and old and needed redecorating.

There were prison officers at both ends of the hall and one standing by the back wall. He was straight: stiff and uptight. The other two were seated behind a desk, checking people through. Prisoners came in groups of three and four, picked up from different wings in dribs and drabs.

We were the last into the room. Waiting for Dad was like waiting for Christmas. The longer it was before he got to us, the shorter the visit would be, and the visits were only between one and two hours. It was way too short a time for the hassle of receiving a visiting order (VO), getting to the prison and going through all the gates, doors and searches. I became panicky. I wanted as much of him as I could get.

We waited.

When he finally turned the corner into the courtyard he looked incredible. I ran up to the windows and pressed my face against the cold bars. He saw me immediately and beamed a massive movie star grin. He had colour in his cheeks and a tan on his skin. His stride was confident. He looked at home in that shit hole. His panache shone through his blue and white striped prison shirt, bright blue jeans and black mock-leather work boots. He had a way of making the worst outfit look good and the worst situation seem easy. It wasn't.

He disappeared from sight while they searched him in a holding room, then at last he came through the visiting hall door. As far as I was concerned, this moment happened in slow motion. He swaggered over to us, gave me a big hug and planted a long kiss on Sam's lips. She flushed.

'Hi, gorgeous. You look fantastic.' He squeezed her leg then looked straight at me. 'Hey, kid. How's tricks?'

I'd missed him so badly I wanted to cry but crying was off the cards in there. 'Where have you been? We've been waiting ages,' I accused.

'One very good reason. Sick bastard. Six screws were escorting the Yorkshire Ripper to the Muppet wing. You know, that guy, Peter Sutcliffe.' I nodded, wide eyed. 'He was kicking and screaming, saying his new mission in life, direct from God, was to kill all screws. Took four of them to hold him down. I was two feet from the crazy freak.'

He showed me the distance with his hands. I'd seen the Ripper on the telly lots of times. I knew what he looked like and I could see him now in my head. He was in the same building as me; a few hundred yards away. I was quietly shitting myself.

'Don't be scared, kid. I won't let him anywhere near you.' Big daddy Frank. Dad smiled at me and ruffled my hair, his attention shifting back to Sam as I moved from fear to frustration that the Yorkshire Ripper was the reason he was late.

'Let's get the worst bit over then, babe.' Dad smiled at Sam. She looked uncomfortable.

'If you get caught I'll be arrested. I don't like this one bit,' she said anxiously.

He wasn't listening. 'Is it in your mouth?'

Dad looked over her shoulder to the two prison officers at the desk. They were busy dealing with a mum and her crying kid but the uptight fucker behind us was watching Dad like a hawk.

A few seconds later the wild kid ran out from under a table and did a commando roll across the yellow lino floor. Rather him than me, it looked filthy. But his timing couldn't have been better. The hawk flicked his eyes on to the boy and scrutinised him for a long moment.

Dad quietly told Sam to lean over to him. She obliged and they started kissing. I hated watching them. The boy was back in his seat and got a clip round the ear for his trouble. I saw Dad struggle to swallow something.

'What is it?' he asked her, pulling away from the embrace.

'Coke. Three grams. Frank, this is crazy. I've had enough of this.'

'I asked for brown,' he complained. 'What am I going to do with coke in here, babe?'

'It was all I could get. We're out of money. No one will

sell to me at the moment. I don't want to do this again. I'm no good at it.'

'Nonsense, you're very good at it and you know it.' Dad calmed her down. 'Guess I'll manage to sell it. It'll get me decent food and some tobacco, at least.' He looked at me. 'So, sunshine, how's tricks? Got any girlfriends yet?'

After seeing that kiss, I couldn't think of anything I wanted less.

While Dad and Sam talked I checked out the other prisoners and their families. I'd watched a scene just like this on the telly. I could hardly believe I was living it. I was in a room full of criminals and a lot of them looked dangerous. This was clearly the point. Everyone was posturing, even Dad. He was putting on his own special show – the swagger and the casual leaning back on his black plastic chair – for the other prisoners, the screws and for me and Sam, letting us all know how well he was coping with his waking nightmare.

Being with Dad was over too fast. Leaving was very difficult. I tried to be big and hold back the tears, but couldn't manage it, nor could Sam. I could see he was upset as well. He held me tight for longer than was comfortable in a room full of heavy geezers and their jailers.

'I'll write soon, kid, send you another VO. You write me first, though, tell me about your girlfriend. I know you've got one. I'll give you some tips.'

Our goodbye was making him shake visibly. I hadn't seen him like that since Granddad died.

I no longer had my father to protect me from the world. I had some good, supportive mates who thought the prison scene was exciting and cool and wanted to know all about it. But they kept their mouths shut at school. This was important to me. It was our secret.

We hung out mainly on the streets of Kensington and

Chelsea. Climbing high scaffolding to eat our takeaway burgers and shakes, we watched the streets below and chucked chips at pedestrians. London looked beautiful from up there but we continued to wreck it on a regular basis. Schools at weekends were the easiest option. It was one good way to release some of the fear and tension and anger. I loved smashing things up, especially if they meant something to someone.

Sam was out of the house most of the time earning just enough money to stop the flat being taken off us. She warned me that men – bailiffs, I hadn't heard the word before – might come round to take the furniture. They did. Whether a bailiff, a copper or a prison officer, most of them had this hard attitude they brought with them. It was a cover up. They were making out they didn't give a shit about how difficult their job was or that what they were doing to other people's lives wasn't despicable. But every once in a while I got a flicker of humanity out of them.

'Why are you taking my telly, Mister? Do you take other kid's tellys? Do you, Mister? Do you still watch cartoons? Which ones do you like? *Mister Ben? The Clangers?'*

They didn't know how to deal with my rapid, innocent questions. They often faltered in the middle of their 'heavy geezer doing a job' routine, trying not to look me in the eye as they hauled more stuff out of our flat. I'd follow them out into the street, hassling them with more and more questions until they cracked.

'Look, son, I'm just doing my job. It's nothing personal. I don't even know you or your mum. My kids like *The Clangers* best. I watch it with them when I get home. If it was my choice, I'd let you keep your stuff, but I got to earn a living, see? Nothing personal.'

Like I said, some of them did give a shit. However tough they looked.

Just about everyone we knew who used to come round and see us at the big flat disappeared after Dad was sent to prison. We'd expected George to disappear; he was protecting business interests and needed to go into hiding. But there were others who used to come round a lot to get stoned and hang out. They'd been good to me. They'd taken me out, played with me, bought me presents. All of them vanished in a puff of smack smoke. The house was full of their ghosts, their voices and their jokes. I wanted them back. It was now a big, empty, cold flat. Sam and I barely made an impact in the huge rooms. I was too scared to go into some of the ones that were less used. Especially the one Dad had been nicked in.

I was getting lonely and bored. After so many months of Dad being inside the pain of not having him around to protect me was becoming unbearable. I had to do something, find someone, to fill Dad's empty space. I began looking close to home for a grown up man I could trust, someone to keep an eye out for me, someone to carry on teaching me how to survive in my twisted, dangerous world. I was heading towards the end of the summer holidays. I had mixed feelings about going back to school. I dreaded all lessons bar English and History. I was looking forward to seeing Leon and my new girlfriend Jacky in a few weeks. In the meantime I had found a new friend – a man old enough to be my dad. He was the house porter and he lived in the basement. He seemed to be the answer to my missing dad problem.

I hassled him with all kinds of questions when he was cleaning the block. His two dogs, Hoppy and Boot, were usually near by. Their names came from one having a busted leg when the porter got him and the other was found as a puppy in a Doctor Marten boot in a skip. All three of them quickly became my friends.

After a few days of me hanging around, the porter offered to cook my tea. I thought he meant a cup of tea and a slice of cake. I was surprised when he dished up a huge plate of steaming hot food at 5p.m.; I usually ate at seven. Compared to Sam's cooking it was dreadful: overdone cabbage and boiled-to-death gammon. It was rough and cheap but it had been cooked for me and that made it taste good.

To begin with the friendship had Sam's seal of approval. The following weekend I was allowed down to see him to watch Saturday night telly. He had bought me four cans of Tizer. After I'd finished the second, he asked me if I wanted some vodka in it. I was twelve years old. It was obvious to me he was trying to get me drunk. My internal radar sent me my first warning. The apparent innocence of our friendship was slowly cracking open and revealing something darker. It was a distant sense of danger. I began to feel there was something a bit dodgy about this man, a bit like the feeling I got around the violent gay teacher at school. The feeling didn't match up with the way the porter was with me, always kind, gentle and attentive. The subtle warnings kept buzzing inside me but I ignored them. They were interfering with the attention I was getting.

'I don't think so. Sam will kill me.'

'She doesn't have to know.'

I nodded at him. This was very cool. I watched him pour the cheap vodka steadily into the can. Mixed with the sweet taste of Tizer it went down easily. I soon found myself properly pissed for the first time in my life. I just about managed to get back up the stairs into my flat. Sam eyed me suspiciously as I headed quickly to bed.

'What's wrong with you, Cas?'

'I'm tired. I want to go to bed.'

'Well that's a first.' She kissed me goodnight.

I think she knew I was lying about being drunk but she

seemed too worn out to get into it. She was working up to fifteen hours a day and still getting a little stoned in the evenings. The stress of what had happened to us, of bringing me up alone was wearing her down, I could see that clearly and I used it to my advantage.

I went to my room and slumped on the bed. The ceiling light swirled above my head and I stared at it. I put on some Pink Floyd, which only made the spinning more intense and my inebriation worse. I turned the music up. I was happy I had another grown up to show me the ways of the world. I was filled with fear and excitement.

I was seeing Mum fairly regularly. She lived around the corner from us in the same basement flat in which she had chosen Jack over me. She was still with him, on and off, but he was rarely there. My sister, Eliza, was born in 1980. She was Mum's third child from as many men. I was happy to have a new sister and I often went round for dinner after school to see her and my half-brother, Paul. We would eat and talk and watch telly – a bit like a normal family. The three of us shared the same sense of humour and we laughed a lot together.

Mum had a foul temper. When she was in a black mood Paul and I kept our heads down. But however angry she got I would still want to stay the night. I wanted to be near her. In Dad's absence she was an important presence. After we went to bed, Paul and I always stayed awake late, talking and telling each other dirty jokes and ghost stories.

Mum was often drunk, stoned or both, but she never failed to cook fantastic meals for us. The food was so good I could eat two plates of it, no problem, even if Sam had already fed me. Being in the warmth and taking in the smells of Mum's basement flat brought back better memories from when I was younger. It smelled like home. There were cushions, throws and candles everywhere. The lights glowed warm orange and yellow. My fantasy version of this perfect home smoothed the rougher reality of what was going on in the rest of my life. It was convenient for me to ignore how chaotic Mum's life really was.

My visits to the porter's much darker basement flat became more regular. Sam was clearly no longer that happy about it but I was off the streets, most of the time, and that was something to be grateful for. At least I wasn't smashing anything up or nicking stuff. I could see she was getting suspicious about my visits to him. I reckon we both hoped that maybe everything would be all right.

My education continued. The porter started showing me art books he'd stolen from libraries. The focus of each was the artist's depiction of sex through history: Neolithic cave paintings, Michelangelo, Raphael, Da Vinci, Rubens, Renoir, Gauguin, Warhol, Bacon, *Penthouse*, *Men Only*, *Readers' Wives*. The progression was calculated and slow. He made it seem like academic education. It wasn't. It was clearly my sex education he was interested in. I knew what he was up to now. But I got to learn about artists I'd never heard of. He showed me a lot of attention. It was what I was used to from Dad, and I wanted it. I continued to ignore the danger signs, it seemed worth it.

Puberty was driving my hormones insane. With his books, magazines and constant talk of sex the porter groomed me into a frenzied state of arousal. At that point I would have had sex with just about anything that moved. He said he understood what it was like to lose a dad. He told me he'd lost his. I believed him. He gave me booze, cooked me food and constantly chatted about loose women and masturbation. He told me how to get the best out of a wank – no adult had ever given me such detailed instruction on sex before, not even Dad. These were things only me and my mates had talked about. Most of us pretended to know what sex was about. The truth was none of us really did. Not at twelve years old. I'd struck an information goldmine in that dingy basement flat.

The porter was thirty years older than me. He had answers to questions beyond my imagination. I didn't tell any of my mates about him. Part of me wanted this oracle to myself. Part of me was ashamed at knowing full well what his ulterior motive was. I knew this man expected payment in return for his tutorial. I was the fee and my time to pay up was getting closer. I put it off for as long as I could.

The time came during the Olympics. Sharon Davies was swimming for England. I loved swimming. I had a major crush on her. She was gorgeous. The porter could see this and suggested I write her a letter. I did, but I didn't get a reply. I was very pissed off and, sexually, very wound up.

'How's the wanking coming along? Still obsessing about Sharon?' he asked me one afternoon. He was very matter of fact about it.

'About five times a day.' I wasn't embarrassed to talk about it.

'You should ease up a bit, son. Spread 'em out. It makes it better when you do. And when you do get round to it, don't always ejaculate.'

'I can't help it. One look at one of those books and it's all over.'

'Use your mind. Close your eyes and think about it as pictures in your mind.' He gave me a smile.

'I'm good at that, making up pictures in my head.' I knew where this was going.

'Come round tonight and I'll show you how. Best to be taught by a man of experience.' He smiled again, no hint of shame.

I was shocked and scared by the invitation but didn't show it. I wanted to learn what to do, but not like this. What else was on offer? He'd been kind to me, looked after me, stood in for Dad. It was impossible to say no.

I've learned stuff from him. A lot, actually. And people usually want something in return for information. Seems reasonable. He wants to talk me through it as I'm doing it. That's what he wants. I know it. He wants to watch me. I'll ask him to keep the lights off. If he touches me I'll kick him in the bollocks. Who would I tell if he touched me? Sam would kill me. She'd call the police. I don't want any more of those fuckers in our house. If only he was a woman. If only it was Sharon. Maybe what he wants to teach me will help me. Maybe he'll help me get Jacky into bed. I want to have sex with Jacky. Christ, I'd like to have sex – full stop. This is doing my head in. I can't go on wanking and never having sex for the rest of my life. I'll go blind. That's what they say, isn't it?

I went round to the porter's flat that evening and stayed late. We watched telly and didn't need to say much to each other. He asked me if I wanted to go to his bedroom. It was dark in there. He worked on me in the shadows. He worked on me with his voice and his lies and his ceaseless encouragement. Was this the kind of dad I wanted? Was this the kind of education I needed? He told me I was a natural. I wanted to please him. I knew how to do that. I followed his instructions in how to hold him, how fast, how slow, when to change rhythm. The smell of acrid sweat and semen made me want to retch but I held it down, I breathed deep to control the panic that was screaming at me to run out of the room and back to my house. I wasn't going to run. I didn't want to piss him off, he was a lot bigger than me and underneath all the smiles and generosity I could tell he had a bad temper. I switched something off inside me to deal with the blackness of the feelings that surfaced inside me in that room. These feelings also excited me. I was confused by my adrenaline and my human arousal. I switched on a part of my sexuality that should have stayed powered down for at least another three years. I had stepped out of childhood into a dark, seedy adult world that was so on the cards for me I thought I may as well get it over with and get on with it. I was getting undivided attention from an adult, and that was what mattered, even if it was all about sex.

I didn't sleep that night.

The following weekend he and I drove to Clapham Common. He was now teaching me more than I wanted to know but I found it hard to stop it. I liked the attention. I just didn't like the feelings that followed. I felt sick and ashamed. I found it hard to look my mates in the eye.

The porter asked me to go to Wales with him. Sam didn't want me to go at first. She was dead set against the idea. Then, at the last minute, out of the blue, she said it was OK. I was baffled by this at the time. I wanted to ask what had changed her mind but I didn't. I think it was some kind of denial that kicked in, a disbelief and casting off of the crazy idea that a grown man would want to have sex with a boy, with her stepson. I will never really know why she said yes, but at the time I was glad she did. I was going on an adventure.

Going to Wales, I knew, would take it to the next level. But I was prepared to do anything I could to hold on to this man's attention, however much the sexual side of our relationship repulsed me. I craved attention. Sam was too busy working and Dad wasn't around.

I offered to do what I thought the porter wanted. The caravan was damp and it leaked. It rained all weekend. Boot nearly drowned in an old drainage pipe. I saved his life. I fished at midnight by a moonlit river. I found a Civil War musket barrel. We ate a chicken that must've been older than I was. I wasn't physically capable of doing what he wanted to do. He stopped trying, saying it was no use. But I didn't want him to think I was a failure, so I gave him encouragement.

The harsh, full moon shone through the net curtain of the caravan bedroom window. The space was lit with a cold, natural blue light. It didn't feel like I was in the real world. I wasn't. It was like having some kind of putrid, sweating animal on me. Everything inside me said this was wrong. I didn't want it. But there was something about having this man on me, twice my weight and twice my height, that was necessary. Unwanted, sickening, painful and terrifying, but necessary. It was about giving in to the inevitable. My gut reactions were telling me to get the fuck out; my mind was telling me this was something I simply had to endure. *Get on with it, Cas. No choice here, mate.* The sooner I shut myself down and accepted what was happening to me the sooner the pain of everything would ease up and I would be able to forget about what I had lost: safety, security, home, childhood, innocence.

I was so out of my depth I was drowning in the shame and confusion of it. I had no idea how to navigate through this kind of murky water. The initial pleasure of attention and learning from this man had turned into a shimmering fear so constant it was becoming normal.

I returned to St Christopher's after the summer holiday was over. I was very sad to say goodbye to Sam. She could see it and she looked like she was struggling with it, too. Now Dad was out of the parental frame she was doing her best to get clean from drugs and alcohol in order to create a skeleton of structure in our lives. I watched her black VW Golf drive slowly away until it disappeared behind a line of poplars.

People at the school – staff and friends – were concerned

by the shift in my personality since the previous term. I spoke to Leon about Dad. He helped. He listened to me and I chose to trust him. A good choice. But I said nothing about the basement monster.

As the term progressed and I spent more and more time around kids my own age I started to realise that I had been properly worked on by the porter. I had been manipulated by a grown up I had trusted. Rage started to build inside me. The rage made me someone you really didn't want to fuck around with. I started getting into pointless fights with kids too big for me to handle. But when I started fighting there was very little that could stop me trying to pound some poor bastard's face in, however big he was. I even enjoyed the prospect of getting a kicking sometimes. The more pain, the better. The big sports teacher was usually the only one to stop me. He would hold me back until I ran out of anger.

I was well on the way to getting kicked out of school again. This kind of violence was a part of me that previously hadn't existed outside of my imagination. I knew it was something to be scared of. The mad stare I'd cultivated at Summerhill by way of warning, with little intention of backing it up with violence, had now become something to worry about. The kids at the school had seen where I could go with it. When they backed off from the fight I was happy and relieved I didn't have to go into a psychotic rage again. I didn't want to have to muster the energy to try and stop something that powerful. But when they wanted to fight, I was ready. I felt murderous, dangerous and out of control.

9

Secrets

Autumn 1980, London to Blundeston

London Underground. My journey starts at Gloucester Road. Outside, she's there. The old, grey-haired lady who sells the Evening Standard. *She's always there. All year round in the finger-numbing frost, the pissing rain, burning sunshine, raging wind. Always there. It's like having some kind of remote grandma. She never looks at me but she knows I exist. She's just getting on with her job.*

She doesn't sell comics, so I head into the station shop. Not the Dandy, *that's for poofs. The* Beano, Whizzer and Chips *and* Mad *magazine: my comics of choice. Sam sends me* Mad *in the post to St Christopher's, that and a fiver or a tenner for sweets. I'm a bit old for comics but I still like them. Fuck what anyone else thinks. I've been reading them for years and they make me feel better. They ease my nerves. I like the pictures. The kids in the pages don't seem to be having too bad a time of it. They have it easy and I like to see that. Something to aspire to.*

This is my first trip alone to see Dad. I've got money in my pocket. Enough for food, comics, Tizer, sweets and some Old

Holborn, Rizla and matches for Dad. He's started letting me roll them for him.

I love staring at people on the tube. Especially the pretty girls. People are smoking. I want a fag but I'm not going to light up. Someone will grass on me or give me another fucking lecture. I open up Whizzer and Chips and get stuck in, only looking up to see each new station as it lights up the train from the dark of the tunnel. This journey is going to take me fifteen stops.

Liverpool Street station is big. I get my ticket and wait for my platform number. It flicks through the black plastic pages of the board above my head. Platform eight. My lucky number.

As I approach the gates I see two British Rail guards standing either side. I recognise the body outline of one of them but I can't remember where from. He's got his cap on, so I can't make out his face. His hair is long and grey and curly. I can't see how big he is under that black overcoat, either. He's talking to the other guard and smoking a cigarette. He tips his head back and blows the smoke towards the roof. I see his face clearly. He laughs but he doesn't think whatever he's heard is funny. I can see that. I know when he's laughing for real. I've made him laugh before, lots of times. He laughed when I made the tough overcooked chicken that must have been older than me walk across the greasy caravan plate singing 'Heart of Glass'. He is holding the gate shut. No one gets passed him without paying.

I looked around for something to charge at him with. I found a bin that wasn't properly fastened down. I tipped it over, snapped the remaining rusty bolt holding it to the ground and picked it up above my head. I had to be quick and quiet. I started running towards the man I knew far too well. He hadn't heard me and was still pretending that the other guard was being funny. I had my blue sneakers on. They kept me silent as I sprinted across the uneven tarmac. I held my breath. The other guard saw me before the porter did. He looked alarmed and gestured to the overweight fucker next to him.

He knew about me and where I lived before I even knew he even existed. From behind grey dirty net curtains, this greasy fat fucker had watched me go out and come home day in and day out. He told me this in the caravan, like it was meant to be flattering, this sexual coward who had worked out the best way to win over the trust of someone as suspicious and damaged as I was. The best way was the slow way. Through the senses. Through food. Art. Music. Porn. Stories. Lies. Education. Touch. Paranoid, he'd changed jobs. This manipulative, evil bastard was going to get a lesson in waste management he wasn't going to forget.

He just had time to turn to face me and widen his eyes in shock as I came down on his head with the bottom edge of the bin. The ripped steel bolt split the area above his left eye wide open. The bin stopped abruptly as it reached his thick skull. There was a lot of blood. His legs gave way and he made a sound like a frightened child as he hit the ground.

His mate went for me so I slammed the bin into his chest hard enough to get him to back off. I carried on with my measured sculpting of my art-loving paedophile's head. Slow, controlled cracks and smacks to his flesh, bones and muscles. The bin was getting heavier by the blow but I was enjoying myself. I was enjoying the adrenaline. I was enjoying seeing his face lose all recognisable features and shape as it crumpled under the impact of the black, standard-issue British Rail bin. His pleas slurred into incoherent coughs, splutters and gurgles as blood and teeth filled his mouth. I was going to prison for this. Might as well carry on and make the most of it. Maybe me and Dad would get a cell together. At least we could hang out. We could look after each other, fight them off together.

But I wasn't going to prison. Not as a convict. Not that

day. I was only a visitor. I wasn't going to run at the abusive bastard and batter him with a British Rail bin. Christ, did I want to, though. Him and his mate would have kicked the living shit out of me. The bin was still in front of me, still half bolted to the floor. I could have picked it up if I tried, ripped it out of the ground and maybe chucked it at him. But I wanted nothing more to do with him, ever. I didn't want to see his pock-marked face look at me again, for any reason. I didn't want to have a conversation about the whole thing in years to come to discover what it was all really about. I didn't want to hear about his own hard times as a kid. No reconciliatory violins for this damaged cunt. I wanted to hold on to the rage I felt that day and use it when I needed to. Call on it when I was in trouble. There was going to be no forgiveness for the man, old enough to be my father, who tried to fuck me in a damp, moonlit caravan in deepest Wales.

I looked up from the bin and he had gone. I wondered if he had seen me and ducked out, not sure whether I would attack him or kiss him hello with a big camp hug, so grateful for having been awoken to my true sexuality. Maybe he had gone for a cup of tea. Maybe he had gone for his regular afternoon wank.

The route was clear. I headed through, barely looking at the remaining guard. The gateway to my first visit to Dad on my own was open. My violent fantasy had given me some satisfaction, some sadness but no regret. I was confused. I had wanted the physical contact I'd had with the porter in the caravan, in the car, in his dark, damp basement flat. I'd wanted it not for the pleasure but for the attention, the affection. It had been some kind of idea of safety in the absence of Dad. If I had wanted it then I deserved everything I'd got. Even if I was only twelve. Didn't I? If I'd had the courage to tell my mates about it they would have been more than happy to come and properly batter the child molester with me. I knew that. We could have brought our wrecking skills to a person who really deserved it.

2 p.m. – same day

It was raining. Coming down in wide, twisting sheets, almost horizontal. The wind around the outside fence was tearing the last golden leaves off the solitary tree by the main gate. The white, steel-meshed fence was as high as a two-storey building. I'd never seen anything like it. This wasn't Victorian. It had been built recently. I tipped the mini cab driver, got out and looked up at the massive fence in awe. There was no chance of climbing it. At the top it lipped over towards me. There were three strips of razor wire running right the way along. You'd have been an idiot to even consider trying to get over it.

I was excited to be there. Another movie set that no kid in school could get on to, except me. There was a tall watch-tower inside the main ground, like a World War Two machine gun post. The weapons inside this one were cameras: a 360 degree span, covering the entire grounds and all the buildings in them. The camera whirred round to size me up. I liked being watched. It changed how I moved. *Am I walking right? Do I look like a criminal? Have I got drugs on me? Guns? Money?* No. Just tobacco and matches. There was nothing to set light to there, except a cigarette. I'd rolled a few on the train and I lit one now. All they could do was tell me to put it out. No one did. A coach pulled up and a load of mums and their kids got off. I didn't want to be part of that group. They looked skint, worn down, miserable.

'Another lesson for you, kid: always look like you've got money even if you haven't. It's all in the clothes, the shoes, the haircut, the aftershave. No one will invest anything in you if you look and smell cheap.'

I had worked hard to look like I had money, but I hadn't really pulled it off. I took a sneaky sniff under my armpits, and headed for the gate. They were definitely friendlier in the country. The man behind the glass even smiled at me.

'On your own, son?'

'Yeah. I've come to see my dad.'

'Where have you come from, then?

'London. On the train.'

I handed him the VO and he looked at me, checking me out, then at the VO.

'Brave lad, all this way on your own. You got any ID?'

My heart sank. No one had told me about ID.

'I've got my scout badge,' I told him half-heartedly. I hadn't been to scouts for months.

'Only winding you up. I doubt you're carrying anything heavier than a pencil. Go on, in you go. Enjoy your visit Chez Blundeston.'

I smiled at him. Bastard thought he was a comedian. I had thought for a minute that I was going to be sent home. That would have killed me.

The door opened. The last gateway to Dad was clear.

I wanted Sam with me at that point but I was also happy to be alone. She thought I was big enough to deal with a visit on my own now and thought just me and him would be good. We'd visited Dad plenty of times. I was used to the routine. I often got fed up with my visits when Sam was there. They always had things to talk about that bored me or I didn't fully understand. The prospect of having Dad all to myself was bigger than the buzz of any birthday.

I was in.

The visiting hall was smaller than Pentonville, Brixton or Wandsworth. They had moved him from one London prison to another before he managed to get down to Blundeston. I visited him in every one of them as soon as I got the chance.

They were all alike: outdated, worn-out Victorian shit holes with the same lighting, stink and staff. When Dad was moved from one to the other we never got any warning. We would only ever find out through a letter from him, sometimes just before we were going to visit. Then we'd have to wait for a new VO, which could take weeks. It drove me crazy.

Keeping the secret of where Dad was from everyone at school was fun most of the time. I liked secrets. They gave me power. But the rest of the time, keeping it all to myself wore me out. Everyone seemed to believe me when I told them he was 'abroad on business'. They thought this was cool and mysterious. Some of the savvier teachers gave me a wry look when I repeated this lie, but nothing further was asked.

Leon was still my only mate from St Christopher's who knew about Dad. But he'd left. His parents had run out of money for his fees and he was now in Pimlico Compre-hensive in London. This place was known to be a nightmare. The thought of ending up there filled me with dread. Money was tight for us, too. Leon and I were still in touch and hung out in the holidays.

I was too young for some of my mates but I was older in this visiting room. I was getting tall and skinny and losing my puppy fat. I looked nearer to fourteen, fifteen even. I was also losing the attention of men wanting to raid childhood innocence.

I strutted across the room and headed for the tuck shop hatch. I got one tea. I would get Dad's later, to make sure it was hot. It could be a long wait for him. At that moment a call was going throughout the prison for all the men with visits. He could be anywhere on site. In the library, where he worked, or running, reading, meditating. He knew I was coming but he still took a long time to come and it pissed me off every time. But when he turned up, my anger melted.

I found a table near to the window and waited. Outside

in the yard there was a sole tree and a brand-new running track encircling it. Dad had written and told me he'd got into jogging. That must be where he did it. The sun broke through the grey and black clouds and shot three wide beams of light on to the tree, the track and finally into the visiting hall. It lifted my sulking spirit. Prisoners were coming past the window in twos and threes. They looked happy.

It was half an hour before he came, alone, in an open-necked shirt and blue jeans. He looked like he was walking into a key scene in a movie. The director's cameras were on him, tracking him slowly. His every move was monitored. Part of him was enjoying it. It was practice for the professional acting career that had never really happened. Practice for his once successful criminal street theatre, the Frank show.

Waiting for the door to open on my side was excruciating. And finally, there he was. He walked over to me, calm, contained, cool. I stood up sharply and hugged him. He kissed me. Dads didn't normally do this to adolescent sons. This was the point.

'How's it going, Cas?' He was excited. Happy to see me. 'Man, you are getting tall and skinny!'

'Good, thanks. You took ages. Yorkshire Ripper been moved here too, has he?'

'Cheeky fucker.' He ruffled my hair. 'I was meditating. Can't break that. Got some tobacco?'

I handed him the opened packet of Old Holborn. He took out the pre-rolled fag, looked at me and smiled. 'Match me, Sidney.'

I knew what that was: a line from Burt Lancaster to Tony Curtis in *Sweet Smell of Success*. We'd watched it together. I had no problem playing Tony. Dad took two long drags to get the tobacco burning. He looked around the visiting hall and nodded at a few of the men. He looked like he was in charge of himself. The guy on the table nearest to us leant across.

'All right, Frank?' He nodded at Dad then reached his hand out to me. 'Fred. Pleased to meet you, son.'

'Caspar. Nice to meet you.'

I wasn't sure it was. The man was covered in tattoos and looked like he'd had his face slashed and kicked in repeatedly. His nose was easily two inches wide. Dad passed him the tobacco and he helped himself to too much. 'I keep an eye out for your old man when he's off with them Buddha faeries meditating,' Fred said.

Dad smiled. 'Fred and I were in the merchant navy together. And most of London's prisons.' They smirked.

Fred winked at me. He was happy. He was being visited by his girlfriend. He got back to his visit.

'So what's happening at school?' Dad asked.

'I hate it. 'cept English and even the guy who teaches that is a bit of a wanker.' I was more interested in what was happening to Dad in prison.

'Sam said you'd been getting into fights.' Dad was more interested in what was happening outside.

'I'm getting teased about being so tall.' Dad wasn't going to hear the real reason. 'They keep calling me daddy long legs and Lurch.'

I looked around. Cigarette smoke was starting to fill the room. It smelled different in Blundeston. Like the country-side was creeping under the doors and through the tiny gaps in the windows. Fresh air was battling to bring in something clean from the outside. After half an hour of chain smoking, the country air lost the fight and I was starting to suffocate.

'Something on your mind?' Dad was looking at me closely to see if I was warming up to tell him a lie.

'I hate school and Jacky won't let me get to first base.'

This was true but was only offered to distract him from

the deeper truth about the porter. I had been steering clear of what had been happening to me in all my visits to Dad since it started. There was nothing he could do about the porter while he was inside. It would be tough for him. But he might have had a go at me for letting myself be tricked.

'Jacky your girlfriend? Great news, kid. At least you're not gay.'

I stopped breathing for a second.

'Don't get me wrong, some of the best gangsters are poofs. Good spenders. Loyal. Very few grasses among them.'

I noticed something out of my peripheral vision. Fred's dolled-up girlfriend was unzipping his flies under the table. She was trying not to make any noise, looking straight into his eyes like she was talking to him about *Coronation Street*.

'I think Fred's bird is wanking him off,' I blurted.

And she was. I could see it happening very clearly just at the edge of my vision. I wasn't going to turn around for a better view, no chance. Didn't want to get caught.

'Man's got to get it when and where he can. Don't look at him. You'll get him nicked. What's first base these days, then?'

'Tits.'

'Have you kissed her yet?'

'Yeah. Lots. She's good. Drives me crazy.'

Fred's hand job was over very quick. His girlfriend didn't bat an eyelid and kissed him by way of completion. She bought her hand out from under the table and wiped it. I didn't want to look any more.

'Take her out.' Dad stubbed out one roll up and immediately lit another. 'Buy her some flowers and some smellies. Take your time and you'll get anything you want.'

'I need a piss.' I didn't have that kind of patience I thought, as I walked away from the table. I was panicking. I wanted to make sure I wasn't gay. I didn't *feel* gay. I'd been seduced before I had had a chance to really find out if I was into girls.

'Sam give you the money for me?' Dad asked as I sat back down.

'Yes,' I replied, nervous and tight lipped.

'Relax, kid. You've got nothing to worry about. Got it wrapped up nice and tiny?'

'Yes.'

Dad nodded to Fred's girlfriend and she squeezed Fred's hand. Fred got up and walked over to the two prison officers and asked them a question. Suspicious, the other officer kept his eye on the room. It was a diversion that he and Dad had arranged that morning. Fred's girlfriend smiled at the officer surveying the room and he enjoyed it. She was good looking.

I put my clenched fist on the table. It was shaking a little so I pressed it on to the table. If the money had been found on me on the way in I would have told them I was hiding it so no one would nick it. Can't trust anyone in this neck of the woods. They might have believed this from a thirteen year old. Drugs were not safe for me to bring in. Not yet. I had put the notes in my palm when I was in the loo. They were wet with nervous sweat.

'I've missed you, kid. You're in my thoughts every day.'

He leant forward and took hold of my hand. I wanted to hear this. I had longed to hear it. But his words had three layers. Maybe they were true, heartfelt. I could see he meant it in his eyes. I could hear the truth of it in his voice. Maybe it was a way of looking convincing. Method acting, moving into an emotional state so that he could hold my hand and take the money. To anyone on the outside it would look believable and in part, it was. But I felt very uncomfortable. A man who was becoming a stranger to me was holding my hand and looking me in the eye and telling me he loved me.

The porter had told me that in the caravan. But this was Dad and although his words were true, I was scared. Scared of getting caught exchanging the money, scared of losing my connection with my father. I no longer knew him as well as I had done. He'd only done eight months of the five-year sentence he'd been given and already there was emotional distance between us. Chances are he would be out in three, if he kept his head down. But he probably wouldn't.

Everything had changed since the basement. Everything had changed since Dad had been ripped out of my life. Each month away from him felt like a lifetime. I was changing physically and emotionally. He only saw my change in two-hour chunks. I was locking myself away, building a high wall to protect myself. Dad was inside physical walls that neither of us could tear down.

I turned my hand upwards and opened my fingers. Three twenty-pound notes were squashed flat between our palms, invisible to anyone else. He drew his fingers together and scrunched his freshly moneyed fist into a ball. He leant forward and kissed me on the forehead. A kiss of thanks. A kiss of genuine fatherly love. It filled my body from my feet to my scalp with a rare warmth.

Before I knew it, the visit was over. I found it hard to let go of Dad. I nearly tripped over three tables as I looked back to wave at him. But I didn't cry until I got on the train.

10

Chemicals

I feel like I'm in prison here. I'm knackered and I fucking hate being told what to do. They know that. Jacky and I split up last week. She said she felt I was more like a brother and wanted to stay friends. Bollocks to her, then. Haven't been in a fight for nearly a week though. That's something.

'One more and you're out,' they told me. 'We don't tolerate violence in this school. You're lucky to get another warning.'

Like I'm supposed to be grateful for being kept in this shit hole.

To my surprise and relief, a few months later I got a call from Sam. The money for my fees had run out. I was having to leave St Christopher's. I was ready to go. To my horror I ended up in Pimlico School. Sam tried to ease my tension.

'It'll only be for a few months, Cas, till I get the money together for a boarding school. I know it's horrible but it's the only school that can take you at such short notice.'

I started in the middle of the week and in the middle of the term. This school was a dramatic change and I was plunged into a hard-nut, multiracial gladiatorial nightmare. I was officially a very small fish. An even stronger seed of resentment, mistrust, fear and anger started to grow in me. I couldn't hide the fear in my eyes. My confidence was shot. There were five hundred kids at St Chris and three times that number at Pimlico. Most of them were tough, street fighting gang kids who would stab you if you even mentioned their mother. I didn't fancy my chances with any of them. Paul had gone there straight from primary. He was shot in the side of the head with a high-powered air rifle on his first day. He survived. I knew I couldn't. I was no longer sleeping properly and was unravelling into a nervous wreck. I was singled out as a freak from the off. Not even the friends I had could stop the bullying. I found it hard to tell them how hard a time I was having.

Any chance I got, I smoked: cigarettes, roll ups, joints, bongs, pipes, the lot. I started drinking heavily. Whatever got me pissed the quickest was best – no matter how bad it tasted or what it did to my head and guts. I understood the true meaning of the word hangover by the time I was thirteen. My fear and confusion were apparent in my face and body from the moment I got up to well after I went to bed. I could see it in the mirror each morning. There was no hiding it from anyone. Unless, that is, I had a good mix of chemicals inside me. Getting stoned came easy and felt natural. Leon, and I got high whenever we could. Morning, lunchtimes and straight after school.

It worked well to begin with. My fear felt in check and I was almost enjoying myself. But after a few months things started to change again. I thought it was down to a particularly strong batch of hash going round. I was developing an intimate relationship with grass and hash. It became what I thought of as a close friend and I relied on it. My drug of choice soon found a way of magnifying my core emotions into some kind of cartoon nightmare. With Dad gone, the porter's sexual initiation, the bailiffs taking the last of what we had and a nightmare at school, I had no solid emotional foundations left, no internal compass to guide me. Drugs were the only thing that could get me through the day, through the streets of London or even a basic conversation. It wasn't long before the drugs and alcohol started to lose their effect.

The more stoned I got the more paranoid I began to feel. I carried on smoking more in the dumb belief that I would reach another level where everything would be all right. I was getting more and more shaky, having regular nightmares, from time to time pissing the bed. I was terrified about what people were saying about me behind my back.

When I could, I still smashed stuff up to deal with my frustration. We heard about a school in west London that had been closed down and decided to pay it a visit. We got through the security fencing without difficulty. The empty corridors spooked us out and to combat our fear we picked up some metal chairs and started wrecking the place. We smashed windows, tables, doors. I found a steel pipe and went berserk. The momentum of our war on the dead school built into a frenzy. We screamed as we smashed and trashed and it felt fantastic. The only thing we didn't do was set fire to the place.

Pimlico School was an accelerator to prison. The school's constant threat of violence and easily accessed supplies of dope set me on the road to full-time chemical use to try and ease my fear and confusion. My buzz was now my sole source of security and communication. I did whatever I had to do to ensure I had a constant supply. When she had it, I nicked money from Sam and any other adult whose wallet or purse I got close enough to. Any cash I had was spent on drugs and alcohol. I needed to eat and drink and Sam was scraping silver together to pay for my school lunches. Dad's lessons in shoplifting really came in handy at this point. I stole whatever I wanted to eat and drink from wherever I fancied. Walking out of restaurants without paying was easy. If anyone tried to follow us we were young enough and fast enough to outrun any waiter. I had watched Dad intercepting mail in the communal post boxes of the mansion flats in Kensington. I learnt how to find the right envelopes containing birthday money, gift tokens, postal orders and parcels from friends, family and mail order companies.

I never quite got round to stealing in front of policemen but I was blatant and arrogant in front of shopkeepers. It was another buzz. If an assistant was working alone in a shop they would often leave me alone; they couldn't be bothered with the hassle. I was resigned to the petty thieving routine and got the best I could out of it.

IN REPLYING TO THIS LETTER, PLEASE WRITE ON THE
ENVELOPE:
NUMBER: MP0815
NAME: WALSH
HMP DOWNVIEW

HELLO CAS,
WHAT A STRANGE PLACE THIS IS. I'LL TRY AND GIVE AN OBJECTIVE DESCRIPTION AS POSSIBLE, STARTING WITH MY CELL WHICH IS TINY. BUT IT HAS AN ENORMOUS WNDOW (ABOUT EIGHT FEET BY THREE WIDE, BARRED OF COURSE). BEYOND THIS IS A WROUGHT IRON BALCONY, VICTORIAN I THINK, WITH FOUR STEPS LEADING DOWN TO A LAWN. SO I SUPPOSE THE WINDOW WAS ONCE A DOOR. TO THE RIGHT IS A LARGE PIT. RUMOUR HAS IT THAT THIS IS TO BE A POND. (HOPEFULLY I'LL HAVE LEFT BY THEN.) THERE SEEMS TO BE A SMALL FOREST BEYOND THE FENCE, WHICH IS ABOUT 20 YARDS AWAY. THE TREES COME RIGHT UP TO THE FENCE WHICH IS PLEASANT BECAUSE IT MEANS BIRDS AND LOTS OF

WILDLIFE, IN FACT I AM VISITED BY TWO SQUIRRELS EVERY
MORNING WITH WHOM I SHARE MY RATION OF PEANUTS.

THEN JUST BEYOND THE FENCE IS A RIDING SCHOOL,
THE STABLE GIRLS LOOK WONDERFUL (AND OF COURSE I'D
MUCH RATHER SHARE MY NUTS WITH THEM). SO I STAND BY
MY WINDOW LIKE SOME OLD COLONEL TURNED SQUIRE
SURVEYING HIS ESTATE. FUCK IT. THAT'S ENOUGH ABOUT THIS
PLACE, I'M REALLY SICK OF IT NOW. THANK GOD I HAVE
INTERESTS IN MY LIFE OTHER THAN PEOPLE AND WHAT THEY
DO WITH THEIR TIME. I'M SO BUSY IN MY STUDIES OF THE
BIZARRE THESE DAYS THAT I HARDLY NOTICE WHAT'S
SUPPOSED TO BE NORMAL. I'M MORE INTERESTED IN WHAT'S
NATURAL.

I COULD WRITE PAGES OF NONSENSE (ERUDITE ONES AT
THAT) BUT I WON'T! I'D MUCH RATHER TALK TO YOU FACE TO
FACE, SO HERE IS A V.O. AND A ROUTE MAP. I'LL CALL IN A
FEW DAYS AND MAKE ARRANGEMENTS.

LOVE YER.

DAD

He had been moved from Blundeston. This letter was the first
I heard about it. He had been inside for almost year and a
half and moved four times. He always wrote in capitals.
Never in the same ink two letters in a row.

It sounded like he was having a better time than I was. I
was now getting my own VOs. It was good that Sam and I
went down separately sometimes. She visited him pretty
much every two weeks whatever was going on and I usually
went with her. She never told me how much she loved him
but I could see it. Sam's actions always spoke louder than her
words.

When she met Dad Sam had plenty of cash and a nice
house. Now Dad was inside and she had lost just about
everything. We had barely enough money for my school

dinners but I nicked what I needed and kept myself going, in line with the lifestyle Dad had got me used to. Sam didn't know a thing about it; she would've killed me.

It was inevitable. We had been kicked out of the big flat and were living in a tiny mews flat near Hyde Park. Sounds pleasant. It wasn't. We were looking after it for a friend, rent free. Sam had three months to find another place. Sam was pretty much all I had but I still gave her attitude; more and more each day. As I grew taller and got more lippy it got harder for her to control me and get me to do what she wanted. After all, she wasn't my mum – not that she'd have done a better job. Whether I thought what she was asking was a good idea or not I objected to it for the sake of it. I was a teenager. A fucked up teenager.

I don't know what I was thinking. I'd had a bad ruck with my girlfriend and had been smoking too much spliff and drinking constantly. I'd been pushing Sam for weeks with my demands. She had, as ever, been pretty patient with me. I was emerging from childhood into puberty and wanted to see how far my new adult boundary could be pushed.

'You're not going out,' she told me for the fourth time.

'Why don't you fuck off?' was my reply.

She went to slap me. I deserved it, I knew that. But as far as I was concerned I was a grown up now and I deserved respect. My reaction was automatic. I managed to catch hold of her wrist just before she struck my face. I kept hold of it and threw her on to the sofa. I leaned over her, without a clue what to do next. I quickly wished I hadn't done it. She looked frightened. I was holding both her wrists. I thought if I let go she might try to whack me again. I was breathing heavily, almost panicking, trying to hold it together.

'Don't ever try to hit me again, understand?'

It sounded like a tough line but it didn't fit the breaking

tremors of my vocal chords. She looked up at me and said nothing. I let go. I felt awful. Scared and hot. My back was sweating. There followed an excruciating silence.

I did as I had wanted to do in the first place and left, slamming the door shut. I had just turned fourteen.

Two weeks before I was due my next visit to Dad I had a dream about him. At least I thought I was asleep. I was lying in bed when I woke up. I turned my head to face the bedroom door, which was open. I could see and feel someone at the end of the hallway looking down at me. There was a bright light and in the middle of it, in a black shadow outline, was Dad. Unmistakeable. He was standing there looking into my room, directly at me.

HMP Downview, 1982

I unwrapped my second Mars bar. Dad was sipping his tea, looking at me closely. I broke the silence.

'Thanks for the letter.'

'No worries, kid. Sorry it was a bit short. Wasn't feeling great that day. Just wanted to see you.'

'Me too. I've missed you. Are the stable girls still here?'

'Every day. Drives me crazy.'

He sounded OK but his good humour was clearly wearing thin. He was trying to cover up but I could see through it. It gave me a strange feeling of power to see into him like that; a feeling of being bigger than him, stronger than him. And maybe, in that moment, better than him. After all, *I* was on the outside and he was inside, suffering. I was nicking from shops and people every day, smashing places and things up, smoking drugs, drinking booze and bunking off school. Most days from 9 to 3:30 my school was a prison, but then I was free to do what I wanted. And since

I was free, I must have been doing something right. I was starting to feel good about myself.

The previous week, after school, a kid had done more magic mushrooms than was good for him. He'd been waiting too long for a tube and decided to jump on to the tracks and run the length of the line from Pimlico to Victoria. He'd just made it to the end of the tunnel when the driver's carriage crushed him between rail and train. I was envious of the attention he got. Even if he was dead. He became a legend. I was starting to feel less good about myself.

But things were looking up. I was about to start a new school.

'Sam's spent ages looking for it,' Dad reminded me. 'It's a good school, in the country, and she managed to get you a government grant for your fees. I've seen the brochure. All them lovely, young country girls to corrupt. You have no idea how lucky you are.'

But I did. I was trying to wind him up. Stoke College was a small private boarding school mainly for the under-achieving kids of rich local farmers. It suited my learning ability at the time. Moving around from place to place, school to school, meant I was dumped in the bottom stream classes. I was distracted, confused and too fucked off to be capable or bothered to do any good in any of my classes. It was all I could do to get to Pimlico on time in the morning and I only did that to stay out of detention and keep the inspectors off Sam's back. Stoke College was going to be my final school before me and Dad were reunited. I had been moved around a lot more than was good for me, a bit like Dad.

'You see me the other night?' he asked suddenly.

I immediately knew what he meant and it sent a shiver down my spine.

'I've been reading this book on astral travelling. Only

way I can get about these days.' He smirked at me. I didn't know if he was winding me up or not. 'Came to the flat to see you. Check on you.'

I didn't know what to make of this. 'I did dream about you, yeah, wanted you to come into my room but you wouldn't.'

'Came as far as I could.'

'Can you do it again?'

'Keep them mince pies peeled, kid.' He winked at me.

I was on a week-long visit for the children of prisoners only. It was organised by the local probation service. We would head to the prison at around 9 a.m., get there for 10 a.m. and be led straight in. We were a low security risk so the usual checks weren't needed. We would have the morning with our dads. Around three hours in all. The afternoons were spent on day trips to zoos and leisure centres. In the evenings we would head back to the scout hall we were staying in. I loved it. We played board games after dinner. *Colditz* was the definite favourite. After a few days Dad and I started to run out of things to say. We played backgammon in silence and he helped me to write some stories. But I enjoyed being bored with him. It was like being back home again, wondering what to do next. The edginess of a two-hour visit and wanting to stop the rapidly moving clock had gone. For that seven days in the autumn of 1982 I felt some kind of normality creeping back in, some familiarity at being with my dad. It was the last time in a long time that we would do this together, free from drugs and free from the fear of the door coming in again. I made the most of it.

11

School's Out Forever

Stoke College, Winter 1982

I can't stop thinking about sex. All bloody day. Lessons are so fucking boring I keep getting a hard on in class. I was with Carrie for ages, on and off. Got plenty of it from her. She taught me loads about how to get a girl going and keep her satisfied. We weren't meant to be having sex, not till we were sixteen. Fuck that. It made me feel better after the porter. Being with Carrie helped put him and his hands out of my mind. The more sex we had the further I got from the basement and the caravan, and the more normal I felt. After we split up I tried to find another girl just like her. No chance. No one's up for it.

Moving from one girl to the next, week to week, month to month has got me a reputation for being a bit sex starved. That's bad news here. The only sex I'm having now is with myself. I've cranked up the dope smoking to make up for it.

Visits to Dad are pretty much every month; every two weeks if I'm lucky. He's been inside for two years and eight months now. The whole thing is really pissing me off. But he stopped messing around with his insider drug dealing and started being good. He got moved to Ford open prison. You're trusted not to do a runner there. It's mainly full of blokes ready for release who the screws think are safe. The gates are actually open and you can walk out any time you like. Incredibly, they come back. Even Dad.

Stoke was a weekly boarding school. Most kids went home at the end of the week. I had been staying with different families at weekends because the trip back to London was too far and too expensive. Moving around all the time was disorientating so I started staying with Mrs T., the school matron, who lived in the village. She was my guardian angel. She never said much but I felt her love and soaked it up. She had five kids of her own and was a second mum to loads of the kids at school. I got extra attention from her because I didn't go home at weekends. She knew I was a troublemaker and kept an eye on me.

One morning Mrs T. asked if she could speak to me. We went into a small room and sat down.

'I noticed the postcard you got this morning.'

Dad had sent me a postcard from HMP Ford. There was a prison stamp on it. He had signed it Frank, and not Dad. I already had an answer to the question I knew was coming next.

'Is Frank someone in your family?'

'He's my uncle.'

'I didn't know you had an uncle. Never heard you talk about one.' She didn't believe me. 'Who's Frank, Caspar?'

I paused and considered my options. Continuing to lie was pointless. I had never told another grown up apart from the porter about Dad and very few of my new mates at Stoke knew. But I wanted people to know. I wanted people to know I was struggling. I saw an opportunity in that room and I took it.

'He's my dad.'

'I thought so.' She smiled. I was surprised. 'Your secret is safe with me.' That surprised me even more. An enormous weight lifted. She opened her arms and gestured me to come over. Without saying anything, I went over and I let her hug me. For the first time in years I was in the arms of an adult outside my family whom I could trust, and I cried.

I had been staying at Sam's dad's house for the weekend. He had a big drinks cabinet and an even bigger wine cellar. I had helped myself to two bottles of whisky, a bottle of vodka, a bottle of red, a bottle of white and a disgustingly sweet bottle of dessert wine. I had wrapped them up in my clothes so they wouldn't clink together. I hid them in my bags when we left and I got them into school. I had a plan. I was going to get as many of my mates as possible as wrecked as possible. We were going to make trouble and I was going to be at the head of it.

The drinking started at lunchtime. I hadn't really drunk spirits before apart from the tequila. I drank lager, cider and wine. I thought the hit was meant to be instant. But I'd eaten a massive lunch and wasn't having much luck with the vodka. I ended up necking a neat pint of it straight from the bottle. The other kids were more cautious, enjoying seeing me walk so blatantly into trouble.

Within half an hour the booze kicked in and I started to black out. I managed to get up to Mrs T.'s office and told her I was feeling 'a bit dodgy'. That was an understatement. She suggested a shower might make me feel better, which I thought was a good idea. I went into the boys' changing rooms on my own. The Mod, a mate obsessed with all things Paul Weller, was in there doing his hair. He stopped his grooming to watch me stagger about, looking for the shower. I found it and stepped in, fully clothed. I let the cold water rain down on me and, for a moment, I thought I was sober again. Within a minute of stepping out of the shower I was back to being wasted. I continued to stagger about in waterlogged clothes, shivering like a wet whippet.

'I'm feeling weird,' I told The Mod. 'I need some more cold water on my face.'

'Let's go down to the river. Come on. I'll give you a hand,' he reassured me. Part of me knew his concern was genuine. Part of me knew he was in it for the story. He loved to gossip and if I had remembered that as I slipped in and out of consciousness, I may have kept my mouth shut. But maybe I chose him at that moment for a good reason.

The river was at the bottom of the garden. It was wide and dark green with algae. On the opposite bank was a line of lime trees heavy with a big spread of autumn leaves ready to drop. I listened to the sound of the wind moving in and out of them and I felt better for it. I laid down on my front by the water's edge. The Mod lay down next to me. I could feel his excitement. I started to splash river water on my face. He watched me closely, sporadically laughing at me.

'Man, you are one crazy motherfucker.'

I ignored him. As the two sensations of clarity from my face splashing and the buzz of the vodka vied for a place in my confused head I felt sadness well up inside me; then anger.

'My dad's in prison. He's been inside for nearly three years. Drugs.' I splashed my face again. I didn't want to tell him about the robbery and violence and fraud. Drugs were cooler and easier for him to understand. But it was out. I felt my stomach sinking the moment I told him. Part of me hoped he wouldn't tell anyone. Most of me knew he would. I was worn out with the lies, worn out with holding it all in.

'I have to go,' he said, meaning '*I have to go and tell someone about this*.' He left me there, on my front, head bobbing up and down, in and out of the water. I took off my glasses and put my face into the murky water. If I stayed there long enough maybe the deathly feeling I had in my guts would go. I wondered what it would be like to drown myself right there. How long would it take before the lights went out for good? Was now the time to kill myself? As the cold water lapped at me, my face went numb. What would it be like, to just stay there, no more worries?

My heart thumped hard in my chest, my lungs panicked for breath. I yanked my head out of the river and took a gasp of air. I wasn't ready to go yet. I rolled on to my back and looked up at the sky. The wind had got up and the clouds sped by. I was in big trouble. The headmaster was going to have to deal with me properly this time.

By the time I'd staggered back up to the main building just about everyone in the school knew Dad was in prison. I had thought I would like the status and the stares. I didn't. I felt ashamed. And then I stopped feeling anything.

I woke up in hospital. I'd had my stomach pumped. I had no memory of it. The headmaster came to pick me up in his big estate car and sat me in the back. The seats and floor were covered in plastic in case I vomited. I felt like I'd been beaten up. The head was pissed off with me, but I also felt some warmth, sympathy even; he couldn't hide that.

My punishment for getting pissed involved several levels of severity. There was my incarceration in a space called the Red Landing in the main house. Every break time, every second of time not in class when I wasn't eating or doing homework was spent on the Red Landing for the rest of that term. If I'd refused the punishment I would have been expelled. The head had wanted to chuck me out as soon as he'd heard about the vodka. He needed to be seen to make an example of me, even if I wasn't the only one who'd got trashed. But he trusted Mrs T. He knew she liked me and kept an eye out for me. She managed to convince him not to expel me. She used her trump card to keep me there, and told Bod, the headmaster, about Dad. Like I said, my guardian angel.

Dad had been sentenced to five years and had done nearly three. He hadn't done much to keep himself out of trouble for the first eighteen months. He could have been out earlier but had fucked up his chances of parole time and time again. He was due for release in eight months, which meant he'd been inside for three-and-a-half years of my life – a quarter of it.

I knew what was coming. He was clearly a terrible influence on me but he was also all I had. I loved him more than anything in the world. He'd taught me everything I knew about survival. I'd had regular contact with him the whole time he'd been in prison, regular letters, regular visits, regular lessons. I missed him all the time, day and night. Apart from Sam he was the one person I knew could protect me in the world. As desperate and hopeful I was about living with him again, I knew I would end up in a lot more trouble than I was already in. More trouble, more crime, more violence and more fear than I could handle. I knew it in my bones. I wanted to be with him but I knew I had to do everything I could to build my own life, to try and create something I could sustain without him. I wanted to do this, needed to do it. But it felt pointless. Why bother fighting it?

I needed discipline to try and get me on the straight and narrow before he got out, even though I hated the idea of it. This meant staying away from him until I was strong enough to stand on my own two feet. As long as I was away from him I could make my own mind up about what I wanted to do. When I was with him, I knew that everything I did and said would be about him and about staying with him. It was wise thinking for a boy of fifteen years old. But backing that wisdom up with action was very difficult.

I had to get myself away from him before he came out.

Summer 1983, Kensington, London

I was due back at Stoke the Sunday night before term began. Sam had been acting weird all holiday. I hadn't seen much of her. She'd had a bath before we left for the station that night. Done her hair and made herself look beautiful. I knew she was going to see a man. My heart hit my feet. I couldn't be bothered to put her through the embarrassment of questions. She'd been visiting Dad every two weeks for over three years. Her loyalty was still there, strong as ever, but now that he was due out, her fear seemed to be getting the better of her. We were both scared. Like me, she was running away.

I knew, right after she dropped me off at Liverpool Street station she would be going to see this new man. He was going to be the wedge between my fantasy of our reunited family life together, perhaps a baby brother or sister, and the continued reality of all the bad shit that had been happening for all those years.

Sam gave me some cash and kissed me goodbye. Her eyes were full of sadness and apology, but she said nothing. We both knew what was happening and there was nothing to say. She was doing her best. I just wish she'd told him before he came out. I could've told him, I wanted to, needed to, but the words wouldn't come. Visiting him two weeks later, the words stuck in my throat. I knew how much she meant to him. I knew how bad he felt about the mess he'd made of everything. I should have told him then and there so he'd have been prepared for the worst. This was going to fuck up all hope of him going straight. This would be the best kind of excuse to get really out of it, and stay like that for a long time. It was to be my last visit, I hoped. The last time I would have to sit in that smoke-filled room while the sun shone on everything outside.

I'd applied to join the navy and I'd hear about my

application in the next two weeks. Dad would be out in five. Hopefully I'd be at sea by then, or at least training at Dartmouth. But I didn't really want to go to sea or that kind of war.

I hadn't told him about the Navy. He would've freaked, then taken the piss out of me and finally he'd have tried to talk me out of it. Besides, when he'd found out that Sam wanted out, I'd be all he had left. If she went, I would have to stay. I knew that already.

'How are your exams going?'

'Just had my mocks. I got two percent in maths and that was for writing my name on the paper.'

'How's English going?'

'We're doing *Macbeth* and I haven't got a fucking clue what it's about. It's like reading Spanish.'

'No worries, kid. When I'm home we'll do some writing together.'

The only studying we were going to do when he got home was the varying weights, measures and prices of illegal narcotics. No chance of As in my exams, just class As for survival.

IN REPLYING TO THIS LETTER, PLEASE WRITE ON THE
ENVELOPE:
NUMBER: MP0815
NAME: WALSH
HMP FORD

HEY.

IT WAS GOOD TO SEE YOU YESTERDAY, KID. SO THIS IS TO BE MY LAST LETTER TO YOU FROM THIS LITTLE PIECE OF COUNTRY HEAVEN. I THINK IN SOME STRANGE WAY I MAY EVEN MISS IT. SOME OF THE SCREWS HERE ARE ALMOST HUMAN. I'VE BEEN ALLOWED TO DO MY JOGGING ON THE COUNTRY ROADS AND

I'VE EVEN STOOD BY THE SEA AND WATCHED THE WAVES CRASHING INTO THE HARBOUR WALLS. HOW LUCKY IS THAT! THE SEA AIR IS FANTASTIC.

YOU SEEMED PREOCCUPIED. YOU'VE OBVIOUSLY GOT A LOT GOING ON WITH YOUR EXAMS, YOUR RAGING HORMONES AND OF COURSE YOUR OLD MAN COMING OUT IN A FEW WEEKS. NOT LONG TO GO, KID. YOU'VE BEEN SO PATIENT WITH IT ALL AND HAVE GROWN UP A LOT SINCE I GOT NICKED. I PROMISE THINGS WILL BE DIFFERENT WHEN I GET HOME. YOU, ME AND SAM WILL HAVE A FRESH START AND WHO KNOWS, I MAY EVEN GET MYSELF A JOB.

THE FIRST THING I WANT TO DO IS GO AWAY, JUST THE THREE OF US, SOMEWHERE HOT AND LIE ON A BEACH AND LISTEN TO THE SEA ALL DAY AND ALL NIGHT, EAT COCONUTS AND MAKE PLANS. AS SOON AS YOUR EXAMS ARE DONE WE'LL DO IT.

GOOD LUCK WITH IT ALL.

I LOVE AND MISS YOU WITH ALL MY HEART.

FRANK

The letter was short. Red ink. Either he didn't have a clue or he was ignoring his instincts. Neither Sam nor I had the courage to tell him. He wasn't even out and my fantasy of how it would all turn out sunny and fine was quickly turning to dirt. I didn't believe in any kind of God but I was praying for a miracle.

I knew that being able to take my O Levels and CSEs and hoping for some kind of a straight life was way too wishful thinking. The moment Dad was released I would go to him; all he would have to do is ask. I wanted to take the exams and I didn't. Any excuse would do and Dad's release after all those years in prison would be the best one I could think of. He needed me around to watch his back. Eleven years working towards 'good prospects and a career' in school and it was all going to be over in the time it took Dad to phone me up and ask me to come home.

12

Smoke and Mirrors

Nine weeks later, Kensington, London

There's the best part of a kilo of cocaine in the bedroom cupboard. It's Peruvian and it's full of beautiful shining pink rocks of pure uncut coke. It's in a green, watertight plastic container, which was designed to keep it bone dry on the hull of the boat. This is the first coke I've done. What a fucking great way to start. I'll be sixteen soon. The navy? Fuck that. What was I thinking! If I'd got through the exams I'd have probably ended up on a speedboat nicking the poor bastards who worked so hard to get this incredible coke over here. Why the hell would I want to do that?

One well-chopped line flies up the tube of the neatly rolled twenty. The rush is quick but gentle. It starts somewhere in my balls and glides up my torso into my throat, and opens up like a slow-motion firework right in the middle of my head. It stops my mind and its bullshit churning; questions, questions, questions. Should I stay or should I go?

One line is fine and keeps me going for up to an hour. Two lines, and everything speeds up a little too much. Paranoid thoughts munch through my head like Pac-Man. A chemical combination is required at this point. Hash smoke and cocaine mirrors. The two drugs fit together nicely – a complete illusion of calm in my body. Fresh Nepalese Temple Ball. I prefer it in joints but a pipe'll do. A line of Peru up my nose and a long drag of Nepal down my throat. The buzz and shudders of too much coke eventually level out. The two rushes meet in my thumping chest and cancel each other out in a reassuring, warm buzz.

I sit down and stare straight ahead. I'm listening to The Eagles humping 'Hotel California' through my quad amp and into my headphones. Should I stay or should I go? The American rock country sound boots out any doubts in my mind, replacing them with an absolute conviction that this is the right place to be.

Dad was in the next room. He'd done so much smack he could hardly stand up. I looked at the coke and watched it sparkle while the music played. Dad was looking after it for George. The moment he'd got out of prison, George, loyal to form, had been there on the doorstep, smiling, with a cockney tear in his eye. They'd hugged and business had taken up immediately, right where it had left off.

I was still in school when Dad was released. I had about two weeks to go to my O Levels and CSEs. I was hating every minute of it. Dad returned home after three-and-a-half years to an empty flat. Sam was gone. There was no note. It took him a week to find her. He called a number George had got hold of and he knew the voice of the man who answered the phone. It was an old friend of his from the sixties. Dad had introduced Sam to him at a party a few months before he was arrested. I had met him too. He was all right.

Sam couldn't speak to Dad, not at first. Eventually they started to look at the practical details of how to deal with the flat, the money and me. They came down to Stoke to take me out for lunch. This was the first time I'd seen them together outside of prison walls since I was twelve. Dad was so stoned he could hardly drive, but he insisted. When they arrived,

Sam looked shocked, embarrassed and worn out. They had been rucking all the way down from London. Dad had been doing most of the shouting. The first and last thing I wanted to do was get into the car with all that shit going on. The atmosphere between them felt filthy and broken. I got into the car and sat silently in the back. Dad drove too fast, too angry, all over the road.

We pulled up outside a pub. He was having a go at Sam about everything, like it was all her fault. I could see he was covering up the fact that his heart was properly broken.

'I want you to buy Caspar a new wardrobe of clothes, up to date, latest gear. Everything. He needs new shirts, trousers, shoes, jackets, underwear, the lot.'

I didn't.

'OK, Frank, please keep your voice down.' Sam was doing her best to minimise the public scene he was intent on making and to get away from him with the least abuse possible. We headed into the pub. I needed a drink.

'And I want the flat. Stay with your new man and pay my rent until I get enough money together.'

He was doing all he could to punish her. Like it wasn't hard enough already. He had enough money. George had seen to that. I was dying with embarrassment and anguish. People had stopped drinking and eating and were watching the unfolding scene.

'You fucking heartless bitch. I can't believe you lied to me.' He whacked back a quadruple vodka lime and tonic. I saw him gulping back tears. 'How long, eh? How long have you been fu—'

'Frank, please. Don't do this. Not in front of Cas. Not here.'

'That's precisely what I'm going to do. He needs to see what happens when you put your trust in someone!'

People started to move away from us. The landlord looked like he was about to come over and have a word.

'Dad, don't. Please. Let's go. I want to go back to school.'

And we left, in silence. Dad was having difficulty walking straight. Sam drove. At the door of Mrs T.'s I said a goodbye that cut into me. I ran up to my room and listened to the car pull away. That was it. There were to be no exams for me, I knew that now. School was about to be out forever.

London – two months later

The spliff was finding it hard to keep up with the strength of the coke I was snorting. Dad was giving me a few lines a day, which he said should have kept me going. I was more interested in taking what I wanted when I wanted it. If I was being loyal enough to stick by him when just about everyone else was steering clear then I deserved some kind of reward. If the buzz started to wear off I would do my best to get more into my system. Dad taught me how to cut the coke and what to cut it with. He began dealing by taking a tablespoon of the pure Peruvian out and cutting a tablespoon of pure vitamin powder back in. The original drug was so strong no one noticed, not for a long time. I was doing the same to Dad as he was doing to George's people, though on a smaller scale.

Dad had been up for three days and nights. He'd finally taken enough smack to knock him out. I had free rein of the flat and was making the most of it. In the big yellow American fridge that Sam had left behind were two large plastic bottles full of emerald green liquid. Dad had told his dodgy Harley Street doctor that he was trying to get off smack. Not even Dad could do the 2,000 millilitres he got every two weeks on prescription and his doctor knew it. He'd only been out of the nick for a week and the methadone was for selling to clucking junkies waiting for their smack to come through.

I had been helping myself to sips of it most times I went into the fridge. The buzz was slow to build and gentle and warm. It evaporated my more intense emotions – the fear and anger – and left me with a sense of completion, a sense of wholeness. An hour after a swig of it I was no longer bothered by the world; I was happy. I had no idea of the strength of the drug or its history. What did I care? I later found out it had been developed by the Nazis during the Second World War as a painkiller for their storm troopers. They soon realised it was good for killing feelings as well, especially fear. And the ultimate bonus was its addictive properties: a good way of keeping soldiers loyal. I was taking it so regularly for so long that I had a methadone habit way before I realised it. I was to discover it was much harder to kick than smack.

It was the methadone that maintained the buzz from the coke, not the spliff as I'd thought. But the methadone had run out and Dad was waiting for the next prescription to come through. Not realising how it had been affecting me, I wasn't initially bothered that he didn't have any.

I had been badgering Dad for ages to give me a smoke of smack. I felt I really wanted it. He had been refusing me point blank. But since I'd started nicking the coke from him and getting more and more manic and jittery, he realised I needed something stronger to level me out.

Finally, as I threatened to fuck up a deal, he took me away from the punters and into the kitchen. He pulled out a neat square of silver foil from a drawer. It had a dried-up blob of brown-black smack in its centre.

'You're messing things up for me, kid. These are new punters and we need them. Have some of this. You're going to have to cut down on the coke. I mean it.'

He held the foil steady at chest height and gave me the well-used foil pipe. He sparked the purple lighter into flame. He was looking down at the foil, melting the crystallised smack back into a thick liquid that would run. I was looking at him.

'Come on, concentrate. When the smoke goes white, take a toke. You know what to do, you've seen me enough times.'

I put the pipe in my mouth and brought my head down. My eyes darted up to Dad for guidance and he nodded at the foil, encouraging me to start. The smoke was thin and wispy at first then the smack started to melt and finally began to move. After a few seconds the smoke residue went a deeper white. Dad increased the angle and the thick black liquid smack on the foil began to run freely pluming smoke that I sucked up the pipe. He skilfully moved the silver square, creating a faded black line where the smack had been, and I continued to follow his lead, eagerly drawing in the smooth white smoke, as it rushed up in front of my face.

I looked at Dad and he smiled at me. His eyes flicked back to the foil and I continued following the smoke and drawing it in. The rush was very much like methadone, but quicker and fresher and even more reassuring. Dad let go of the lighter trigger and the flame went out. I carried on sucking. The smoke continued to plume and disappear into the pipe for a few more seconds until the last of it was in my lungs.

'Don't say anything to anyone, kid. They wouldn't understand, believe me.'

He handed me a cigarette and I took a drag on it, pulling the narcotic smoke further into my lungs.

'Now, let me carry on with business. Go and watch telly in the bedroom. Enjoy yourself.'

I was happy to do that. That's where the coke was.

*

Dad had said he was going to pay for me to go to a crammer to study for the exams I missed. I was into the idea at the time, when it was the deciding factor for me leaving Stoke, but now I was at home getting stoned I couldn't be bothered. Dad didn't push the idea any further either. I had officially flunked out of school and really didn't give a shit.

I went to visit Mum a fair bit after I left school. We got on, as long as I didn't hassle her about anything. She hated being hassled. When she was on form she was a riot but her darker moods, mostly related to too much alcohol and spliff, were getting worse. I now preferred to head home when the moods hit. I'd tried to talk to her about the porter. She gave me this shocked look when I told her, and briefly tried to console me, then changed the subject to her latest harvest of homegrown grass. We could talk about most things but paedophile abuse was off the cards. She gave me her wisdom on straight sex and drugs and life, usually when stoned. When we were alone together we were more like brother and sister; she treated me pretty much like an equal. She was good to me when I wanted to talk about Dad and Sam and I still stayed with Mum from time to time. Her cosy basement flat in Tite Street was a bolt hole, some respite from a dangerous world. Many years later she told me that she was so shocked she didn't know what to do. So she did nothing.

Dad had met a woman while he was hauling a filing cabinet up the stairs to our flat. True to form she was a model and she was stunning. She was a lot younger than him. She was seventeen years old. He was forty-two. I thought she was about the right age for me, not him, but her designs were clearly on Dad. He'd been out of prison for three months. I thought it was too soon after Sam but I could see why he wanted her. Kate was beautiful; I found it hard to keep my eyes off her.

Dad had become a teenager again. They couldn't leave

143

each other alone. He was happy. I was happy for him but seriously pissed off that I was re-living the trauma of hearing my father having sex every night. The coke kept him young enough to keep up with her.

Within a couple of months they started arguing and an old pattern re-emerged.

We had a party one night and I was left to deal with a flat full of stoners I didn't know or trust. Dad and Kate were gone for two hours. He was always longer than he said he would be and it always worried me. He said they were going to get some cigarettes. It should've taken ten minutes. The stoners slowly drifted home until I was sitting in the flat on my own. I had been doing too much coke again and couldn't find his stash of smack. I didn't fancy the methadone, it took too long to kick in. I was out of spliff. I was watching a VHS pirate of *Blade Runner* for the fifth time on a static-filled screen. I could just make out what was going on. The inside of my cheek was sore from constantly chewing and biting my flesh. That was the coke. I was rocking on the edge of the sofa trying to console myself. The window was open and I could hear the roar of the October wind in the trees outside. I wanted to be back in the country. Drunk by the river seemed far better than where I was.

I heard the key in the lock, jumped up and went into the hallway. Dad and Kate were standing there smiling at me, both still dressed in their his-and-hers party gear. He had a look on his face somewhere between a naughty schoolboy caught nicking sweets and Jack Nicholson on acid. I couldn't quite believe what I was seeing. I wanted to run out of the house.

I scanned them both from head to toe. There was a scratch on the side of Dad's face from his ear to his mouth and a huge bruise covering Kate's right eye. The white of her eyeball was reddening with her own blood. The crisp whites of their matching outfits had been transformed into something out of a Stephen King climax. Her white lace outfit was torn in several places and was fifty percent red with blood. Whose it was I had no idea. The side of Dad's jacket was ripped from armpit to hem and the left arm of it was spattered with blood and mud. Their expressions, staring out at me from specks and flecks of blood and dirt, were horrifyingly comic. Kate waited for me to say something, then burst out laughing. I felt very shaky. In response to my obvious shock, Kate spoke.

'We got into a proper fight with some arseholes whistling at me. Fucking wankers didn't see that coming, eh, darling?'

She ran her hands through Dad's matted hair.

'No, babe. You fight like a lunatic.'

'I need to clean up.' Kate headed into the bathroom and locked the door.

'Fucking hell! What happened?' I asked Dad.

'There were some arseholes who fancied her, that bit's true. I got her away from that. There were too many of them. Even for me. She was kicking off about wanting me to kick the shit out of them. When I tried to calm her down she fucking started on *me*! I had to hit her with a dustbin lid six times before she stopped coming at me. Every time I whacked her and knocked her over she sprang up like that robot in *Blade Runner*. Frightened the fucking life out of me. She's got some arsehole that one, no doubt about it.'

Two weeks later, Dad and I were in the flat alone. Kate had gone to stay with a mate in the country. There hadn't been any smack around for the last ten days and the methadone had run out. Dad was making good money on cutting the coke but its strength was starting to be affected and he'd had to slow the scam down. I was finding it hard to sleep. My limbs were aching and I felt like I had a cold coming on. The flat had one bedroom. I slept in the sitting room. My back was aching from being on the sofa for so many weeks and I didn't want to sleep on the floor. I went in to see Dad.

'Can't sleep,' I told him. 'Can't switch my head off and I feel like shit.' I sat on the edge of the bed. Dawn was breaking through the curtains.

'Does it feel like a cold?' I nodded. 'You're clucking, kid. Get into bed with me. You're not to have any more gear. Ever.'

My first withdrawal had started. At least I had Dad to help me. If anyone knew how to get through it, he did.

13

Welcome to the Real World

Winter 1983, London

We're in a new place on the Fulham Road. It's better. It's bigger. There are two doors to get through to get on to the street, which makes me feel a little less paranoid. I usually keep my shoes on day and night and sometimes when I'm crashed out on the sofa. Shoes on and upstairs window open. I've got my escape route over the roofs worked out. I haven't done a complete test run but I know I can get on to the roof of the cinema and that should be far enough.

It's all the coke and all the punters that's doing it. Business is booming. We've made about fifty grand in profit in the last two months, mostly on smack and a little on coke. Dad has a way with the punters. He's good at this kind of business. He knows how to turn them on and make them feel special. They like buying from him. Our competition up the road is supposed to be an arsehole. We've taken a lot of new customers off him. Dad seems to like everyone who comes in here. He's pretending. I can't. I can't stand most of them and I'm sure the feeling is mutual. They interrupt me working on Dad for more gear. He usually ignores me when they're here.

There are five of us living here now. Me, Dad, Kate, Dan and Natalie. Dan is a bit of a prick. He has a six gram a day habit and has shown me how to insert two needles in his arms at the same time: one in the right, one in the left, crossing his hands and taking hold of each plunger with the opposite hand, suicide junky holding his weapons of choice, ready to shoot. He can do this and not pass out. That much smack in one go would kill most people. He puts a gram in each syringe and only looks vaguely stoned after the plungers are sunk home.

Then there's the French model, Natalie from Paris who can hardly speak a word of English. I don't know what she models, she looks dog rough most of the time, like she's just got out of bed. Her breath stinks.

Dad and Kate are out buying the next batch of smack and I'm in the house with Natalie and Dan. I'm supposed to be 'keeping an eye on things'. Dad has warned me to keep a close eye on Natalie in particular. Dan clearly fancies her and Dad says he'll do whatever he can to get into her knickers. His only chance of that is to give her her first hit of smack. This would be a bad idea. She's already had two lines off Dad today and is hassling Dan for more. Dan's happy to be hassled and is showing off.

'Right then, why don't you let this master in the art of jacking up the finest China white show you how it's done girl, eh?'

He couldn't keep his eyes off her tits. To be fair, they were great tits.

'Dan, I don't think this is a good idea. She's never had a hit before.'

'Don't you worry your little head, my son. I know what I'm doing here.'

'You put a gram in each hit. Even if you put a quarter of what you normally bang up it'll probably kill her.'

'Like I said,' he was grinning at her and she was grinning back, 'I know what I'm doing.'

I watched him closely. I had no confidence in him whatsoever. I watched him pour the small pile of smack into the spoon, add the liquid then the vitamin C, to help break down the heroin, burn the base of the metal and let it bubble gently. He certainly knew how to prepare a hit. Natalie cooed in appreciation.

I hadn't moved on to needles and had no intention of doing so. I deluded myself into thinking that as long as I stuck to just smoking smack I would be all right. I saw injectors as proper junkies, and they were to be scorned. Truth was there was little difference between foil and needles. Injecting was a quicker, sweeter rush and carried a greater risk of OD but my habit at the time, smoking smack on the foil, was around three grams a day. This was three times the average smoker's habit and twice the amount that went into a three hit a day needle habit. I refused to admit I had a problem. There was usually enough smack around to keep my withdrawals at bay. The closest I'd got to cold turkey at that point was a few sleepless nights, a runny nose and mildly aching limbs, and Dad had seen me right. I hadn't been away from heroin or methadone for more than a day for the last six months. At the time of Natalie's inaugural hit I had just smoked half a gram of smack on my own. I was feeling good.

Her eyes were glued to the spoon and followed Dan's every move as he filled the syringe and flicked the air bubbles out. She looked hungry for it. He wrapped the silk scarf gently round her arm and tightened it. He turned the underside of her arm upwards. The pressure squeeze of the silk tourniquet made a thick, deep-blue vein slowly rise under her bone-white skin.

'Lovely veins, girl. Lovely. Look at that, you're a natural.'

He tapped her wrist three times and brought the biggest vein up higher. He stroked her skin longer than was necessary. The thickest vein bulged up for attention, and the needle went in easily. She swore in French.

'Easy now,' he reassured her.

Anger flashed across her face but quickly melted as the plunger was pushed home. Before it reached the hilt of the cylinder, true to French cliché she let out a long sigh and three surprised words. 'Ooh la la.' Her eyelids started to droop. She glided back on to the sofa. A rasp of air left her lips.

'For fuck's sake, Dan. I told you to go easy!'

'She's all right, just enjoying the buzz and why not? While I enjoy the view. You're gorgeous, aren't you, my little French flower.'

He stroked her stockinged leg. She didn't respond.

'She's not all right. Look at her! She's turning fucking blue. Look at her!'

The deepening blue started in her lips. I watched in horror as it crept out into her cheeks. Her breathing had slowed almost to a stop. She looked deathly beautiful. I yanked her up off the sofa and shook her. She gurgled a bit but continued to go a deep hue of blue. I shook her harder. It made no difference. I started to panic. She was clearly OD'ing and that could not happen, I'd been given clear instructions.

I shook her so much she almost threw up. I could hear it rising in her throat. It didn't make it out of her mouth, and settled back down into her stomach. I'd seen people fall asleep on smack before, including Dad. I'd watched their breathing change and the colour in their cheeks fade but I'd never seen anyone like this before. Only an idiot would fail to see she was dying. Her heart was slowing down and if I didn't do something soon it would stop.

I started slapping her. Tentatively at first, then I got a feel for it and slapped her harder. I got a response and the colour in her cheeks started to fade back to a mottled pink. I hit her across the face over and over again until she said something in French that I thought meant fuck off. I carried on hitting her until her cheeks were almost back to pink. I almost started to enjoy it.

'Fucking hell, kid. Go easy, you'll ruin those Parisian good looks.' Dan's input.

I heard the door downstairs slam shut.

'Shut the fuck up,' I told him. 'Go and get some cold water.'

I hit her again, twice, but this approach had stopped working. I could feel her slipping deeper into what was obviously a coma. I tried mouth-to-mouth based only on what I'd seen on the telly. My whole life felt as though it was based around what I'd seen on the telly. I put my lips to hers. She was beautiful. I could see it now I was closer. Her breath smelled of puke. I reeled back and dry retched a couple of times. I got myself together and began to blow into her rank mouth. Her chest started moving up and down.

'What the fuck is goin' on here, kid! I'm gone five minutes and some fucking French cunt is turning blue in my front room!'

'It's OK, Dad. I've got it.' I didn't turn to look at him.

'Fucking right you've got it. That dopey French tart dies in this flat I chop her up and she goes in the Thames. I mean it! I'm not going back inside!'

The scene was utterly ridiculous. I felt like laughing right into her mouth. The mixture of panic, adrenaline and danger was overwhelming. I knew Dad meant what he said. It scared and excited me. I continued to blow air into her lungs.

After about thirty seconds I felt something dart into my mouth. I thought it may have been a chunk of puke but then realised it was fleshy and warm. Her tongue. Her eyes weren't open but she was regaining some kind of consciousness, wrapping her tongue around mine properly French kissing me. Her eyes snapped open and I felt her lips curl up against mine as she started to grin. My mouth-to-mouth had clearly worked. She was back and she was very, very stoned. I reared back across the room and wiped my mouth.

She lurched off the sofa and came at me with open arms. I needed to get away from her. It was my house, but I got out. I just about managed to shut the door on her grinning, stoned face.

Leon was on the edge of my social scene. He was into finding highs that were less physically dangerous. He was mainly into spliff and coke. We got stoned together and I was a good source of good quality coke for him. He steered clear of smack and tried to get me to do the same. I liked his concern. I felt cared for, but I ignored him.

I was having a great time, regularly going shoplifting and joy-riding with my mates. It was a miracle we didn't kill ourselves in the cars we nicked and hammered around London in, day and night. Leon was my closest friend. He lived in a world that was straighter and more stable than mine. I loved going over to his house and being inside the normality of it. Sometimes I came close to feeling like a normal teenager around him and his family. But not often.

Dad had started doing business with a guy called Mat. Mat wasn't into smack but he was into dodgy antiques. There was money to be made shipping over Buddhas and mythological animals from Thailand. Mat was doing the trips for Dad. They made good money doing this business together.

Mat was a rare, safe adult in my world. He knew a lot and helped me to organise my otherwise empty and chaotic days.

He became a mentor. We smoked dope together and talked. He got me thinking about what else I could do with my life apart from crime and drugs. I didn't come up with much, but he was one of the few grown ups I would listen to when he told me what he thought the best course of action was for me, especially when I was arguing with Dad. He had authority and experience and he saw I had potential. I was inspired by the way he dressed, the way he walked and talked. His confidence was clear. He was clean and sharp and knew how to make money, even if he was breaking the law most of the time. He hustled with dignity and grace. A bit like Dad, but he wasn't my father. This man got my trust and attention. It was a shame he got greedy and decided to rip us off.

Mat and Dad took two Thai ducks they'd bought from a skilled craftsman in Bangkok to a famous antique auctioneers in London. They were given the seal of approval and the dodgy wooden ducks were dated 'early nineteenth century'. Dad and Mat bought forty more pairs and shipped them over. They both agreed to stagger the sales across London. The auctioneers' 'genuine article' seal of approval made selling easy. They took them to shops at least five miles apart. There was to be no flooding of Thai ducks on the London antique market. But unknown to us, Mat had bought another sixty pairs and was preparing to flood the market throughout the rest of the country.

Mat had properly fucked up and when Dad found out I was unable to see Mat again. If he'd shown his face back in London, Dad would have cut it wide open. He promised me that.

I was missing Mrs T. and my mates at Stoke. I decided to go to a party down there, with Leon. School had been out for nearly a year and I was keen to find out what everyone had been doing. We passed through Stoke on our way. I saw Mrs T.'s house. Leon pulled the car over and I got out and headed quickly over to the house. The curtain twitched. She opened the door before I could knock. She looked at me and could hardly speak.

I hadn't realised how stoned I was and how rough I must've looked after eleven months full-on using. I jabbered on to her about all the things I was doing with my life. She didn't believe a word of it. It wasn't what I'd expected. I thought she would have been pleased to see me. She looked devastated. I said an awkward, confused goodbye and walked back to the car, slower this time. I'd let her down. I'd let myself down. The wild party went some way towards blocking her face from my mind.

London – two months later

Whatever Dad had hoped or planned for went out the window the moment Sam left him. I think it was the excuse he was looking for. I didn't really buy the promises he made and the dreams he had when he was inside but I wanted to. It was safe for him in there. Three square meals, somewhere to exercise, a bit of small-time dealing, enough to keep him stoned. HMP *wherever* was a place to meditate, read and relax; somewhere in the country. Most prisoners made fantasy plans. But re-entering the real world, chasing a pound note and keeping the police from the front door was a lot harder than dealing with screws at a cell door. Dad said he wanted to be a monk. HMP Ford was as close as he got.

The initial warmth I felt between us in the first few months after he got out was long gone. He was now hassling me to get a job.

I was meant to meet a new punter on the Gloucester Road early one morning; too early. It was a young posh bloke and he needed to be vetted before Dad would let him in the flat as a regular punter. It felt good to be trusted. I was moving up the ranks and getting more interesting work; less of the grocery boy more the proper dealer, with some credibility. But I overslept and the punter got pissed off and went elsewhere. Dad was furious. He was blowing it out of proportion and I realised he was making a point that to be a good worker I needed discipline and respect. By fucking this deal up I'd shown neither.

He went on all day about it. I tried to placate him with cups of tea, made him a bacon sandwich, asked him if there was anything I could do. He had only slept for an hour the night before. The hour I was supposed to be getting up. He was seriously moody. He snorted coke all day and he got more and more agitated.

'You wanna help out? Come to Harrods with me. We're going shopping.'

Dad's shopping trips rarely involved paying for what was in the basket.

'You're off your face, Dad. You're not in the best state to concentrate, are you?'

His childlike response was to take two Ativan and down them in one. Ativan is a powerful sleeping pill, a nasty drug, one in a long line of powerful downers often used by depressed housewives. Getting addicted to those was worse than smack. The withdrawal led to major panic attacks. But Dad had the resistance of an elephant to drugs. These pills wouldn't knock him out, they would calm the coke jitters, but they would also slow his reaction time down to the comical. Ativan was not a pill to pop before shoplifting a place with some of the best store detectives in the world. Dad wanted to punish me. He wanted to have some fun, to liven things up.

I tried to resist the shopping trip. I dragged my heels all

155

the way to the Brompton Road like the angry, sulky teenager I was. But there was no getting out of it. We started on the ground floor. Harrods was heaving with rich middle-aged women and tourists. Dad asked a shop assistant for a big carrier bag. I knew that was a mistake. It alerted the attention of a plain-clothes store detective right by us. The pursuit started.

Dad was now properly out of it. The Ativan had beaten the coke hands down. His eyes were drooping and he was actually nodding out. He waltzed through the store like a camp lord, plucking items off racks. Everything was tagged. I was dying of embarrassment and I wanted it to stop.

We went to the changing rooms and headed down to the end cubicle. My job was to keep an eye out for the detectives. Dad didn't really want the clothes, he was clearly just making his point. He had brought a pair of wire cutters with him and was systematically clipping off the electronic tags and putting the suits, shirts and trousers in the big Harrods bag. I noticed someone looking down the aisle right at our cubicle, right at me. I told Dad.

'Don't be ridiculous. You've had too much coke. You're being paranoid. Keep looking.'

I did. One person looking at us became two, then three then four. I told Dad when each new pair of eyes appeared and each time he told me to shut up and keep looking. He wanted to get us busted. I could have just walked away but that would have spelled sure-fire disaster for Dad and I had nowhere else to go, nowhere else to live.

Harrods bag now laden with clothes, we walked out. I could feel two people walking very close behind us. We got through the electronic security barrier and we were nicked. We were led through the labyrinth of back corridors to a shitty little office. They sat us down, telling us both that we were in a lot of trouble. Dad got out his wallet.

'Look, I've got five grand in here. I can pay for the lot right now. I forgot to pay. I was going to. Downstairs. Why would I steal these clothes if I have all this cash?'

He took it out and waved it at them.

'Beats me, mate. The wire clippers and the pile of tags in the changing room say it all. You're still nicked.'

We were taken to Chelsea police station and put in a cell together. We had both been searched but they hadn't accounted for fashion. Dad was wearing a grey pair of pixie boots. Somehow he managed to make even those look good. On the outside of the left boot was a tiny zip pocket. The top of the boot was turned down, revealing the fluffy inside and covering the zip. Dad had hidden a gram of coke in the zip pocket. He arrogantly stuck his boot on the bench, took out the coke and made a line for us both. Snorting coke in a Chelsea police station cell almost made the farcical shopping trip worthwhile.

Dad told them it was all his doing and was charged with shoplifting. I got a caution. I was off my face and laughing for the first time that day.

We had both been doing a lot of coke and not nearly enough smack to level out the edginess. I hadn't slept in two days and my nerves were in shreds. Dad and I had been bickering, sniping and scowling at each other all day. After weeks of stoned procrastination we were finally painting the front room. Leon was helping out.

'Here's the paint for the main coat. Whatever you do don't knock the fucking thing over,' Dad snapped at me.

'You've said that about twenty times in the last ten minutes. I heard you the first time.'

'Less of the lip, kid. Get on with the painting.'

He carried on nagging me for the next half hour about not knocking the paint over. Then it was his turn to get up the ladder. To my surprise he took the pot up with him. He was smug, looking like he knew what he was doing. He got to the top, got two strokes of Apple White on the wall, and knocked the pot off the ladder. The paint went up the walls and all over the brown carpet. I burst out laughing. Leon stayed quiet. With a completely straight face, Dad spoke without looking at either of us.

'Painting's over. Give us a hand, will you?' It wasn't a request it was an order.

'You knocked it over. You clean it up,' I said, still laughing.

He gave me a look I'd seen him give to others but never to me. I stopped laughing.

'I'm going out,' Leon told us. And he left.

'I'm going out, too,' I told Dad.

'You're not going anywhere. You're helping me clean this shit up.'

I didn't reply. After three-and-a-half years without him I was already sick to death of being around him. I had a 'fuck you' fire in my veins and decided there and then that I was going to move out. I left the room, closing the sitting room door behind me. I packed a bag.

'What are you doing in there, kid?'

I heard concern in his voice. I still didn't answer. I headed for the hall. He followed me to the door. I went to open it. He put his arm across me and held it shut.

'Where are you going?'

'Out.'

'You're not going anywhere.'

'Move your arm, Dad.'

'If you walk out that door I'll . . . I'll cave your fucking head in.'

He was holding a lump hammer by his side. This was insane. I sobered up at once. Dad was strung out from too much coke and a serious lack of sleep. He wasn't himself but he had still threatened me. If I stayed I would have to put up with more arguing and paranoia. If I tried to leave he might attack me. He didn't want me to go and this was his way of pleading with me. But I'd had enough. I was leaving, and that was more than he could deal with.

'Please move your arm, Dad.'

He dropped his exhausted head and moved his arm. I walked out, intending never to come back.

I headed to Fiona's house. She was my new girlfriend. I had met her through my brother, Paul. She was a bit younger than me, a model and came from a very straight, wealthy Asian family. I was in love. I think she was in awe. I was two years older than her and had money to spend – on her. I'd taken Dad's advice about the wining and dining of women.

I got to her house at about four in the morning and woke her up with stones at her window. She let me in and I told her about what had happened with Dad. She thought it was tragic and romantic. I thought it was pathetic and sad.

But after twenty-four hours of hanging out with this stunning girl I started to feel very rough. Lack of smack. A snotty nose had turned into a streaming cold. I was running hot and cold sweats and my legs ached so much I was finding it hard to walk. Lemsip wasn't doing it. With no methadone in my system for over a week and now no smack for a day and a night, this was the longest I'd been without any opiates since I started doing drugs six months earlier. I hated what I was feeling and it was getting worse by the minute. I was ready to do anything to make it stop. I needed something to level me out and Dad had what I wanted. I reluctantly headed back home. He had me just where he wanted me.

On a rain-soaked afternoon I returned to a flat packed full of antiques I hadn't seen before. They were lined up in the hallway and stacked in the sitting room, bedroom and kitchen. Dad had been busy.

He was hunched over a large piece of foil, white smoke pluming around him as he missed most of what he was chasing.

'What's all this?' I asked angrily.

He lit a cigarette and took his time before speaking. 'You stayed away longer than I thought you would.' He picked up an ancient gilt lampshade. I flinched. He noticed. 'George put us on to this antiques runner and this is what the little tiger came up with.'

'What the hell are we going to do with it all?'

'Sell it, swap it, use it around the house. Sure we can think of something.'

I was withdrawing and he could see it. I was doing my best to hold it together. My pride wouldn't allow me to ask him for any smack. Not yet. He wanted to re-establish the ground rules and let me know who was in charge. He picked up the square of foil, the pipe and the lighter and sat down next to me. He handed me the pipe and I took a long, silent smoke. My limbs began to loosen and my breathing changed. After a few seconds the cold sweat on my back began to dry. My anger towards him melted. I was happy for him to be back in charge. It was easier that way. He pulled the foil away, a little too soon. I wasn't fully back on track.

'Can I have some more? I'm feeling really rough.'

'Later. That'll keep you going.'

It was just enough to keep me going and it would keep me connected to him, not wanting to leave. It was his insurance against having to do everything on his own. Tough as he was, he hated being alone. The phone went. It was George's antiques runner. There was a problem.

'You fucking *what*!' Dad shouted into the receiver. He continued to listen. I could see incendiary anger moving across his face. He prepared to speak. 'So, *this* is what you're going to do. You call your sister back and tell her you brought the stuff here to sell. Give them the name the house is in, Terry Marsh. I had nothing to do with this, understand. I wasn't there. Tell her it's here and I had nothing to do with it. Come and get it out and take it back. I won't be here. The keys will be under the mat. If you fuck this up and get me nicked I will break both your legs. That's a promise. Do you understand?' He waited for an answer. 'Good. Now get to it, you little prick.'

Terry Marsh was one of Dad's made-up names. He put the phone down and looked at me. 'We're going to have that extra smoke, now.'

'What's going on?'

'The little prick told me everyone was away. We were robbing his fucking parents' house and we were seen taking the gear out the back door. No one could make me out, so he says. We have to get out of here for the day, kid.'

After clearing out all traces of foil and drugs, we left. We took our business door to door, driving from one end of London to the other. The punters were happy not to have to come out on such a cold day. So grateful, in fact, that half of them gave us a smoke for our trouble. We were passing the time at punters' houses while the stolen antiques were, we hoped, being rescued from our flat in Fulham.

We had several types of punter, all easily classified. The Hooray Henry/Henrietta was Dad's favourite. They were generally polite, generous and loaded. Their class, dress sense and education reminded him of his aspirations and made him feel less seedy in his work. They made up seventy percent of our client base. He loved posh women. He told me Henriettas were better and ruder in bed than their working-class counterparts, especially when stoned. 'They have more time, more money. Their disciplined upbringing means they push the boundaries in bed. Dirty, lovely, rude, tarts.'

Then there was the office worker. I could never figure out

how they kept a nine-to-five, five days a week office job together, despite a smack and coke habit. These bright, intelligent punters, sharply dressed in Savile Row and Givenchy, were the most punctual. They turned up like clockwork between 5 p.m. and 7 p.m. every day, coming straight from their jobs in the city to buy enough gear to keep them going for the next twenty-four hours. The coke would keep up the competitive adrenaline edge needed during day and the smack helped them come down and relax in the evening.

Rent boys and hookers were very professional and generally very quiet. They were quick to buy their drugs, seldom complained about the size of the deals and were quick to leave. They bought narcotics mainly to numb the nightmare of their daily schedule.

The working-class punter was a rarity in our house. Dad didn't encourage their drug purchases but the ones he worked with provided business links that were often lucrative but dangerous. They were frequently violent and unpredictable. I came home one day as Dad sprung out of the front door in full boxing gear and bamboo-knuckled sparring gloves.

'Where you goin', Dad?'

'That little toerag Kevin hasn't turned up with the money again. He's going to get a dig to remember.' Coked up and wide eyed, he sprinted up the road like a greyhound running for a rabbit.

Dad wasn't fussy enough about the people he did business with and this caused him more trouble than he admitted. In some way he was being loyal to his working-class roots and not forgetting the shitty side of the street he grew up on. The working-class punters were often small-time crooks with 'big-time charley potato' attitudes – they really thought they were the business – and best avoided.

There were some very well-known people buying drugs

off us on the Fulham Road. Celebrities. Musicians, actors, models and varying ranks within the aristocracy. They were all defined by how ordinary they were, the huge quantity of drugs they could consume and their general lack of affectation. They seemed resigned and committed to their daily drug use. They were friendly, waited their turn and treated me with respect. Good breeding and good manners. One famous face gave Dad his brand-new five series BMW as collateral for three grams of smack and a gram of coke. We drove the car for a month. It had heated seats, quite a big deal back then. Another would regularly come and score off us by helicopter, landing at Battersea heliport. He would call just before he left his big house in the country and we would watch him flying over our flat, turning up ten minutes later on his custom made Italian motorbike.

The old hippy was the rarest of all customers and the most interesting. They would usually arrive in beads and headscarves, anything colourful and chic that made them look different and got them noticed. They usually bought coke for a 'party they were throwing for some friends'. They never admitted to having a smack habit and if they bought any it would be for the coke comedown 'at the end of a long night'. Dad had a very different way of communicating with them. They would often stay beyond closing time and he would reminisce with them about long-dead friends and the good old days when it was 'so much easier to make money'.

I couldn't see anything easier than the work Dad was doing. We were making a fortune. Selling drugs was a natural progression from Dad's genuine pleasure in being the centre of attention and in control. He was the king of his narcotic realm and he carried out business with professional, respectful charm. Unless someone fucked him about. But punters knew not to do this. He would give credit to those he trusted and he would enjoy the extra power it gave him over them. He was the most popular, charismatic and generous dealer in the area. I was proud of him and could see the obvious benefits of running a business in the way he did. For most of our customers it was as much a social call as business. I got respect by default. Even when they didn't like me, and I could always tell, they smiled and nodded and didn't give me any attitude.

Dad brought his freebase kit with him wherever we went. On that door-to-door day he made several batches. Freebase was an early form of home-made crack cocaine. It could be made in two ways that I knew of: one was with bicarbonate of soda. The other was created with liquid ammonia. The process separated the impure, cut coke from the pure, uncut coke. The pure coke formed into a rock which, when rinsed, could be smoked. I was never any good at chemistry at school but I was very good at making freebase. For me, learning was all about application and desire, and I had plenty of that for the finished product. This incredibly powerful drug would be the death of our booming business.

We headed back to Fulham late that evening. Business had been good but Dad was nervous. He didn't know what to expect and was hyper alert. We walked up a side street, slowly. I followed his lead and pace.

'Keep your eyes wide, kid.' We walked on to the main road.

'See anything unusual?' he asked.

'No.'

'Look again.'

I scanned the streets and saw two men in a doorway. They had been there before but I hadn't noticed them.

'What do you see?'

'Two men. Over in that doorway, watching the house. They look dodgy.' We carried on walking towards The Goat in Boots pub.

'What else?'

Suddenly more pairs of men started to appear in front of my eyes, like an invisible cloak had been lifted.

'Two by Europa Foods, pretending to look at the deli counter.' My heart was beating four times as fast. 'And two more walking towards the flat.'

'We need a drink,' Dad told me. We walked into the pub.

We sat and watched the three pairs of plain-clothes police biding their time out on the dark, wet street.

'What are we going to do, Dad?'

After our second drink he wiped his mouth dry and looked at me. 'I need you to let them in and if it's still there, let them take the gear. The little prick has clearly fucked it up.'

'But they'll arrest me!' I felt about ten years old.

'They won't arrest you because you've done nothing wrong. You let them in and tell them he gave you the antiques and you thought they were clean. You had nothing to do with the burglary.'

'Why don't you do it?'

'I've just got out of nick, kid. Just being associated with stolen goods is enough to fuck my probation. I'd be back inside before I got to court.'

I didn't want that. Where would I get my smack from?

'I'm scared.'

'You've got nothing to be scared of, kid. You've done nothing wrong. All you have to do is let them in and give them the gear.'

He kept saying the words over and over, like a mantra. 'You've done nothing wrong, kid. If they ask, tell them the place belongs to Terry Marsh.'

I felt like I was being worked on by my father but refused to believe it. Finally after another half an hour and four more vodka lime and tonics I agreed. I left the pub, slightly pissed, not looking back. I ignored the heat of the stares of the men watching the flat. I got to the front door and let myself in. Hairs all over my body were on end. The antiques were still there. I was in a cold sweat. I got into the house and sat on the bed. Within thirty seconds the buzzer went. I was shitting myself. I pressed the intercom.

'Hello?'

'It's Nicky.' It was a woman's voice. We supplied to three different Nickys. Two women and a man. It sounded like one of the women. This was very bad timing. I buzzed her in. She wasn't alone. I heard a load of footsteps coming quickly up the stairs. I stood behind the closed door, my body shaking.

'Who is that? Where's Nicky?'

'I'm Nicky.' It started as a man's voice then turned into the woman's voice I'd heard on the intercom. Then I heard laughter. Male laughter. 'Open the door, son.'

'I'm not opening the door. You just fucking lied to me. What the hell is going to happen when I let you in?'

'Open the door or we'll kick it in.'

I'd had this feeling before. It was a battering ram moment and I couldn't face going through with the violence of it again. I opened the door. There were eight policemen and one woman, all plain-clothes. We hadn't spotted them all. Six rushed past me. The last two took hold of my arm, twisted it behind my back and cuffed me. I was led upstairs.

'You're up to your neck in it here, mate.'

'I didn't nick this stuff, I'm just letting you in so you can take it back.'

'Very thoughtful of you to tell us it's nicked.'

I was led down the stairs and into the street. People were staring at me. I knew things were only going to get worse. I looked across the road into The Goat in Boots. Dad was gone. I was driven down to a small police station in Oxford near to where the robbery had taken place, and locked into a one-man cell.

Oxford Police Station

My first hours in that cell were a nightmare. The withdrawals had already kicked in on the way down in the unmarked police car. Being locked in a concrete cell seemed to accelerate the symptoms. Every inch of flesh on my body felt like it had been taped down with sticking plaster. The most basic movement was like wading through hot, stinking mud. I didn't even have the energy to crawl. My levels of self pity and desperation were off the scale.

No one spoke to me. They could see I was starting to squirm like a dying insect. The smile on their faces when I pleaded for some methadone said it all. They wanted to see me sweat a lot more before they took me out for questioning.

My mind would not switch off and would not stop thinking about smack, smack, smack. There was nowhere to put my focus in the cell, nothing to distract me. Nothing to watch, nothing to read except the illiterate graffiti on the yellow walls, the same shade of yellow they'd had in Wormwood Scrubs. All the room had in it was a blue plastic mattress and a shit stinking toilet. I paced around, sat by the door, on the bed, the loo, beneath the tiny window three feet above my head. I kicked the iron door several times and realised the pain of the impact on my bare feet at least distracted me from my withdrawal for a few seconds. I masturbated compulsively, each orgasm saturating my body with a few endorphin-filled seconds of pleasure. As the last of the smack finally left my body my nerves and flesh screamed for a hit. I couldn't bear being in my skin any longer. I felt like dying.

I listened to the voices and noises outside the cell and tried to make mental pictures from what I was hearing. A canteen trolley, keys in locks, a drunk shouting, kicking, sobbing, a distant radio playing, cars and lorries a long way off, and every once in a while the siren on the latest squad car dispatched to deal with another criminal.

I couldn't sleep. I stayed awake, pacing and fidgeting, muscles gnawing at my bones. I was given some food and a cup of tea. I threw up the bangers and mash as soon as I'd finished eating them. I fell asleep to the sound of birds waking.

Late that afternoon I was shaken awake by a worried-looking man wearing glasses. I was drenched in cold sweat. There were three wide-eyed faces peering down at me.

'There you are! Good. We were getting a bit worried. Been trying to wake you for nearly three hours. Thought you were a gonner for a minute there, young man.' It was a police doctor, flanked by two uniformed officers.

My pores were leaking toxins and I stank of piss and semen and sweat and fear. I was properly ashamed of myself. 'Can I have a cigarette?' were my first words.

After some rotten food, which I kept down, and two fags I was taken into a room and my questioning began. It had been all I could do to get up off my wet plastic mattress, out of the cell and down the station corridor. I wasn't going to get any medication until *after* this particular ordeal. I was trembling from head to toe from fear and withdrawal.

After a couple of hours of relentless questions they realised they had no solid evidence on me in connection to the burglary. They knew who my dad was and asked me a lot of questions about him. I said he had nothing to do with the burglary and I didn't know where he was now. They found no record of Terry Marsh. I could see they didn't believe a word of what I was telling them. But what could they do?

The antique runner clinched my release. They had nicked him too and were holding him in the cell down from me. It turned out he was the weeping drunk. He had admitted to the burglary and said he'd done it alone. His parents weren't going to press charges. He was cautioned and was free to go.

I was given two paracetamol and released without charge or apology. The runner and I were released at the same time. I should have beaten him up for my trouble, and for Dad, but I didn't have the strength. Besides, he looked pitiful. I was actually glad of his company and our complicity on the train back to London. We had both survived.

I got back to London and phoned Kate at the flat. She told me Dad was staying at one of George's flats. I headed over to him. My withdrawals were now past their worst but I was still desperate for a smoke. I was let in by George's girlfriend, headed downstairs and found Dad squatting on the kitchen floor toking on a freebase pipe. He looked up at me with a lung full of smoke and smiled.

'Hey, kid,' he squeaked. He held the pipe out to me in a gesture of peace.

'Have you got any smack?' I asked. He could see I was struggling. He shook his head.

'This is it for now. Got plenty of it, though. Much as you like.'

I knew the coke would heighten my withdrawal. I was looking for the muscle-soothing effect of an opiate, something to slow down my jittering muscles, something to help me sit still and stare at the wall. The amphetamine hit of the base would magnify the restlessness in my bones but it would get me stoned and perhaps take my mind, if not my body, off the excruciating pain.

Nothing was said about the bust. He asked me if I was all right but not about the details. No apology, though he had guilt on his face. Neither of us wanted to discuss the fact that he had put me up to get nicked. He had lied to me to keep himself out of prison. If he'd told me in advance what was going to happen to me I wouldn't have gone through with it. But however fucked up it was, we were both out and we were together. I took the pipe from him and started smoking.

14

Rise and Fall

We have the best part of sixty grand in the bank. How the fuck Dad has managed it I don't know. I thought we were doing half the drugs ourselves.

Dad gives good deals and it's always quality gear. It doesn't mean we're not ripping the punters off. The drugs on sale are cut by up to fifty percent of their original strength to increase profits. What we get from Mahmoud, our dealer in Dalston, even after he's done his own downgrading, is that good, that pure, that we can afford to cut it. Be silly not to. We reduce the purity and we still sell some of the strongest gear in Fulham.

We were in the final stages of organising our trip to Thailand. And Dad was hoping never to come back. He wanted to go legit, or as near as possible, by the end of the year. The drug money was going to be invested in more mock antique ducks, Buddhas, mythological rabbits, deer and golden painted birds of paradise. This line of dealing was a sure start with good profit margins and a step away from narcotics and prison.

When Dad's drug shop was shut for the day, he would tell me how much he hated dealing to what he called 'emotional casualties'. He told me our time dealing was limited. It is for everyone. Selling drugs on that scale is all about timing; taking it right up to the edge and making as much money as possible before stopping, before getting busted. If the dealer isn't using the product there is more chance of keeping to a deadline and budget and getting out before the police come in. If we hadn't been getting stoned, the fake antique business would have been possible.

Dad had decided to shut up shop for the Christmas holidays. Three days without answering the door and having to watch him act. Music to my ears. Just me, him, Kate for a day or two – and all the smack and coke I could smoke. London at Christmas is a desolate place. Without all the traffic and people it was almost bearable. A good excuse to stay in and take a lot of drugs.

Dad and I went out for a drive on Christmas Day to get some fresh air. We had taken too much coke and had popped some strong downers to ease the edge. We were both finding it hard to keep our eyes open. The streets were empty of people and traffic. After a few minutes cruising just off the King's Road in our Renault 5, I fell asleep in the passenger seat, head against the window. I woke up very suddenly to a wide arc of yellow sparks on the other side of the glass, followed quickly by an excruciating screech of metal on metal. A sound much like the crash in France. Dad had also fallen asleep and had drifted the car into a long line of parked cars, ripping and scratching into their expensive, Chelsea bodywork. He was actually still asleep after scraping into the first three cars and I had to scream at him to wake up. After it had gouged a final chunk out of a Mercedes Sports, our wrecked car came to an abrupt halt on its own. Dad got out, dazed, looking at the damage.

'What the fuck happened, kid?' He asked me, like it was my fault.

My door was now jammed shut. Panicked, I scrambled out of the driver's side and ran off. Dad told me when he got home that he had knocked on the doors of a series of houses nearest to the wrecked cars and had paid the owners in cash for the damage.

The three-day break we had taken for Christmas drifted into a week. After near-constant base making and smoking we finally ran out of coke and had to venture out to buy more. After ten days away from the momentum of constant customers, something in Dad visibly gave up. Our doors to the dealing didn't reopen for business. The phones stayed unplugged. Kate moved out and stayed at her parents'. In a stoned haze, the outside world started to recede. The only reality was the sitting room, telly, stereo, candles, foil, free-base, pipe and our replenished and seemingly endless supply of drugs. My buzz and hunger for freebase was levelled by the opiate of smack in a way I had only dreamed of. Too much smack left me dribbling and nodding, unable to say anything much more than 'Have you seen my tropical fish?' Too much base left me erratic, paranoid and volatile, constantly checking the street for dangerous men in doorways. The two drugs smoked together were made for each other: all the problems in the world, up in one incredible puff of very expensive smoke. I've never been able to get my head around the insanity of how much we consumed from that Christmas onwards. Recently, with a clearer head, I did the maths.

It broke down to something like this:

- One gram of cut coke usually gave us a quarter of a gram of pure, smokable base.
- Out of every 28 uncut grams (one ounce) freebased, we got back around seven smokeable grams of base to smoke a day; four for Dad, three for me. This cost

us a £1,000 per ounce which came to around £7,000 a week.
- Total: £42,000 of coke smoked in just six weeks.
- The smack was around the same price for us to buy, and we smoked about two ounces a week between us. That came to £2,000.
- £2,000 a week came to approximately £12,000 of smack smoked in six weeks.
- Coke and smack smoked in six weeks between me and Dad: a grand total of £54,000.

Along with our minds, the profits were well and truly blown. Thailand – Dad's Happy Ever After – was out.

Dad's attitude to our rapidly folding business was suicidal in its recklessness. He was on a mission to fuck everything up and I followed along more than willingly, behind him – as long as there were drugs to prop me up and shut me up.

Dad had fallen out with our dealer in Dalston. Our supply of coke had been dry for a few days and we had just finished the last of the smack. It was a cold, empty space and in that moment I knew it was all over. So did Dad but he said nothing. 'I'm going to see Mahmoud,' he told me in a pissed-off monotone.

'How long will you be?' After just two hours without drugs I was already starting my withdrawals.

'Couple of hours at most.'

The thought of two more hours without smack cranked up my fear of withdrawals and I shivered. 'Will you call if you're gonna be any longer?'

'I won't be. Don't worry about it, kid.'

Dad left the flat. I watched another weird art film on Channel 4. It was cold and the blow heater wasn't making much impact. I got into Dad's bed and fell asleep. When I woke up it was dark and I was feeling much worse. It was raining steadily against the window outside. Dad had been gone over six hours and hadn't called. Scared, I reluctantly rang Mahmoud and got a voice I didn't recognise.

'You're looking for Frank you say? Yep, he's here. He says he's going to be a while and why don't you come over.'

'Um . . . it's Sunday. There aren't any buses.' I wanted the conversation to end.

'Get a cab.' And he put the phone down. Something was clearly wrong. My increasing withdrawal and my need to know what Dad was up to was way too much for my curiosity to resist. I got dressed and left the house with a cold fear that was only just beaten back by my need for smack. I was desperate for a smoke to ease the sweat on my back and the increasing aches in my legs. When I got there the front door was open. I could see people in the hallway. No one I recognised. My gut told me to get out fast. I turned on my heel. I took two steps away from the door when I heard a woman's voice call to me.

'Hi there. Can I help you?' She was a policewoman.

'No, it's OK. Wrong address,' I lied.

'Have you come to see Mahmoud?'

'Er, no.' I lied badly.

'No need to make a fuss on the street, eh? Come in and have a chat. Just a few quick questions.'

It felt like I was back at school. I did as I was told. As I walked in, the street light faded and the brightness of the hall light hurt my eyes. The lampshade had been removed. There were lots of police in the house. The junkies had already been arrested and taken to the station. My legs started shaking.

'Stand there, love, legs apart, rest your palms on the wall in front of you.' She patted me down. It was the first human contact I'd had in weeks. I welcomed it. 'Now drop your trousers and pants and bend over.'

'I'd rather not.' My left leg was trembling uncontrollably.

'We can do it here or at the station. It's up to you. If you're clean, you can go.'

I did as I was told. I hadn't had a bath for over a month. I smelled bad and felt ashamed. She didn't seem bothered. Two policemen walked past and laughed at my naked, skinny arse.

'Got yourself a handsome one there, Trace.'

She ignored them. 'You're a bit young to be mixing with these kind of people. Were you here to buy drugs?'

She asked me this while she parted my cheeks, looked up my arse and around my balls with her white rubber gloves. She was gentle about it, like a monkey looking for lice. Part of it turned me on. The other part left me speechlessly embarrassed. Admitting to being there for drugs would have been stupid, no matter how obvious it was. 'No,' I said, trying to keep it together while she continued looking for narcotics that weren't there. 'Well, what were you here for then?'

'I was trying to find my dad.'

'Your father?' She was clearly taken aback. 'What's his name?'

'Frank Walsh.'

Telling her his name was a mistake. But I wanted to know what had happened to him.

'Oh, right. Him. He's at the station. Slippery bugger. Tried to escape twice, even jumped over the garden wall. Bill over there had to knock him to the ground to calm him down. Very determined not to come quietly, your father.'

I looked over to 'Bill'. He was massive. He had a kind face but the body didn't match. He was whistling while loading up kilo blocks of smack into a big clear plastic bag with two other plain-clothes officers.

'Well, you're clean, in a manner of speaking. Give me

your name and address and you can go. I'll know if you're lying, believe me.'

I wanted to lie but I couldn't. I gave her my real name and address and immediately regretted it.

'We'll be keeping in touch,' she assured me.

After five quick minutes in that rank, drug-infested hallway, I was out. The air on the street smelled sweet. I was so shaky I had to walk at half speed to stay in a straight line. I felt like an old man and looked like a tramp. I had no money for a cab and there were no buses. I walked the seven miles back home in the now pissing rain. I was shivering from lack of smack and soaked to the skin. After just fourteen months on the outside, Dad was gone again and I was alone. A year on smack, a year of dealing and I'd had enough of everything. I was running out of reasons for living.

Two days later

I got home and sat in front of the telly with no idea what to do next. There was no food in the house. I had no money. I was forced to go back to shoplifting for what I needed. Mars bars and baked beans, mainly. I had no access to drugs. No one would come within a mile of me now. Business was over. I was in the middle of my worst ever withdrawal and could barely walk to the loo.

I finally managed to get hold of Kate. She came round to see me with two 150 mls bottles of methadone. They were to last me up to three days and would help me come off smack without too much of a crash. She stayed about ten minutes. We didn't say much. She cared about me and this was her way of showing it. But she needed to stay out of the way for the foreseeable future. She needed to make sure she wasn't implicated in the business in any way. She gave me a sad look and a hug and left. I put the stereo on in an attempt to fill the emptiness in the house and to block out my rising fear of being alone. I looked at the bottle of methadone and held it up to the light. The gloopy emerald liquid inside was going to take away my withdrawal. I took a swig and screwed the lid back on. Nothing happened. I took another swig and another and another. In ten minutes the bottle was empty. Within half an hour I felt the opiate rush warmly through my bloodstream and into my head. I felt better. Much. I lay back on the bed and listened to The Steve Miller Band. I was still skint, alone and desperate but I was stoned. Everything was back on track.

Between songs I thought I heard something downstairs. A click in the lock. I sprung up and turned the stereo down. The front door opened and clicked quietly shut. Was Dad back? I stood up on the bed praying it was him, knowing it wasn't. Someone was coming up the stairs. Frozen to the spot, I stood and waited. Out of the darkness of the stairway I saw a man in a suit reach the landing. He was tall and well built, he had a kind face. It was Bill from Mahmoud's house.

The methadone had given me false courage. 'How did you get in?'

'Your father gave me his keys. Said I could look around.' Dad would never have done that, not willingly. 'I've just come round for a chat. Few questions about your dad's line of work.'

I didn't want to talk to him but I was desperate for company. The methadone was increasing in warmth and intensity – opiates always gave me the confidence I never had. The familiar ease that the drug always promised crept into me. Why not, I decided. I hadn't spoken to anyone in days.

'I haven't got anything to say.'

'Well, a few days down the station may help you change your mind on that.'

It would. There was no way I was going back into a cell. 'Why don't I make us a cup of tea?' he suggested.

I gave up the pretence of bravado and sat on the bed. Bill headed down to the kitchen and five minutes later came back in, two cups of tea in his hands and a sympathetic smile on his face. Dad had warned me about this moment, about the kindness and the warmth. He said there was a new kind of policeman around. One that liked to work alone, not in the routine good-cop-bad-cop cliché. This kind of policeman was smart, ambitious and dangerous. Not someone to be messed around with. I wondered what was happening to Dad at that moment. Were they beating him up? He would be sick in his cell. His withdrawal would be peaking. But he was used to it. He'd done it a dozen times. And there I was sat on the bed, stoned, drinking tea with the aptly named Bill.

'You're a bit young to be involved in all this.'

'Everyone says that. I'm old enough.'

'Your dad get you involved in it?'

'In what?'

'You know what I'm talking about.'

I had no idea how much he knew about the dealing. Keeping my freedom was a priority, this man could take it away in a heartbeat.

'Do you mean the antiques?' I faltered.

'We know he's been dealing and there are plenty of people willing to back that up. It seems business hasn't been so good lately.' He paused for a sip of his tea. I wondered if he was bluffing. 'Was he involved in the robbery of that house in Oxford?'

'Didn't they get their stuff back?'

'Yes, but we still haven't caught the second burglar. The family are keen to see someone other than their son prosecuted. He's a rich-boy troublemaker but he's still their son. You still seem to be the best lead, even if there isn't any direct evidence. It'd be a bad thing if you got arrested again and locked up for something you didn't do, wouldn't it? Just to make some posh folk in Oxford feel safe and happy again.' He paused for a moment. 'We know your dad is Terry Marsh.'

He knew exactly what he was doing. I liked this copper but my mind was racing, looking for a way out. Dad had stitched me up with the antiques. The police weren't giving up. I wasn't going back inside. The methadone was doing the trick, covering me in a false sense of safety and hope. In that newly stoned moment, everything suddenly felt like it was going to be all right. I decided talking was definitely the best medicine. I wasn't going to do another three days cold turkey in another shit stinking cell. Dad could handle it. I couldn't and wouldn't.

Each word that came out of my mouth put another nail in Dad's coffin and I knew it but being in the moment, enjoying the buzz, the first decent company in weeks, getting it all off my chest was more important. I told Bill about Dad's connection to the Oxford burglary, about the dealing we did together. I talked too much about everything I hated about dealing: the people, the hours and the fear. I painted a bad picture of my father. I was enjoying the sound of my own voice. The more I told Bill the less likely it would be that I would get put in a cell again. Bill was listening intently.

'Mind if I make some notes?' he asked me.

I didn't object but the official nature of pen to paper made me nervous. It also made me more articulate. It felt like a performance and I was playing up to my audience of one. I was milking the drama and darkness of my life; like I was living inside a Greek tragedy and I needed rescuing from it by someone just like Bill. I paced the room as I spoke. I put the consequences of where my statement would lead to the back of my mind. I knew the trouble it would cause Dad but I was doing this for me not him. Maybe at some level I was getting back at him for stitching me up with the burglary but this wasn't a conscious thought at the time. At that moment with my new mate Bill it was a matter of survival at any cost.

Bill continued to take notes, nodding and making sympathetic, understanding noises from time to time. Incriminating words flowed out of me. 'Would you be prepared to go to court to back this up?

'Yes.' I wasn't. I wanted him to go now.

He put his notes away with a smile on his face. He gave me a few fags and left me alone in the cold flat. I had become the grass Dad had always told me not to be. I had dumped him in it up to his neck. I had crossed the line but I was too stoned to think any more about it. All I wanted to do was enjoy the buzz, alone.

Three months later, Fulham, London

I walked out of the flat in Fulham and left the landlord to clean the place up. We owed him over £5,000 in rent. The place looked like a squat and smelled like a dog kennel. The only trace of the style it once buzzed with was a few sticks of incense and a wall hanging. I'd sold the stereo, the video and the TV. That was the final push for me to get out. I couldn't stand the silence any longer. With the worst of my withdrawals over, I got up one afternoon, got dressed and walked out, glad to see the back of the place.

I thought about going to Mum's and decided against it. I couldn't be around her for more than two days without getting into an argument. Asking Sam if I could stay with her and her new man was out of the question. I was too proud to ask my friends. I toyed with the idea of Mrs T. but knew she wouldn't have me in the house, not after my last visit. I had one option left. I went to my aunt Grainne's house. She was still living in our old family house in Fulham. It had been Granddad's place and he left it to Grainne and Dad when he died. Dad took his share in cash and blew it. I was conceived there when Mum and Dad were homeless.

She saw the state I was in and agreed to let me stay a few weeks. I was surprised she was so welcoming; I hadn't seen her in years. I had my own room and was back on three square meals a day.

It had taken about five weeks to level out from the withdrawals. I was back on spliff and booze and that, for the most part, was doing the trick. I was hanging out with Leon again. I felt like I had come back down to teenage earth. Grainne became another mother to me. She and Dad had fallen out but she wouldn't see me out on the street. Grainne took me to visit Dad. After the raid at Mahmoud's he'd been transferred straight from his police cell in Clapham to HMP Wandsworth. Familiar territory. He was serving the rest of his previous, unfinished sentence and was also on remand for the Oxford antiques job, one stolen car, unpaid rent, stolen credit cards and cheque books, two bank accounts in false names and, last but not least, dealing in class A drugs. Bill had found several former punters of ours who were happy to talk about Dad and his dealing in order to stay out of cells as well. With or without my big mouth, Dad wasn't going to be out again for a long time.

He was pleased to see me, and he wasn't. 'Hey, kid.'

He kissed me and squeezed the back of my neck. He kissed Grainne and she sat quietly next to me. They didn't speak to each other.

'Well, I'm in a right fucking mess this time. Do you realise what you've done, Cas?' He rolled a cigarette. He didn't offer me one.

I was almost speechless with shame. 'I was stoned. I'd been on my own for days. He was being nice to me. I wasn't the only one.' I deliberately didn't apologise.

'You're going to have to go, kid. You can't back that up in court.'

'What do you mean, "go"? Where?'

My arse cheeks gripped tight at the prospect of going on the run. He looked at his sister.

'Can you get him into a kibbutz? Out of the country. Anywhere.'

'Doubt it. Don't have enough money.' She thought a moment longer. 'I've got a friend in Devon who may be able to help.'

My future was arranged for me in front of my eyes and I didn't have a say in the matter. The visit was short. I knew Dad still loved me. He would, no matter what I did. But I could see he was angry. If I went to court and was questioned about the statement I made, his sentence would be doubled. We hugged and I left, trying hard to conceal my tears. He didn't. I saw them sparkle in his eyes. He wiped them and kissed me goodbye. My aunt didn't say much on the way home. She was thinking about what to do with me.

Summer 1984, London to Devon

The train left Paddington station and headed for Exeter St Davids. I had a good seat. As the fields and rivers started to appear, my body relaxed.

Grainne was into her magazines.

'Nobby's a bit of a weird name, isn't it? Is it real?' I asked.

'He was in the navy. It's a nickname for sailors.'

'If someone called me that at school I'd belt them. Is he a nutter?'

'He could be, if he's messed about, but he's calmed down a lot. He's got three kids.'

'I didn't know there were going to be kids there.'

'And a wife, Joanne. They're a nice family.'

'You said he was a gangster.'

'I said he was a retired gangster.'

'Is he . . . hiding . . . in the country? I mean is he on the run, as well?'

An old lady on the seat opposite stopped reading and looked over at us. Grainne lowered her voice and expected me to do the same. 'He retired to the country. Anyway you'll be able to ask him all the questions you like when you meet him. Just don't talk about guns. He doesn't like it, not in front of his family.'

'How do you know him?'

'We met in the sixties.'

Which I translated as her having slept with him. I didn't ask any more questions.

I went to find a window to hang my head out of and have a spliff. The cold rush of wind stripped away my stress and woke me up. For a moment I forgot where I was going and why. I looked at the passing countryside and I felt calm.

The handover was weird. Grainne spoke to Nobby for well over an hour. He then took me on a walk around his land, just the two of us. He wanted to know about my interests. What trouble I'd been into. About Dad. Every time I answered a question I felt he was completely focused, sussing me out to see if I was safe enough to have in his house. I was being interviewed. I was nervous around him. He seemed nice enough but however long ago it was, this man had been involved in guns and violence. Grainne told me he'd made his money in scrap metal. Scrap metal and crime usually went hand in hand.

I passed the interview and was in. Grainne had got in touch with Sam about my need to disappear. I hadn't wanted to get her involved but I did want to see her. With Dad in prison she once again stepped in to help. She and her new man had agreed to part fund my stay in the country. The rest of my food and board would be covered by my working on the land. My strength had come back and I was up for it. I got fit and it was the closest I'd been to nature since Stoke. For a while it felt like everything was going to level out. I helped around the house, cooked, fed the chickens, went for long walks and made friends with kids in the area. None of them knew the real reason I was there.

The intention had been for me to stay for a few months, while things cooled down. It was completely unrealistic on all fronts. Dad hoped the police would get fed up looking for me and get on with the trial with the evidence they had. There was no real plan for me other than to get me out of the way for as long as possible and hope for the best. Grainne kept us up to date with what was going on in London. Things didn't cool down. The police were still looking for me. I was told not to sign on the dole, open a bank account, talk or send letters to anyone I knew in London. It would be very difficult for the police to find me. My hiding rolled into six months, then nine. I was getting bored. Unable to get spliff, I upped my drinking. One night I was left to babysit Nobby's kids. I got so drunk on his home-made wine I passed out and the kids put themselves to bed. That went down badly. Nobby began to see me as a liability and I became unwelcome.

I'd had no contact with Dad all this time and I was missing him badly. There was a high court bench warrant out for my arrest and Dad's stay in prison was extended while they searched up and down the country for me.

Sam and her man couldn't afford to keep sending money so it stopped. I had to start looking for a way to get money to cover the cost of food. Working on the land wasn't covering it. I went to Exeter and signed on. That was stupid.

My love of food and cooking was the only thing I could

think of harnessing in order to make a living. I had dreams of cooking on yachts in the Caribbean. I needed to learn more about it. Nobby and his wife convinced me to go to the local technical college where there was a catering course. I'd preferred the idea of going to France as Sam had done when she was a teenager to learn how to cook good food. But I ended up in a shit hole on the outskirts of Exeter that was alarmingly like Pimlico. I got a grant and started that September. I hated it from the moment I got there. We were taught how to make Florida cocktails, fish soup and French fancies. I cooked on instinct not from a recipe book and a teacher shouting abuse at me. My 'fuck you' attitude resurfaced and most of the lecturers took a dislike to me.

I finally had to leave Nobby's place so I started to look for digs in Exeter. A kid in my class told me there was a room going in his parents' house. I had nothing to lose. I went round.

The house was pure suburbia – pebble-dashed walls, beige wood-chip wallpaper, white plastic double glazing, pictures of flowers in plastic frames, and a microwave for all home cooking. The mum was nice, straight, smiley. I fancied her. I agreed there and then to take the room and to move in the following week. As I was leaving, the dad came home. I heard the car door shut and felt nervous about meeting him. I was always more nervous around men – the threat of violence, the threat of unwanted sexual attention. I was standing by the door waiting to leave. Through the frosted glass I made out his height and weight. I could see his white shirt and black trousers. Something felt wrong. His key went in the door and it opened.

'Hello, dear. This is Caspar. He's going to be moving in next week.'

I couldn't believe what I was seeing. The dad was a policeman in full uniform. I tried to break into a convincing smile while a sweat broke out on my back and the familiar hot rush of smack withdrawal seemed to be back. It was fear.

'Hello there. Nice to meet you, Caspar. My name's Gary. I'm sure we're all going to get along famously.'

I nodded my head and smiled, made my excuses and left.

I reckoned it would arouse suspicion if I changed my mind so I moved in anyway. Dad's voice echoed through my head. 'The best time to commit a crime is right under a copper's nose.'

I stayed for six months. Gary and his wife were very kind to me. I never felt comfortable in that house, though. I stayed in their other son's room while he was away at university. All his stuff was in there. I felt like I was invading his space. I was. Gary liked me and I let a friendship develop. It was ridiculous. It couldn't last, I knew that.

When I'd signed on while I was living at Nobby's, I'd given the social security office a different name and had made up a National Insurance number. To my relief and surprise it had worked and my claim was approved. I told them I was of no fixed abode and picked up my giros from the post office. But when I applied for the college grant I decided to put my real name on the application. I began to create a paper trail of my movements. I knew it was a dumb thing to do but part of me was tired of running. As far as I was concerned I could've been in hiding for years. I couldn't face it.

Just before the end of term, on a Friday morning at about ten o'clock, Gary came into my room. He was in uniform. The look on his face was a mix of anger and embarrassment. He had a set of handcuffs in his left hand.

'You know what this is about, don't you, Caspar?' I thought briefly about jumping out of the window. 'Why didn't you say something, for God's sake?'

I felt bad for him, having me under his roof for over six months, treating me like a son. This would have made him a laughing stock at the station. He looked at the floor and rubbed his forehead. He looked distressed. He raised the handcuffs, looked at them, then at me.

'I don't need these, do I?'

The least I could do was go quietly.

A marked police car came to pick me up. The kid and his mum were in the sitting room when I left. They didn't come out and say goodbye. I wouldn't have either. I was taken to Exeter police station and put in a one-man cell. A call had been made to London and two plain-clothes officers were on their way down to get me. One of them was Bill.

Bill came into my cell with his disarming smile. I couldn't help liking him. We didn't say much. I followed him to the main desk, got signed out and felt strangely happy to be in the back of his beat-up old Vauxhall.

Bill drove slowly back to London. We moved through suburbia and into the high streets of the city. I was taken to Clapham police station. Another single cell, a cold stone room with nothing in it save a blue plastic mattress and a rank toilet. It never got any easier. After two days I was moved to Ashford Young Offenders Institution and held there to stop me running again before my court date with Dad.

15

Judge, Jury and Executioner

Autumn 1984, Ashford Young Offenders Institution

For a one-man cell, this is big. It's way too warm. The pipes are hot and every night I wake up covered in sweat. At least I'm not clucking. The ceiling is too high to hang yourself from: there's nothing to tie a rope to anyway. And they've taken my laces out of my shoes, in case I try to throttle myself.

There is never any silence in here, always something going on in the corridor or out in the yard. Day and night. I'm not sleeping properly. If I stand up on my bed, on the iron bar at the end, I can see out of the barred window. There's always loads happening after final lock up. I can make out the floodlit compound. The cell windows face each other in a massive square. Kids are chucking lit toilet paper out of the windows. They do it every night. 'Mickey! Mickey!'

I can't see a face, only hear the voice.

'Yes, star!' comes the reply.

'You got some candy for your bro?'

The Asian-sounding kid has tied a loo roll to a torn sheet and is now swinging it in ever deeper sweeps to reach Mickey's cell,

189

*which is on my left. It glides silently past my window. I couldn't
grab it if I wanted to. There will be spliff or gear in that loo roll,
each end plugged up with more loo paper. I could murder a smoke.*

Kids talked to each other through the night, telling each
other about their girlfriends, release dates, convictions,
arguments, being stitched up, fights. None of them spoke to
me much. I was lonely but, more than that, scared of getting
beaten up. Given the choice, I preferred to be ignored. There
were dangerous, violent kids in there.

I had made a connection with one Polish guy in the
coach on the way in. He had given me half a packet of
cigarettes. He couldn't speak a word of English but his gift
said it all. Apart from him my only contact had been with
prison officers. Most of them had been sympathetic. They
could see I wasn't going to give them any trouble. I was worn
out and terrified. I felt like I'd had my 'fuck you' attitude
kicked out of me.

I had no idea when I was getting out. On my cell wall
someone had written what they were missing; what they
were going to do when they got out: *'Get home to my girl, roll
a massive spliff and watch some bad ass horror. Eat me some fried
chicken and get down to some sweet home lickin'.'*

Some of the writing on the wall was better than the cowboy
thriller I was reading. I got hold of a biro and graffitied my own
hopes and dreams on the Victorian brick walls, scratching in all
the great things I would do when I got out. Everything I had
done to death and taken for granted over recent years suddenly
became extremely desirable. I ached for a beer, a spliff, a
woman, a television. All I had left was masturbation and even
that was getting boring. Everything of value had been taken
away. Even a cigarette became gold dust in the cells and on the
wings. I could see how Dad could make so much money inside
with so little to exchange. People were desperate.

I never liked school dining rooms. The intensity, the staring eyes of curious girls and aggressive, territorial boys. It was all about who was going to sit next to who and who was going to be seen by the whole school to be hanging out with the coolest kids. I hated getting left on my own. The canteen at Ashford YOI had all this angst and then some. It was all male. Violence was in the air. Every new kid was scrutinised. I didn't get invited to sit next to anyone. I had no front or swagger to carry me along and just about everyone could see it. I got my tray of food. All I could see in my head was that canteen scene in *Scum* and I was waiting for the whole place to kick off and erupt into an explosion of food and chairs and tables. That would have been something. At least I could have got lost in it and joined in. No such luck. The room stayed seated and the young offenders ate their breakfast resentfully. It was seven thirty in the morning and I wasn't awake. I sat down at the end of a long table. I parked myself, kept my head down, and tried to not be seen.

'Ere, you're a big skinny fucker, aincha. What you in for, then?'

The kid who spoke to me seemed all right. He was eating fast with his mouth open. What was I in for? Keep the answer simple and tough. Word would move around the prison very quickly about the type of crime you had committed. There were a few no one would ever admit to and if anyone found out you had done one of them, you would be dogged and tortured by it for the rest of your prison life.

Never ever admit to the following:

1) Sex offences, including rape, children and animals
2) Grassing *anyone* up, especially friends and family
3) Stealing a pound of bacon from Tesco.

Nicking from Tesco was at the other end of the scale and not nearly hard enough. Your crime needed to carry weight but not shame.

'Wassamatter star? You fucking mute or something?'

He swore at me but it wasn't aggressive. Swearing as often as possible was about being cool. If you spoke like a posh kid, you would be singled out for serious suspicion and probably get beaten up. I had a posher voice than any of the kids on my table – the result of a mostly private education – and I was trying to hide it. I was becoming paralysed with confusion and fear. What to say? How to say it? I had grassed my father up and gone on the run to avoid backing it up in court. I ate faster to delay having to speak, despite the fact I wasn't hungry.

'Well, he's hungry, eh, lads! Plenty of eating for a skinny fucker.' He laughed at himself and a few others laughed with him.

I lowered my voice as much as I could and kept it short.

'Drugs. You?' I didn't look up. That's how Charles Bronson would've done it.

'Robbed a petrol station. Poured diesel over the cheeky fucker's head for giving me shit. Should have set 'im on fire but I didn't.'

Most of the time it's hard to know who's telling the truth in prison but for some reason I believed this kid. He looked very capable of setting someone on fire.

'What kind of drugs?' he asked me. I was hating the attention.

'Smack and coke.'

'Fuck me, lads, we got another junky on our table!'

He applauded me, as did a few others. I smiled reluctantly and breathed a bit deeper. The bell went. I was saved.

My nerves were jangling inside my body like a smashed-up piano. I jumped every time a door slammed or there were any sudden movements. As I was escorted back to my cell two kids passed me, one of them singing me a song:

'Ooh . . . le freak! Aaaah . . . freak out!' I caught my

reflection in a glass partition. My hair was standing on end, I was sweating profusely and my prison-issue clothes were all the wrong size. My trousers were too short and swinging round my ankles, my boots were too big and hurting my feet. My blue and white striped shirt sleeves were halfway up my arms. I looked more like Coco the fucking clown than a wanted criminal.

I left Ashford in what they used to call a black Maria: a prison transport van. This one was a truck and was white with blacked-out windows, much slicker looking than the old version but no more comfortable. The truck could hold twenty. Each of us was put into a single, locked cell just big enough to sit in; more like a cage. The windows were too high to look out of. In any case, we had to stay seated and cuffed. I desperately wanted to see the outside world, some countryside, some buildings, anything. I eventually heard the rising sound of city streets. Traffic. Voices. After two hours in the box the truck drove down into what must have been an underground car park.

Me and the other prisoners were led out into a basement cell complex beneath Horseferry Road Magistrates' Court. We ended up in a big holding cell and we all took up separate positions a safe distance from each other. The only bit of furniture in the room was a long bench running right the way round the cell walls. Years of graffiti was scratched, written and burnt on to the door, walls and bench. There was so much of it, layer over layer of angry words, dirty jokes and surreal ramblings, I couldn't read half of it.

Not talking to anyone while waiting in a locked room for over three hours is a hard thing to do. There were seven of us in there. I needed to create a silent hard-nut image. The need to talk showed up the fact that I was scared shitless.

We were finally called out and I walked into my first court appearance. Despite the fear, it was exciting. The room was huge. High ceilings, bright strip lighting, long lines of desks covered in masses of paperwork and two barristers in wigs and black gowns. A wooden-looking woman sat poised by a weird-looking typewriter. There were three police officers and two prison guards. The magistrates' bench dominated the room with its throne-like chair sitting proud between two smaller ones. I was led to my spot, a Perspex partition with a hard bench in contrast to everyone else's comfy chairs; as if they hadn't made enough of a point already about my low-life status. Bill was there with another plain-clothes copper I didn't recognise. My barrister was a woman. I hadn't been introduced to her. She came up to me, leant across the partition and forced a smile.

'Good morning, Mr Walsh. Just answer the questions you're asked truthfully. This is going to be short.' She was severe, sharp and no-nonsense. As she walked away, fear rushed through me again. That hadn't been much of a pep talk.

I was asked by the grey-haired magistrate to confirm my name and address. 'Caspar Walsh. No fixed abode.'

And that was it. They set a date for Dad's court case. It had been on hold the whole time they were looking for me; that, at least, made me feel important. The magistrate gave me a stern word about having wasted police time and government money and warned me that if I did it again I would get a custodial sentence. He then released me on bail. That was a big surprise. I was out.

I had six weeks till Dad's court case.

It was time to get stoned.

I had no money. Shoplifting was not a good idea. I couldn't risk getting caught. I was panicking that I wouldn't be able to find enough cash to be able to eat. I made a call to an old mate from Stoke. We had been close at school. I had spent some weekends at his parents' farm. We'd watched TV, got pissed and eaten the great food his mum had cooked for us. Untroubled, peaceful days. I called him from London and told him what was going on. Some of it, anyway. Just enough to elicit some sympathy and a place to stay while I figured out how to get some money together and how to get hold of some decent spliff. For the time being I would be happy to do some heavy drinking with Ian, for old times' sake.

He picked me up at the station in his new car. It had been three years since I had seen him. He was doing well for himself. He was pretty much the same to look at but he had grown up and got sensible. I didn't feel I could have quite the same laugh with him as we had had when we were at school. We hung out for three days and got drunk, remembering Stoke and going through some of the good times and some of the shit times. His mum said I could stay as long as I liked. I loved the idea. I could see Ian wasn't into it.

'It's not cool for me to stay, is it?' I asked him.

He looked at me and tried to smile. I could see it was difficult for him. 'I would love you to stay mate but . . . no.'

'It's cool. I understand. It's been a great weekend, it's been great to see you again, really. I miss the good times at Stoke.'

I did understand. I was saying the right thing. I knew I had to go but I was scared and could feel my isolation and confusion growing. I had absolutely no idea what to do next and no idea who to turn to. Part pride, part realisation that I'd burnt a lot of bridges.

Ian took me to the station and gave me a hug. He handed me a tenner and we said goodbye. That was it. I was heading back into London and didn't know where I was going to stay. It had been three weeks since I'd left my family house in Exeter. Catering school was over. I was completely at a loss as to what to do with myself. I was embarrassed at the state I was in. I thought again about Grainne, Mum, Sam and Leon – but I couldn't bring myself to ask any of them if

I could stay with them. Pride and shame were stopping me from asking for help.

I went to a hotel in Earl's Court. I stayed for two weeks. What a fucking dump that was. I had signed on, so my rent was covered. The thirty quid a week I got to live on I spent on booze and spliff. I was scratching around for food, stealing mostly from the hotel. I shared a room with two other men. A cell on my own seemed a better option. They were in their fifties, both drunks. There was violence in that hotel, on a regular basis. My bunk mate was either sorting it out or causing it. One night I heard screams upstairs, a woman being beaten up. I was paralysed with fear in my bed. My bunk mate headed upstairs. I heard him knock on the door, followed by a moment's silence then a loud thud that could only have been a big person hitting the floor. My bunk mate returned a few minutes later with blood splattered across his dirty white vest and all over his unshaven, haggard face. He said the blood wasn't his. He was well pleased with himself.

'That'll teach the fat, drunk fucker to beat up on women.'

He was fat and drunk, too. The only difference was he beat up on men. I left the following day. I would rather have slept on the street than have stayed a moment longer in that place. The night before Dad's court case I ended up in a derelict house. Talk about feeling sorry for myself. A perverse part of me enjoyed the drama of it.

On the day of the court case I scored two grams of speed and an eighth of black hash. I couldn't afford coke and I'd wanted weed. The case was at the Old Bailey, court three. I hadn't seen Dad since I'd gone down to live with Nobby the previous year. It had been the longest I'd ever been away from him. I'd got used to it.

I knew we wouldn't be able to hug or talk. I was determined not to let him down again. I was going to deny everything I'd said in the statement to Bill. That would make things up between us and maybe he would get released.

My barrister was there. She looked a bit pissed off with me. I'd tried to smarten myself up but had done a bad job of it. I went into the loos. I had about fifteen minutes before I was due in court. I'd already snorted a gram of the speed and smoked two joints before arriving. That was probably what was pissing my barrister off – she could see I was out of it. I was all over the place. I thought another few lines of speed would sort me out and help me lie with greater confidence. I took a line, then another, thought 'fuck it' and finished it off. Smoking was out of the question. I had taken so much speed my face was now wet with narcotic sweat. I thought I was ready for my big moment.

Dad was already in court when I walked in. I tripped over something on the floor that wasn't there. Dad smiled but he looked nervous. I waved at him with false confidence and jerked a half smile. I was led into the witness box. The judge looked severe. When he saw the sweat on my face and my jittery behaviour he raised an eyebrow. Bill was there, too. He was becoming such a feature in my life I was almost reassured by his presence. If he hadn't been so set on locking Dad up for as long as possible I would have waved to him, too. I took the oath on the Bible and proceeded to answer the prosecution's carefully constructed questions. Most of them were based on my original statement made to Bill that night in Fulham. As it was fed back to me in the courtroom, I systematically retracted each page I had signed. I tried to explain why I had said what I had said.

'I was under a lot of pressure from the police. I was confused. I was sixteen. I was withdrawing from heroin. I was scared. I didn't know where my father was.'

I had been convinced I was finding a smart way out of the web I'd woven for myself. It was my first public piece of theatre. I had the jury, the whole room, rapt in sympathetic concentration at my reams of bullshit. I was on a roll. I was enjoying myself. The judge looked exasperated by the time it was taking for me to meander through each of my answers. He interrupted me several times to keep me on track.

'Mr Walsh,' the judge warned me, 'may I remind you that you are under oath and that it is an offence to lie against that oath, punishable by a prison sentence . . . sometimes a long one.'

I hadn't realised I was doing such a bad job. The speed was making me jabber and ramble.

As the drugs wore off, my confidence began to falter and I realised what a mess I was making of the whole thing. I looked over to Dad. He had his head in his hands. That's when any confidence I had left drained out of me. The sweat was running down the side of my face in skinny streams. I wanted desperately to get off the witness stand.

The prosecution finally finished. The defence stepped in and tried to salvage the car crash I'd made out of my Q+A. She did a good job considering but the jury didn't believe me. From my stoned ramblings, I'd made the mistake of wanting and getting their sympathy. This was obviously bad news for Dad. I was later told by my barrister that they'd pitied me and could see I was confused. They blamed Dad for this completely. I left the court and went straight to the off-licence. I spent the last of my dole money on cheap vodka.

A lot of the length of Dad's sentence was down to his previous convictions. The rest of it was down to the jury believing everything in my statement made to Bill and nothing of what I'd said in court. They believed everything about our business. Bill was good at his job. He shook my hand after the Old Bailey fiasco. He was grateful for my chaotic performance. Any anger he had felt towards me about my disappearance vanished with the four-year sentence Dad was given by the sharp-eyed judge.

16

Mr Nowhere Man

Summer 1986

Grainne's in hospital. She's been good to me, like a mum. She's given me money and fed me and talked to me when I've been down, which has been all the time. This isn't personal. I haven't got any choice. I mean, I can't think of where else to get money from. I know there's a telly in her house and that it will get me at least an eighth of black. The window's open. Grainne has a nice house. Someone's supposed to be keeping an eye on it for her, while she's in hospital. She's got cancer. I think she's dying. You leave a window open like that and someone is bound to rob the place. I'm going to get the telly, leave, and close the window, make sure no scumbag stranger tries it on. I'll pay her back when I get some money. She'll understand, she always does. I have to be quiet, though. It's dark and the neighbours might see me and think I'm that scumbag.

The telly is upstairs. She's got too many cats, place stinks of them. Smells of that yappy little white poodle she used to have, too. It used to shit everywhere, when it was alive.

Fuck. The telly isn't here. It was here last week. I've got to get something. *Hang on, this red trunk, there's bound to be something in this. It's full of junk. None of it's worth much. The dealer won't give me fuck all for it. What if I take the trunk? Take the whole thing. I mean, all of this stuff together has got to be worth at least thirty quid. Yes, I'll take it. Good one.*

It was very heavy. I got it down the stairs from the bedroom without making much noise. I had to stop for plenty of breaks. I got it through the window on the ground floor, but made a lot of noise. I made even more noise staggering up the street with it in my arms, like a big red treasure chest; then across the common. I got a cab but had no money to pay. I thought I'd get the dealer to pay for it, it'd only cost a fiver. He wouldn't mind. Get the trunk in the cab, the cab to the dealer's and the spliff in my hand. Sounded reasonable. Grainne wouldn't mind, I thought. But, actually, she did. And when they found out, her sons did as well. My cousins were big, and they had bad tempers.

I got to the dealer's and he couldn't believe it. I was so pumped up with the drama of it that I managed to convince him to pay for the cab and have a look in the trunk. He clearly just wanted me out of his house.

'What the fuck am I going to do with all this junk, man?' he asked, sifting through Grainne's trinkets, paperwork and glass jewellery.

'Come on, the stuff in here is worth at least fifty quid,' I argued. 'Look at the trunk. You could get thirty for that on its own. I'm only looking for an eighth. An eighth, the cab fair and a few cigarettes. I'll roll us a joint.'

'I don't need a joint, mate. I've got plenty. What's this?'

He picked up a small wooden box. It looked like it had something important inside. Maybe some money. I snatched it from him. I opened it up and inside was a small plastic bag. Inside that was something grey and crumbly. I opened the bag. It was full of ash and small pieces of hard, white stuff.

'Is it gear?' he asked me, suddenly more interested.

'No.' I knew what it was and my heart sank. 'Shit. It's my aunt's dog.'

'What?'

'My aunt's dog's ashes. It died before she went into hospital. Fuck. My cousins are gonna kill me!'

'Well, you can take the fucking ashes with you, mate. I'll have the wooden box, though. That's nice, that is, I'll keep my spliff in it. I'll give you a teenth, the cab fair, a packet of fags and the change in my pocket.'

A sixteenth of black hash for my trouble. It was a pathetic amount. But I took him up on his offer and left, feeling dreadful. I went to the common, sat down and rolled a joint. I had to get the ashes back to Grainne's house, make it look like whoever took the trunk had found the ashes, had an attack of conscience and left the dead dog behind.

The following day I went back. There were some builders working two doors down. They were eyeballing me. Someone else had already been at the house. The window was now firmly locked. I had to get the ashes back in. The upstairs window was open a little. If I threw the bag through the window maybe they would land on the upstairs landing and I could get it to look like the robbers had left the ashes behind.

I took the bag of ashes out of my pocket and looked at it. It was light. I had been good at throwing the cricket ball at school. I lined up my eye to the half-open window and lobbed it. It hit the window ledge and came back to me. I threw it again.

The next throw hit the window itself. By this time I had the full attention of the builders, who'd stopped working to see what I was up to. I was attracting too much attention.

One more go and I would have to leave. I threw it too hard, off centre, and it hit the red brick wall. The bag exploded and the ash rained down on me. Most of it landed on my shoulders and head. The builders were now laughing. I was frozen for a moment, unable to believe what had just happened. How could I have done this to my aunt? She'd done nothing but good by me. It was ridiculous and tragic. I'd become a junky for spliff. I couldn't afford smack. My housing benefit and dole just covered my rent and food. I had sunk to doing the desperate, nasty stuff to get spliff. This was what most junkies would do for smack, rob their own family.

My cousins found out from the neighbours what had happened. They were given a description of someone who could only be me. Tall, skinny, black-framed glasses, matted hair, black leather jeans, Converse All Star trainers. I'd been watched as I'd staggered up the road with the red trunk in my arms.

A mate told me that one of my cousins was going around saying he wanted to stab me. My cousins and I had always got on well. Like Grainne, they'd looked out for me. I liked them both, but this was a piss take too far. I kept my head down for the rest of that summer and barely had a smoke for weeks. My aunt died in the autumn. I never apologised to her or made it up to her in any way. She'd had a tough life. I didn't have the courage to say goodbye.

Winter 1986

To compensate for Grainne's death I started to see more of Mum. She cooked me meals. We smoked a bit of dope together, talked and drank wine. She was struggling to hold her life together but she was still good company, most of the time. She'd moved into a new place. I liked it. She'd brought

202

all the wall hangings and rugs and lights with her from Tite Street. It was a home from home. Paul was around a lot and we hung out and smoked together. He was growing up fast and getting into his own drug taking. Excessive behaviour ran in the family.

Eventually I got off the dole and into a job. All I could think of was catering. I liked pizza so I got a job in Pizzaland. I stayed there for a few months then moved up in the world to Pizza Express. I was living on my own in a bed and breakfast box room in Wimbledon, smoking dope and drinking and going out on Saturday nights. I just about made the rent each month; it felt like a big achievement. The regular work, the routine, the roof over my head were all doing me good. I was rarely late for work; I wasn't going to risk losing my job and being on the street again. I was motivated by my need to get as far away from what had been happening to me as possible. When I got out of the way of the 'you're not cool enough' snobbery around the people I was working with, I got to like them. We hung out more and more. I was invited to parties and was spending less and less time on my own. I was starting to feel like a member of the human race, almost normal. The harsher memories were starting to lose their edge.

IN REPLYING TO THIS LETTER, PLEASE WRITE ON THE
ENVELOPE:
NUMBER: CR96356
NAME: WALSH
HMP SWALESIDE

HELLO DARLIN CAS.
ARE YOU REALLY WELL? I HOPE SO. PHYSICALLY YOU LOOKED
GOOD WHEN I SAW YOU, SO I THINK YOU'RE PROBABLY
FEELING MUCH BETTER MENTALLY (THEY ARE CONNECTED

ARE THEY NOT?) I AM SO HAPPY YOU HAVE WRITTEN AT LAST. IT MEANS SO MUCH TO ME.

YOU ASK IN YOUR LETTER HOW THINGS ARE WITH ME? MY WORLD HAS BRICK HORIZONS. I WILL NOT LET THEM MAKE ME UNHAPPY. AT THIS MOMENT I AM LISTENING TO MOZART ON THE RADIO. MY IMAGINATION IS STILL INTACT AND WORKING WELL. I HAVE MY BELOVED BOOKS. I ALSO HAVE A JOB SO AM UNLOCKED A LOT OF THE TIME AND I DON'T GET THAT LONELY ANY MORE.

A BEE HAS JUST LANDED ON MY ARM AND I THINK WE ARE LOOKING AT EACH OTHER. HE'S GOT BORED AND BUZZED OFF. THANK YOU, BEE, FOR GIVING ME NICE THOUGHTS.

I'M GOING TO TRY AND GET SOME MONEY TO YOU.

WOULD YOU LIKE ME TO SEND YOU A LIST OF BOOKS I THINK YOU MIGHT LIKE? LITERATURE IS ONE THING I DO KNOW ABOUT AND LOVE. TRY PHILIP K. DICK. REMEMBER 'BLADE RUNNER'? HIS BOOK IS CALLED 'DO ANDROIDS DREAM OF ELECTRIC SHEEP?' ALL OF HIS STUFF IS MARVELLOUS. HE HAS SO MUCH TO SAY. HELP, I'M RUNNING OUT OF SPACE (BUT NOT TIME).

FROM A CRAZY BUT LOVING DAD.

LOVE YOU VERY MUCH.

XXX

Green ink. Same prison-issue paper. Blue, lined and double folded. I smelled it and was reassured by the memory of all the other letters expressing love.

By the time I was fifteen Dad had me reading books on metaphysics, the cosmos, science fiction, western and eastern philosophy, poetry and astral travel. Most of it completely spun me out. I believed him when he said the secrets to life could be found in books. I just couldn't figure out what most of the books were saying or where exactly the secrets were hidden. His way of writing to me often pissed me off. I wished he'd just speak to me directly, not through a poem or a smart proverb. But I got the message that he loved me.

I didn't get it together to visit him much after that letter. I was missing him but I still felt bad about the court case at the Old Bailey. He'd clearly forgiven me. I don't think he was ever really pissed off about it. He knew he'd played a big part in the whole thing.

I'd found myself a girlfriend, the manager of the Pizza Express where I worked; French, gorgeous, with very a bad temper. She taught me to cook proper French food, when she wasn't chucking it at me. Being with her was more of a route to regular sex and company than anything long term. The constant drugs and alcohol and sex were keeping me nicely distracted. For a while, at least.

Being off smack and crack felt good but I was still hooked on getting high. I was smoking a lot of spliff and had got into double strength lager and cider. This stuff was lethal and as strong as spirits. It wrecked the lining of the strongest stomach. I kidded myself that as long as I was off spirits I was OK. But the beer was so strong it gave me an ulcer in less than three months.

During the second year Dad was in prison I noticed cracks of depression start to appear inside me. My mind was slipping back into a state of intense confusion, fear and paranoia mixed with something else, a total lack of motivation and direction. Even though I was working and seeing friends, even though I had a girlfriend, I was starting to spend a lot of time alone again. The more time I spent on my own, the more twisted my thoughts started to become. However fucked up his fathering was when he was out of prison I needed Dad to tell me what to do next. Without him, I didn't have a clue where to go or what to do.

It was distant at first. If I got stoned enough I could block it out – just. But it kept moving closer, like it was hunting me. I was finding it hard to concentrate at work and was making a lot of mistakes. I became scared I would be sacked, and that I'd have to go back to robbing my own family. The thoughts forming in my mind were starting to frighten me. My fears about what people thought of me and how I was going to continue to survive were blown out of all proportion. The volume in my head – a kind of white noise – was cranked up so high I could hardly make out what was happening around me. I was constantly distracted. Cars and trucks would rumble past me and I would jerk and jump in fright. I couldn't follow the simplest things that were being said to me at checkouts. Under the bright supermarket lights I would flush with embarrassment and sometimes have to walk out, leaving my shopping on the conveyor belt. Phone calls from mates worrying about me became a source of distress, so I stopped answering the phone.

An inability to cope wasn't new to me, especially when I'd been clucking. But I wasn't clucking at this point. I started to experience longer and longer periods of acute confusion and fear. I couldn't concentrate on anything for more than a few minutes. A movie on the telly was out of the question. It caused me intense anxiety to watch anything with a storyline. I tried to hold on to what was being said, to piece it together into something that made sense. But the words I heard continually unravelled and broke up into scattered sentences and, to my surprise, into angry, violent images. Channel hopping was the only way to get some peace. Hanging out with friends was now an embarrassing, unwanted event. I was unable to keep a conversation going for any length of time. I had never been short of 'chat', so my mates noticed it. I didn't have the ability to explain what was happening to me. Most of my life I'd had a few voices going on in my head at any one time. These were just my regular thoughts, figuring out what to do by talking to each other. I was used to that. But the inside of my head had now become overcrowded. These new voices would argue harder and more aggressively than before. They would shout each other down, trick me into doing things I didn't want to do. One voice became particularly powerful. It made it clear to me that it was with me for the long haul and for my own good. 'No fucker can be trusted, Cas. The safest place for us to be is alone, mate, in this room, smoking dope and drinking Tennants Super.' I believed it.

There was a link between my sliding mental health and all the spliff and smack I had consumed. When I was hooked on heroin any flicker of the psychosis going on in my head would vanish. It was one of the reasons I refused to stop taking heroin. I knew I had a physical addiction to it and that that was dangerous, but it had also kept a darker part of me hidden in a corner of my mind and I was glad of that. Now, something unwanted was growing inside me. It was feeding on my lack of smack and growing fear.

I started smoking even more spliff in the twisted belief that it would deal with my rising insanity. I was continuing to make mistakes at work and the customers were getting pissed off with me. To pay for my increased spliff intake I made a very poor attempt at nicking some money from the till. I was caught and sacked on the spot. Soon after that I got dumped by my girlfriend. I was skint and alone in my room in Wimbledon.

I'd been in this position before. It was familiar and almost welcome. The invading sense of paranoia increased with my intake of spliff. It loved my isolation and insecurity. The spliff ran out and I no longer had the energy to get out of bed to get more, even if I had had the money. I stopped going to see Sam and Mum and Paul and my mates. I didn't even see the other people that lived in the house. It was a lifestyle choice. I was more comfortable on my own.

Miraculously, Dad had kept his nose clean in prison this time around. He got parole after two of his four years and was due out in six months. The time away from him had ended up drifting by in a pointless haze of dead-end jobs, getting stoned, mere survival. It was like I was just passing the time, waiting for him to come home. I wanted him with me and I didn't. When he got out he would be back on the smack, double quick. That meant I could get some in me and be back in with a chance of fighting off my insanity. It seemed like a danger worth stepping into, worth getting another habit for. I was craving the false security of heroin again. I was prepared for the nightmare that went with it, anything other than being in that room alone. It was a way of life I knew well. I believed getting high on opiates meant I could get some control over the chaos of it all. I was completely deluded.

Spring 1987

One night I was watching TV alone in my tiny room; Bruce Willis in *Moonlighting*. I was desperately trying to work out what was going on with the plot but my mind was now regularly slipping in and out of chaos. If I got to the end of a show and had a vague idea of what the story had been about it was a sign I was on the up, something to celebrate. The end of the episode that night had left me hopelessly confused. I was pissed off with Willis: his looks, his charm, his money. I was sitting on my single bed, in a tiny room in the middle of suburbia. No money, no style, no prospects. If I wasn't so crazy too, Dad would've laughed. It was a long way from how he had always lived his life and taught me to live mine. My mind had broken up into glass shards of painful memories, some real, some imagined. Surreal, violent and comical images of death flickered on and off in my head, like a cheap neon horror movie.

I gave up on Bruce, got up and looked out of the window. I could see across the gardens into the cool, spring night. The orange glow of the city streets beyond filled me with fear and a feeling of hopelessness and desolation. I couldn't see a way out. I wanted my dad. I wanted my mum. I'd had enough.

I sat back on the bed and took the rope curtain tie-back off its mock brass hook. I turned the TV and the lights off and left the curtains open. The half darkness in the room was blue, much like the caravan in Wales. I looped the tie-back round my neck and started to slowly, ritually tighten it. I had no real idea what I was doing or whether it would work. I pulled it tighter and continued to twist. I gasped, my vision blurred and I passed out.

I woke up on the bed – how much later, I don't know – and tried to crawl into the tiny space beneath the sideboard at the side of my bed.

I spent the next two weeks trying to work out how to kill myself. A train, a roof, a bridge? Why the hell would anyone want to jump off a roof or in front of a train? What a fucking selfish mess it would be. All that pain and fear and stress to the driver, to the suicide's family. I had heard that the train driver who ran over the kid from school in the tunnel at Pimlico Underground had had to retire early. It was the third death under one of his trains. Suicide affects other people. That's what stopped me. I didn't want to do it to my mum, to Paul, to Sam, to my mates, to myself. If anyone would understand the need to end it all it would be Dad. I didn't want to do it to him, either.

I had just about enough energy to get to the post office to cash my giros. That kept me from getting kicked out of my room. The rest of the time I stayed in bed and watched telly. I was losing strength by the day.

Dad came out of prison in the middle of my mental tail spin. I avoided him for a few weeks. He eventually found me and called me at the house. Most of me didn't want to speak to him. A small part of me did. Desperately.

'Where have you been? I've been trying to find you for weeks.'

It was such a relief to hear his voice. 'I've been feeling bad.'

'How do you mean?' He was genuinely concerned.

'Just bad, Dad.'

I went to meet him at a pub on Wimbledon Common. It was busy; more people than I'd seen in months. He bought me the first proper meal I'd eaten in nearly five weeks. We sat on the common and watched the sun go down. It was peaceful. My mind was almost still. It was pointless resisting the inevitable. I couldn't cope alone. There was nothing else for me to do but to join him again.

Besides, he needed someone to watch his back.

17

End of the Road

December 1987, Lots Road, Chelsea, London

I am hating every fucking minute of living in this flat. Yellow, dirt-stained lino floors, with deep stiletto marks indented. Filthy magnolia walls. Bare light bulbs. Nothing but smoke-stained net curtains at the windows. A cracked concrete patio out back with dried dog shit everywhere. On the kitchen wall someone has scribbled in blue biro: 'Ladies, go walking lightly in your high heeled shoes!'

This is a hookers' flat. It's not being used for sex punters at the moment. Dad and me have got it now. There's only one bed. He turfed me on to the floor a few months back when he got kicked out of his flat in Earl's Court. He said I had plenty of mates to stay with if I wanted a bed. I don't.

I can't imagine anyone wanting to have sex in this shit hole. Let alone pay for it. Better than a car, I suppose. But I've seen the hookers. The only real colour in here is my fish tank and my five tropical fish: one Siamese Fighter, three Neons and a big-eyed goldfish with fin rot. The goldfish and Siamese ruck all the time. They take it in turns to chase each other around the tank. With no telly, the tank is my only entertainment. I can watch it for hours, as long as I'm stoned.

The flat is now set up for just that, and for our dealing. I'm also working for the two hookers who own it. They live just off the North End Road, not far. Latisha and Sadie, not real names, of course. A punter of Dad's, a sweet Scottish girl called Susan, gave me their number. She said they were looking for a sticker boy. Dad said it was easy money and that it might lead to better things. I doubted that from the start.

I would go to Latisha's on Tuesday and Thursday mornings at about 10 a.m. I'd collect up to 500 stickers, depending on how many I had left from the previous day. Each one was handwritten in different coloured felt pens. The handwriting was flowery like the writing the girls at Stoke used to scrawl on the desks. The sentiment of the text wasn't that different.

Sexy Sadie for sweet soul time. Latisha gives stern love.

Three days a week I would cycle to the best-positioned public phone boxes in central west London. My patch stretched from Olympia to Sloane Square, down the length of the King's Road and back up to West Kensington to get my wages. I was a hard worker.

When I got to the phone boxes I'd place the stickers wherever they could best be seen. I did this whether someone was in the phone box or not. It was always risky. I got shouted at a lot, punched twice and arrested once.

The copper had been chasing me down the King's Road for ten minutes without me realising. I was cycling from box to box doing my job. He was on foot, doing his. Each time he got near me I was off to the next box. When he finally caught up, completely out of breath, he grabbed hold of me. I'd had a feeling something was up but I didn't really give a shit. I had a gram of smack, a pipe and some foil on me. I managed to hide the packet of smack in some filthy tissues I found in my pocket while he inspected the foil. When he and his back-up team loaded me into the van I swallowed the packet. This was difficult. I had to moisten it with my saliva and chew it slowly enough not to be seen. I didn't get stoned. I did get a caution.

Working on the King's Road for two hookers, after having grown up on it and played along it as a kid, was severely depressing. The magic of running in and out of shops and derelict areas, nicking stuff and smashing things up with my mates and harassing women only a few years before was gone. Junkies and alkies can go decades without really wanting to stop, without reaching the end of the line and realising that they've had enough. But I'd already reached my rock bottom plenty of times. I was twenty years old.

The hookers' flat we were dealing out of smelled of burnt smack, freshly cooked freebase and jasmine joss-sticks. Each day was much the same as the next. I was so stoned most of the time I hardly even noticed the seasons passing.

I would sit down at 3 p.m. each weekday afternoon and take out some foil, open up a packet of smack and prepare a smoke. Routine was important. I worked in the mornings, with the stickers. Lunch at the White Horse pub by 1 p.m. Hot food and two bottles of strong lager in a pint glass, with a dash of lime cordial. Same pub, same drink, different lunch, five days a week. After lunch, back to the flat for my first proper smoke of the day. I took care of the clucking junky punters from 4 p.m. till 7 p.m., so I would have about one hour to smoke the daily cluck out of me, at my leisure. Dad would arrive around 6.30 and start the night shift. I hated dealing. I hated the people, the hours, the money. I dealt so that I could smoke all the drugs I wanted. My fee was being stuck in the grim hooker flat, like a prisoner. If the punters came at ten to four I would tell them to come back later. If they whined that they were sick and promised me a line of smack if I let them in early, I'd tell them to fuck off and make them wait longer. I didn't need their smack, I had my own. Besides, theirs was cut and mine was stronger. When I was dealing I had power and I used it. I was a bastard to buy drugs from.

The smack was well and truly back in my system. My depression was nowhere in sight. The smack put the suicidal, depressive feelings on pause. So not only was I physically hooked on the gear but also psychologically. It was something to keep the depression out of sight and out of mind.

Business would be completed by 10 p.m. At that point, Dad would usually head out to see Kate and often not come back, which meant I would get the bed. Kate couldn't shake her love for him. Much as she'd tried to move on in the two years he'd been away, she'd stood by him and she was clearly happy to have him back in her life. So, more often than not, I'd be left alone and would order a pizza and four bottles of beer: same pizza, same beer every night, delivered right to my door. Routine. The bad food, the booze, the drugs, the stress and the constant fear wore an ulcerous hole in my stomach. Over time, the smack smoke settled and stuck fast to my lungs. At night I'd wake up in the middle of a coughing fit, struggling to breathe. I had to be careful how much black and green phlegm I hacked up to clear my lungs. If the coughing got too much I'd throw up. Blood was constantly seeping into my stomach through the ulcer. The vomit was always a thick, congealed mass of brown, stinking gloop: a mixture of pizza, blood and smack. This was the gauntlet I ran every morning simply to breathe clearly enough to get a decent enough smoke in me to stop the withdrawals from the few, short hours without smack. Sometimes I'd wake myself up in the middle of the night just to smoke the shivers away before the morning came. Then I'd start the whole thing all over again. Routine.

*

214

I noticed that Dad had started limping. He refused to get it checked out at first. He hated doctors and hospitals. He told me it was an abscess. He'd had them before. It had been caused by the smack he'd been injecting into his muscles. He was too scared to put needles straight into his veins – I sympathised with that – and this was the price he'd paid. He started walking with a stick, then ended up in a wheelchair. The abscess was the size of an egg and growing and the poison under his skin was milky white like venom. I drained it by hand three times a day and dressed his wounds with great care. The poison kept building up and its toxicity started to knock him unconscious. I finally managed to convince him to go to hospital. I took over the business as soon as he was in his hospital bed. It seemed essential. Bad move. I didn't want the responsibility. I did want the extra drugs. Left to Dad's smack and my own devices my habit doubled.

I was scared of needles, too. I went from smoking two to five grams a day. I visited Dad each day in hospital, taking with me his four gram parcel of smack. Each time I got there I'd find him sucking on the laughing gas he'd asked for to relieve his pain. The smack was already dealing with his discomfort, he just wanted something extra purely for recreation. Walking into his ward and stepping behind his constantly drawn curtain was a joke. He'd lie there pretending to be Dennis Hopper in *Blue Velvet*, face covered with a yellow plastic gas mask, laughing insanely.

'You got the gear, kid?' he asked through the mask.

I always had the gear. That was why I was there.

The smack was being held at a flat in Clapham. The flat belonged to a customer. He was happy to exchange his expensive home for a regular supply of uncut smack. He also fancied his chances at nicking some when we weren't around, his shifty behaviour made that obvious to me. Every day I had to take a minicab across the river to weigh up and bag up the day's orders. He would watch me closely while I went through the process. I was always careful not to let him see where I hid the main batch; there was every chance we'd be cleaned out overnight.

I told him, 'I fucking hate dealing.'

'Why don't you stop?' he suggested.

Seemed simple enough, but I knew I was too hooked – on the smack and on Dad – to just walk out.

One afternoon the doorbell went. My heart stopped. The junky answered it and let in the callers. To my panic-stricken astonishment he let in two uniformed police officers. I was so terrified I could hardly breathe. The room was a dealer's cliché. Weighing scales, foil, small plastic bags, white paper packets ready for the weighed smack, matches, tubes, the lot. I didn't look at the police as they walked past me. I didn't even say hello, I couldn't speak. I just fiddled around pointlessly with the paraphernalia in front of me, waiting to be arrested. They walked past me, said hello, and continued into the garden.

While they were out there, I put everything away.

They had been called out to check on something going on in next door's garden. They weren't expecting to see anything unusual in our flat and so they didn't notice anything unusual as they walked past. I hid the gear and left, still expecting to be arrested. Their patrol car was parked right in front of the flat, blue lights flashing. I thought I was going to have a heart attack. I got into my waiting minicab and asked him to get a move on. It felt like a message to get out of the business. I knew then and there that I wasn't cut out for this line of work.

When Dad was discharged I had to wheel him back the mile and a half from the hospital to the hooker's flat. He had a walking stick in one hand, a fag in the other. As we walked past people in the street he waved the stick at them, shouting like a mad colonel, telling them to 'get out of the blasted way.' Hilarious for him. Humiliating for me.

The abscess was serious and flared up again a few weeks later. He refused to go back to hospital so I had to look after him at home. The pus was slowly poisoning him. It was my job to drain it from his left buttock and put a sterile dressing on. I did this three times a day. After half an hour of my manual drainage work he would usually pass out from the pain and poison, that and all the smack he had smoked to get him through the ordeal of me touching it. He was very helpless in that state. I was the grown up, taking care of the sick child. I felt useful and I did it with love.

Dad quickly realised how much my habit had increased while he'd been in hospital. Now he was back in charge I wasn't getting nearly enough to stop me being sick, and I was getting angry. He caught me stealing from him several times. As a solution to my increasingly erratic, angry behaviour, often taken out on the punters, he took me off main dealing detail.

My body was in bad shape, but no insanity or suicidal urges seemed a fair price to pay. I was on a constant low-level withdrawal. I know there was a part of Dad that liked having this kind of control over me.

Kate was three years older but none the wiser and still on drugs. Much like me, she had stuck mainly to spliff and booze until Dad got out of prison for the second time. They got back together and she got back into smack. Dad had this effect on a lot of people.

A few months later, I woke up to a room full of smoke and the TV on fire. Dad was on the bed. I was on the floor. We'd fallen asleep with a candle flickering. The candle was the culprit. I shouted at Dad, panicked and ran into the kitchen to get some water.

217

'What the *fuck* are you doing, Cas! Stop!'

I had been about to throw a pan of water over the plugged-in telly. Dad stopped me blowing myself up. We started arguing about who had left the candle burning. The argument turned into a full-scale row. I got up, took a bottle of methadone with me and left. It was three in the morning and I had nowhere to go but I was feeling stubborn and decided not to come back. I cycled around the streets looking for somewhere to crash. I eventually found a basement cellar off the King's Road. I had a concrete floor for a bed, only a small comedown from usual. It was late May, so just warm enough. I stayed there for a few nights with my bottle of methadone, using it more as a sedative than something to ease my encroaching withdrawal. I needed a lot of methadone to feel level. I got up in the mornings and carried on my sticker work, feeling and looking rougher and rougher. Dad thought I was staying at a mate's house. After four days away, and the end of the methadone, I went back to the flat.

One day, when I was alone in the flat, Leon came round for a rare visit. He was concerned.

'Cas, listen to me. You have got to get your shit together. You're going to get busted. I know it and you know it. Come on, man, get out of here!'

I was touched by his concern but it didn't change anything.

Leon was smoking a little dope, maybe the odd line of coke here and there at parties, but that was it. Smack was off the cards for him and all my other mates. I'd crossed the line again and they were scared for me.

'Come on, Cas, you don't want this. I know you don't. I'll put money on this place getting turned over inside a month.'

I tried to distract him by talking about my fish, but it didn't work. He left. He looked worried. I could see his concern but I couldn't feel it. He sometimes turned up at lunchtimes and we would smoke a joint together. It was always good to see him. He wouldn't touch the smack and I was ashamed to do it in front of him. But that didn't stop me. He was worried for me, too. Everyone around me seemed to be warning me to get out. The summer passed without us being busted.

January 1988, Holland Park, London

Simon and I were standing outside his flat in his car park. It had started to rain.

'You're going to prison, Caspar. You know that, don't you?'

I wondered if he knew something I didn't.

'Has someone grassed me up?' I asked him angrily.

'Call it instinct. Feminine intuition, sweetie.'

Simon was the campest man I'd ever met. He had a thick, black moustache and a body like John Travolta in *Grease*. I'd been living at his place for two weeks. He was neurotic about most things but cool about me being in his flat. He was one of Dad's best punters and we both liked him. When tempers had flared time and again at the hooker's flat, it had made sense for me to get out and find somewhere else to live. He had a good heart and was one of the few gay men who didn't try it on with me. I trusted him. He was agitated that day but I cut him some slack. He was still in shock. His kitten had climbed into the washing machine the night before and had been put on spin cycle number five.

'I'm not going to prison.'

'I'm not sure you'll have much say in the matter. You've been dealing smack with your father for the last six months. They only have to bust one clucking junky and they'll put you away for more years than you could cope with, darling.'

If he was trying to scare me, it worked. I knew I was breaking the law, lots of laws, every day, all day. I also thought the last two busts were as bad as my luck could get.

Simon looked down at the floor. 'Oh, God, darling, much as I hate to say it I'm afraid you're going to have to move out. I'm doing far too much coke right now and my paranoia levels are through the roof. I'm getting palpitations. I'm grateful for the drugs for the rent but I have my reputation to think of.'

My heart sank. I was going to end up back on the street. I had no one else to stay with.

'Oh, darling, I am sorry. You're up to your neck in sleaze and completely out of your depth. I keep thinking you're a grown up when you're just a kid.' He stroked my hair and I let him. 'It's a tragedy of Greek proportions. But you do have a choice, you know? You can get out of this awful mess. You don't have to end up like your father. Heaven forbid.'

I ignored the pop at Dad and the pep talk. I needed to sort out my living situation. The rest could wait.

'Do you know anyone I can stay with?'

'I have a girlfriend in Hackney, Tabitha. Mad as a cat but a heart of gold. Far enough away for you to stay out of trouble. It may even keep you out of prison.'

The problem with me staying out of trouble was that it meant staying away from Dad and from my access to drugs. Neither was an option. I was too much of a coward to go through another withdrawal.

Simon put a piece of paper on my back and scribbled down her number. The contact was reassuring. I tilted my head back and looked up at the trees and sky. Rain splashed into my eyes. Simon's full stop was conclusive. I needed to make a decision.

*

I moved into Tabitha's house, which was more like a squat. She was OK, she made me laugh and she grew her own weed. I would commute back and forth between her place and then Latisha's to pick up stickers, and then head to the flat to do my smack shifts. I was seeing less and less of Dad. He was losing his motivation with the business and spending more and more time with Kate. It was like we were treading water, repeating old patterns, selling to get stoned, with no plans for the future. My habit had doubled since I'd been allowed to collect the weekly batch from North London before taking it to Clapham. It was near Tabitha's house. I cut the smack at her place – using the skills learned from Dad – before I gave him the gear. He trusted me. I made the most of that trust and did the same with the coke. I also made up three fictitious customers and regularly paged Dad from a public phone box pretending to be these made-up Hoorays, asking specifically for me to meet them and sell them either coke or smack. Dad was chuffed with the good use of this new technology and didn't care that he had never met these punters or that they wanted only to be met on the street. I would walk back into the flat after paging him and feign surprise at having been asked for personally by 'Toby', 'Tamara' or 'Harry'. Dad happily gave me the gear to sell to these non-existent Hoorays. I would head off to the local toilets with the gear and get stoned at my leisure. I stole cash from his wallet and paid him for the drugs with his own money. It was a sweet trick. He had absolutely no idea what I was up to and it felt good.

After the best part of a year of dealing from the hookers' flat in Lots Road and working for the hookers, I started noticing unusual things going on. At first it was the feeling that I was being watched. It was partly paranoia, brought on by the coke, and partly real. I kept seeing pairs of men and women walking around outside the hooker's flat, trying not to look obvious. Some sat in cars, some stood talking quietly to each other. Maybe it *was* just the coke, I tried to convince myself. But they had the same feel about them as the police who had busted me for Dad's antiques haul. I chose to block them out. I chose not to believe what my eyes were telling me.

I was in the middle of my first smoke of the day when there was a knock at the window. Two raps, then three more. My stomach lurched. The automatic response to a knock at the window was fear, no matter how stoned I was. When the coded knock was completed with a final set of two taps I knew it was Dad. The fear turned to excitement, like when he used to pick me up from school. It was followed quickly by disappointment, when I remembered where I was and the life I was living.

I put the foil away. I was still feeling rough. I hadn't had enough. Dad walked in.

'Hey, kid. How's work?'

'Some bastard held a phone box door shut on me when I was putting a sticker up. Couldn't get in. Told me to fuck off and get a proper job, said he was calling the police. I nearly smashed him in the face.'

'Prick. When are you going to college?'

'Dad, for fuck's sake, please.'

We were living like criminals, selling class A drugs, working for prostitutes, ripping people off whenever we could. And yet Dad still had the same aspirations any father would have for his child. He wanted me to study, to go to college, university even. He wanted me to get a good education, get myself out of the life we were living and into something better, something more honourable and worthwhile. All I had to do, it seemed, was simply rise out of the dark mines of crime by studying.

'You need your O levels, kid. Working for hookers is OK

for a stopgap but you're going to want something more stimulating. A career.'

'What, in drug smuggling? Can we have a smoke, I feel rough. I haven't had any since this morning.'

'You're a terrible liar. You should become a policeman.'

In silence, he slowly took out his bag of smack, foil and matches and prepared a smoke for us. He deliberately took his time. He said it was more Zen to do it that way, more respectful, more spiritual. I just wanted the smack as quickly as possible.

Thirty minutes later I was sitting on the floor, huddled over my foil, a can of double strength lager by my leg, a joint and a cigarette burning in the ashtray. After so much drug consumption getting a good buzz was becoming tricky. It was all about finding the right combination of liquid, smoke and breathing. I took a chase on the foil, a puff on a joint, a puff on a cigarette and a swig of lager. I held my breath.

And then it washed over me. I'd been looking for that elusive buzz for almost two weeks. It hit the spot beautifully. The sensation rushed through my head, my chest, into my belly and radiated out into my aching limbs. I was still holding my breath. Hold, hold . . . and . . . exhale. Hardly any smoke came out; it was all in my lungs. Everything got better. I was all right. I could breathe. My muscles stopped twitching and my flu symptoms vanished. I could think again. Some space for the dialogue in my head to unravel.

What the fuck am I doing here? I don't want this. Even Wimbledon was better than this. Was it really? You've got no choice and you know it. I don't want that crazy psycho shit in my head again. Smack'll take care of that. I'm stuck then, is that it? Yes you are. I want this shit to stop. I mean it. Let's be honest here, it's not going to stop, is it? No. Guess not. I'm not going into treatment. No fucking rehab and no meetings. No chance. The only way this is going to stop is to get busted. Simple, I need to get busted. I want to. I don't want to. Please God don't let that happen.

God has got nothing to do with it.

I would have to be physically taken out of this situation to stop it. That was the only way.

I got back to my new chemical combination and tried to shut the voices out.

Two hours later

'I've got some stickers to pick up. I'll see you in a bit,' I told Dad.

I kissed him goodbye. I tried to hug him, too, but after I got little response I gave up. He didn't *feel* like he used to. He was colder and harder. It was the smack. I was resigned to my drug-induced cocoon.

I got my mountain bike from the back garden. It was cold and wet outside. The last thing I wanted to do was cycle to a hooker's flat in West Kensington.

I got to the New King's Road. I was stoned but I knew how to ride. A man appeared in the road ahead of me. He didn't wait for a red light. He was waving to someone behind me and I swerved to miss him. He walked towards me. I swerved again and he started to run right at me. Why the fuck was this man running towards me? Clearly a nutter. I swerved again, he lurched forward, panting, and caught hold of my jacket collar. He wrenched me off the bike. I heard screeching tyres behind me. He put my arm behind my back, held it there to control me, rushed me out of the road and slammed me into a wall.

'You're fucking nicked, mate.'

He was enjoying himself. I had smack on me and hooker stickers. I was fucked.

'What's your name?' he asked me.

Adrenaline gave me Dutch courage.

'Who the fuck are you?' I shouted into the wall.

I knew damn well who he was. The screeching tyres belonged to an unmarked police van. A uniformed police-man picked my bike up and slung it in the back. An unmarked car pulled up. This was all happening very fast.

'What's your name?' he repeated.

'Toby.'

'Stop pissing about, you little shit. What's your name?'

'Caspar.'

'Caspar who?'

'Caspar Walsh.'

'That's more like it. Well, Caspar Walsh, as I said, you are officially nicked.'

'What for?'

'You know damn well what for. Supplying class A drugs. I'll read you the details at the station.'

He twisted my arm tighter and turned me in the direction of the unmarked car.

At that moment another group of policemen were battering down the red door of the hookers' flat. Dad was out the back, trying to throw his big bag of smack and crack over the wall. The end wall of the garden was the back of a warehouse and way too high to lob things over. Besides, he simply didn't have the strength in his skinny junky arm to chuck it over. He ran back into the bedroom, flipped the lid of my fish tank, thrust his hand into the cold water and buried it under the gravel.

The police entered, shouting and yelling, like they always did. There were two other people in the flat with Dad, terrified clucking punters who did as they were told. Dad sat quietly on the bed, dirty green water dripping off the ends of his fingers. As the police frantically searched the flat, the bag of gear made its way from under the fish tank gravel and floated, gently, Zen-like, to the surface.

Back on the street I was being forced into the back of the unmarked car. Just like in the movies, we pulled away too fast. Just like in the movies, the cuffs on my thin wrists were too tight.

It seemed I should have been careful what I'd wished for. My silent prayer had been answered.

18

Stone Cold Turkey

I've been moved around from police cell to police cell over the last two days. I wasn't told where I was going, but I knew from the distances travelled in the back of various vans that I was still in London.

I reached the peak of my withdrawal yesterday and can hardly walk. I've been constantly retching and vomiting and shitting. Now I'm in a very big holding cell. Bigger than anything I've been in before. There are a lot of men in here and I need to control my bodily fluids. The centre of the room is open and bare, an expanse of battered, green lino. Two strip lights buzz above my head, one is flickering on and off like it's dying. I know the feeling. There's no natural light and it stinks of sweat and fags and tea. I think it's underground. Why are they always underground? Again, there's a wooden bench running along the walls, right up to the cell door. The solid steel door has very little paint left on it. Decades of scratched words, kicks, punches and head butts. That looks like dried blood on the scarred metal. I have to get out.

There are about twenty-five geezers in here. All kinds: blacks, South Americans, Chinese, Middle Easterners, Eastern Europeans, all shades of white. I'm scared of every single one of them. Surely this isn't right? I mean, all these headcases in the same room together. The police must know the chance of it kicking off in here are seriously high. Or maybe that's their strategy so they've got some violent entertainment to wile away the tedious day. Over in the far corner there's a white guy and a black guy. They're standing close and they're whispering to each other. Both of them are in white paper suits. I've seen that on the telly. It means they've either raped or killed someone or have been fucking around with bombs. I know I have to look cool in here, otherwise I'm going to get a kicking. But every unexpected noise makes my body convulse with fright. People laugh at me when they see it. I would, too, if I saw a 6 foot 5 inch pale, skinny junky's arm jerking out at a right angle every time a door slams.

I don't know where to put my eyes. I know I'm not supposed to look at anyone but I want to. I want to know what they've done, especially those geezers in the paper suits.

The door was opened every ten minutes or so and up to five of us taken out. They were doing it alphabetically. It felt like school roll call. 'Walsh' was always last. This was as frightened as I'd ever been. I did not belong in there. The guys around me looked comfortable and easy in their surroundings. I needed a cigarette. But I wasn't going to ask anyone for anything.

Finally, my name was called. I had never been so glad to see a man in uniform.

'Come on, move through. Stand over there and get in line. No talking.' Barked instructions from the officer.

A lot of the men in the holding cell started to naturally drift into suitable pairs. I didn't feel drawn to anyone. I shuffled up the queue until I reached the head of it. An officer with a Polaroid camera stood in front of me, bored.

'Stand on that white line and look up. That's it. Smile for the camera. Come on, for Christ's sake.'

The flash went off and my left arm flew out at a right angle. The guys in the queue behind laughed.

'Bit jumpy there, mate.' The copper looked at the Polaroid. 'This isn't your best side, I'm afraid.'

He showed it to me. As the image developed I got a shock. I hadn't looked in the mirror for months. It didn't look like me at all. It looked like I'd been dug up.

A week later and I was still feeling shaky, the usual flu-like symptoms of a runny nose, sneezing and aching limbs. The pains were still intense, but much more bearable. I was now managing to hold down my food and had enough concentration to read a bit, which helped me pass the time.

I was due in court at 9 a.m., which meant being woken up at five in the morning. Before my eyes had properly focused, they shoved a greasy fried breakfast in front of me. I wasn't hungry but I ate it. I was taken out of the cells and walked into the back of a waiting prison van. We drove across London, stopping off at stations along the way to pick up more of the same. Each stop took a ridiculously long time. This is why we had been woken up so early.

We finally got to the courts. They took me in at basement level then up to the first floor. It had massive windows all the way along the corridor. I could see down on to the street below. People were walking by. They were going about their business just twenty or thirty feet – and a whole lifetime – away. I was told to stop outside a cell door. It was near to the courts for quick access. I hoped I'd be alone in there. No more white paper suits, please. The key clunked in the lock. As the door opened, there was something familiar in the air. My heart skipped several beats. There he was sitting cross-legged on the blue plastic mattress. Dad looked comfortable. He smiled at me.

'Hey, kid. It happens to the best of us.'

'Dad! Shit. Do they know who you are?'

'I hope so, they just nicked me,' he joked. 'They must've fucked up.'

We shouldn't have been in a cell together.

'What happened?' I asked. I was shaking.

'They let me out on bail. Wanted to see where I went so they could nick everyone. They busted me as I was coming out of the bank. I had all my money on me. Bastards loved every minute of it.'

They had known he would try to skip bail and leave the country, hence the trip to the bank, but they wanted more evidence, as much as they could get. They were fed up with his non-stop criminal merry-go-round. They wanted him off the streets for as long as possible. The money in the bank was something by way of proof of his criminal activity, but fortunately for us there were no more drugs than those found floating in the fish tank. More drugs, or links higher up the chain, were what they really wanted, along with as many statements as possible from our eclectic selection of customers. The police had waited in the flat after they had taken Dad and the two punters to the police station. They systematically let in every customer looking for their daily gear and took them away for questioning. The working girls and boys were the most honourable and kept their mouths shut all through questioning. They always did. They understood the street rules on grassing. The celebrities usually talked first and fastest, followed closely by the Hoorays and Henriettas. The hippies generally said nothing, on point of principle. They were for the most part anarchistic and the police would get little or nothing out of them. That said, there was still enough evidence laid down in the statements of clucking, frightened junkies to put my dad and me in prison for a long time.

I couldn't believe it. Dad had been planning to leave me alone. He had been planning to leave the country. I felt sick at the thought of it. I sat down slowly on the bench. My muscles stiff. He put his hand on my shoulder.

'You OK, kid? You look dreadful. Lost a lot of weight.'

'Never been this bad before. Aren't you sick?'

'Full of methadone. It'll be here soon, though. You'll be feeling better and I'll be writhing about on some nasty cell floor, shitting my pants and chuckin' my guts up. Think of yourself as ahead of the game.'

I lay down on the bench. Suddenly, I couldn't keep my eyes open. But when I shut them my thoughts moved about faster than I could cope with. I hadn't slept properly for days. Dad reached over and started to massage my thighs. He knew just where to rub and it felt good. I had never wanted to be held so much in my entire life. The deep ache of the cold turkey was easing but my legs and arms still felt like someone had repeatedly given me dead legs and arms. Punch after punch after punch.

This was the first real physical affection he had shown me in years. This was how I remembered him. But it felt final. We may as well have been going to a funeral. He knew we were in a lot of trouble. After ten minutes or so he cleared his throat.

'Are you ready for this?'

I didn't have to ask what for. I knew what he meant. He meant, was I ready to go down. Was I ready for prison? I waited a long time before I answered. 'Yeah, I think so.'

But I wasn't. I was lying for him. I wanted him to be proud of me. I wanted him to know I was going to be all right. I wasn't ready for any of it. This wasn't the way it was meant to be. Fuck this, I thought. I wasn't going down his path. I was too scared. I was going to do whatever I could to stop the nightmare from continuing. Fuck smack and fuck the depression. If I ended up in prison, if I got a long sentence, it would mess me up for good. I would get my head kicked in and be raped, no doubt about it.

'I'm looking at ten this time, kid. Way too close to the last one.'

'How long will I get?'

'First conviction for dealing class As, with a good word from me . . . about four.'

Four fucking years. I wasn't doing four years. No chance.

I didn't say any of this to him.

'Plead guilty,' he told me. 'It's your first proper bust. I'll write a letter to the judge telling him you're not to blame, I am. You'll get a lighter sentence.'

'What about you?'

'I'm going guilty. If we go not guilty there'll be a jury trial and we'll get sent down anyway. They've got plenty of evidence and statements, and the sentence will double. Best not to piss the judge off. Especially when it's so obvious we were up to our necks in smack.'

We didn't say any more to each other. There was nothing more to say.

We went into the courtroom together, in silence. The prosecution read out the charges. Conspiracy to deal class A drugs. Possession of heroin and cocaine. Even I got bored of hearing my name read out over and over again, with more and more details about our charges. It turned out that our friendly neighbourhood watch had grassed on us, just as she'd promised.

I'd got locked out of the hookers' flat one night and been forced to knock on the neighbour's door to see if I could climb over the back wall. The place was full of women. They were having a hen party.

The owner eyeballed me up and down. 'You're our new neighbour, aren't you?'

I nodded.

'Well, darling, the last tenants were a couple of prostitutes, the ones before that were crack dealers. The place is cursed with scumbags; let's hope you don't follow suit, eh?' She winked at me. 'If you do I will call the police immediately. Seems fair enough, don't you think, girls?'

I nodded again and the women behind her laughed like a bunch of posh hyenas.

'Of course,' I said in my best voice. 'Can't be having that kind of thing going on round here, not in Chelsea.'

I'd smiled at her and was allowed to climb her wall.

I'd forgotten about that conversation. True to her word, she'd seen what was happening in our flat and grassed us up. We'd been watched for three months. It was called Operation Scorpio. It began on 22 April 1988. The police only had enough funds for surveillance on Wednesdays and Thursdays. But those two days had given them plenty. The list of charges put together by the chief inspector was long and tedious. All I wanted to do was sit down.

Me and Dad were remanded in custody and a court date was set.

I had come of age, so it was mainstream prison for me now.

I was due to do my remand time at HMP Brixton but, luckily for me, there was a prison officers' strike on. I was marked down for a police station in the West Midlands and marched on to a coach full of prisoners. All the seats were taken, except one next to the only headcase on the coach. He was covered in dark red flecks of what I later worked out was dried blood. His face, beard, snow-wash denim jacket and trousers were covered in it. He looked like he'd been in a car crash. Or one hell of a fight. My cuffs were undone and I was told to sit down next to him. The guard took my left arm and his right arm, pulled them across our bodies and cuffed us together. We may as well have been having a cuddle, at least it would have eased the biting pain of the metal cuffs.

This guy smelled like he'd been on the streets for months. As well as the blood, I made out yellow piss stains on his jeans. It was all I could do not to throw up on him. He told me he'd jumped off a bridge while on acid. Thought he could fly. He was angry, though thankfully not with me. I think he liked me. He was angry with the coppers on the coach. Every time they walked past us he growled at them, like a dog. Finally he fell asleep and slowly pulled my left arm across to his right side so that the cuffs dug deeper into me and our clinch became more intimate. I didn't dare pull my arm back and risk waking him up. At one point he snapped his eyes open and asked a passing copper for a fag. When he was refused he started shouting, threatening to kill all the guards – right in my bloody ear.

Two prisoners were smoking spliff in the back. It smelled sweet and delicious to my clucking nose. The police either didn't smell it, which was doubtful, or were ignoring it, which was much more likely. Our escorts wanted a quiet journey. I was dying for a smoke.

That journey to the West Midlands went on for three and a half hours. The cuffs on my wrists didn't stop hurting for a single second.

On arrival, I was given a two-man cell. The guy in it with me was a drunk going through the delirium tremens. He was seeing animals and insects coming out of the walls. I was seeing a lot of the inside of the toilet bowl. The average heroin withdrawal lasts around two weeks and I was just over halfway. The dregs of it reared up in that cell, in one last attempt to humiliate me and teach me a lesson. It stripped away the final shreds of my dignity. My system was chucking fluids out top and bottom. I would eat my food and immediately throw it back up. While I was throwing up I would feel wet shit backing up in my bowels and have to get my arse on the seat, quick. Up and down, backwards and forwards, head in the bowl, arse on the seat for two days solid.

The cell smelled like a Third World sewer. My cell mate was very understanding. He didn't say much and would pretend to be asleep a lot of time. I knew he was awake. It must have been a nightmare to listen to me retching and groaning and vomiting day and night. We respected each other in our private, shitty detoxifications and didn't say much about it. The drunk got released after four days and I was back on my own. I had grown attached to him and had welcomed the company. I missed him.

Our exercise was in a caged yard fifteen feet by five feet. One hour a day. Masturbation was the only decent way of briefly getting away from the pain and frustration of my aching legs. The anger at my situation led me to a new, pain-killing discovery. I would get so wound up I started to punch the thick, brick walls. The pain in my hands distracted me from the pain of my withdrawal. I punched the walls so many times and so hard my knuckles disappeared, replaced by blissfully aching blue bruises. By the end of the week I was a physical and emotional wreck.

A doctor had prescribed me some pills for pain relief. He suggested I write to a treatment centre. If this was prison, then rehab now seemed like a good option. Anything to get out of my cell. I wrote to two treatment centres, gave the letters in to be sent off and returned to my withdrawal.

The Stourbridge police guards were easy on us. They gave us pizza, cigarettes and chocolate. They let us watch telly through the bars in the holding area. One night I was watching *Legal Eagles*. I was enjoying it. I was off the smack and could make out what was going on. Something to celebrate. We were interrupted by a banging on the door. The telly was switched off and a group of heavy-looking police officers, sent from London, came silently in.

A Brummie policeman I'd made friends with came up to me. 'You're in court in the morning. Get your things together. There's a minibus to take you back.'

I did as I was told and headed back to my cell to collect my things. He followed me. He lowered his voice. 'Best keep your head down from now on, son. Those guys are animals.'

'Who?' I asked.

'The boys from the Met. Different breed altogether. There'll be no pizza down there. Best of luck to you. You deserve better than this.'

It must have been about two in the morning when we got to Camberwell in London. Why the police couldn't have come for us earlier, I don't know, but we arrived at the holding cells tired and pissed off. I'd been warned that it would be like a zoo, full of animals. And that was about right. No one said anything to us about where we were going next or what was happening. All we knew was that we were due in court first thing the following morning and none of us would be getting much sleep. The police weren't concerned that we presented our best side.

We were led past the reception desk and down a flight of stairs. I could hear voices and shouting from below. It seemed a long way off. We kept on going down, at least two flights below ground. It was like going into some kind of bunker. Or hell. I could hear water sloshing about. My senses were spinning, trying to work out what was going to happen next.

'Hey big daddy, papa baby. We got ourselves some sweet new meat coming down, special delivery!'

It was a poor impersonation of a woman's voice, still quite a way off, but becoming clearer. We got to the last few steps and I could see water on the floor of the passage ahead, about three inches deep.

'What's going on?' I asked the copper in front of me.

'Some bright spark shoved a loo roll down the toilet. Flooded the whole ground floor.'

I could smell shit coming out of the blocked toilets. We waded through the water, flecked with filthy bits of toilet paper and carried on down a series of corridors. My feet were soaked. We finally reached the first of the cells. All the centre hatches were open, probably to get some air into the pokey boxes. Or to get a good look at the new arrivals. They were just about big enough to see a face through. The man behind the first cell door pushed his face right up to it and large lips blew kisses at whoever was passing. I was the first.

'Where's my daddy day care, baby? You gonna come here to sweet baby Jane and give me my medicine?' It was the woman's voice I'd heard a few moments earlier.

The man's lips were painted with a deep red lipstick. It had been put on badly, some of it smeared around his mouth as though he'd been kissing someone hard. The faceless, red lips kept puckering and blowing kisses at me. It sent a shiver down my spine. I kept moving.

As I approached it, the third cell door along exploded with three violent kicks. 'When's papa gonna get his poontang then, eh?' The man behind the door screamed in a fake American drawl. More faceless lips. 'I'm getting *really* fucking lonely and *really* fucking horny in here!'

He carried on kicking. I could make out a moustache, bad breath and a lot of anger behind gritted, snarling teeth. As he spoke, he spat saliva out of the hatch. I was glad he was behind a locked, steel door. But for how long?

The lipsticked face behind me crooned a soft, camp response. 'Ooh, baby, if they unlocked these doors I'd be down on that big beautiful cock of yours in a second. You wouldn't even have to wash it.' Followed by the manic clapping of excited hands.

The policeman behind me whacked the transvestite's cell door with his truncheon. The metallic bang made my arm fly out. I wasn't sure if all this was a show, by way of a welcome, or was for real. Another shudder went up my back as I continued on down a set of steps to the final corridor. Mine.

I could feel the moustached man's voice directed at my back. 'We got ourselves some sweet hometown girls tonight. Look at the swing on that beautiful arse.' He was talking about me, I knew that for sure.

'Stop here,' our escort ordered.

There was someone already in my cell, a one-man cell with a blue plastic mattress on the floor for me. My cell mate came to the door and looked through the open hatch. The door was unlocked for me.

The shouting and whistling and obscenities continued into the night. I felt constantly under threat and terrified. It was a nightmare I couldn't wake up from.

It turned out that I was two days early for my court case. I managed to make a call to Mum and she came to visit me. I wasn't allowed out of the cell. The guard opened the hatch. I hadn't seen her for ages. I felt like a child behind that door. I was still a child. She handed fruit and chocolates and sweets and cigarettes through the small hole. They wouldn't let us touch each other. This was the deal with holding cells. Keeping us locked up was all they were interested in. I wanted to hug her. I wanted her to hold me. She reached her hand through the hatch and stroked my face and started to cry.

'Oh, Cas. What have you done, darling? Look at you.'

Those ten words were enough to make me break down in front of her. I cried for the first time in as long as I could remember. My inability to hold her, my imprisonment, my powerlessness all merged into one and I felt my knees buckle. I pushed them against the cell door to keep myself upright, and kept talking. We had five minutes. That was all they gave us. When she left I collapsed on to my mattress and cried into my stinking, grey blanket, apologising to my cell mate over and over.

That night I was unable to sleep. The withdrawal was almost out of my system but the sleeplessness could stick around for weeks. I pressed the buzzer to get an officer to come to me. I'd already called him out an hour earlier.

'What do you want now?' He was pissed off.

'Can I have a light?' We weren't allowed matches in case we set fire to our cells or ourselves.

'You just had one.'

'I can't sleep,' I told him.

'Well if you keep buzzing me for fucking matches this will help you sleep, I promise you that.'

He was holding a battered wooden truncheon in front of my face. I had no doubt that he'd give me a good kicking if I gave him any shit. The same went for the rest of the guards. They looked uptight, like they needed to let off steam. I took the light for my fag and made it the last of the night. I was due in court for the bail hearing in the morning.

Next day, Dad was there too. We were charged with the same crimes so we had to be in court at the same time. I walked, escorted, into yet another courtroom. I never got used to the feeling of fear and respect those rooms commanded. They are imposing places. The severe atmosphere intimidates and that affects everybody's behaviour. It's always the same. There is a tight ritual to the way everything is done. The lights are bright and normal movement becomes restricted to wooden gestures, with theatrical posturing from the barristers. The judge is the only one who ever seems vaguely relaxed. I was told by my counsel exactly how to behave and what to do just before I needed to do it. I did my best to oblige.

Dad was in court already, sitting silently by himself, like

he was meditating. He looked content, resigned to what was going to happen. He looked over to me and smiled. He nodded twice and looked back down. I saw the judge sitting in his big leather chair. Everyone was going about their business. The judge was reading a letter. He smiled, shook his head a little and rubbed his chin. Dad watched him while he read it, looked right at me and winked. I had no idea what he was winking about. The judge's smile turned into a chuckle.

I entered the dock. The prosecution read out the charges and objected to both our requests for bail. My brief declared I'd been accepted into a treatment centre in Wiltshire. That was the first I'd heard about it. My letters had obviously got through. It would have been nice if someone had told me. There was just one snag. There was a waiting list and the speed of my placement was dependent on monies being available. I had no money. Whatever happened, I would get a place sooner or later. I needed it to be sooner.

The judge refused Dad bail on the spot. He granted me mine, on the proviso that I get into treatment as soon as possible. I couldn't believe it. I was free.

Dad had one stop off to make before he went back to HMP Wandsworth. He had to go to the Chelsea and Westminster hospital. It was just up the road from where we used to deal and where I'd first got busted. Dad hated hospitals. He always had. But his abscess had flared up again. I really wanted to visit him in hospital before he got shipped to Wandsworth but I was too confused and angry with him to go. I had finally begun to blame him for what happened to us. For what had happened to me.

The condition of my bail was that I stay with Mum. It had been a long time since I'd slept at her house. It felt strange. Suddenly she was being the mother I'd been wanting all my life; she was back in charge after all these years. She was taking care of me. She had been doing her best to work with the demons of her own addiction and put them to rest. She was making slow progress but it was steady and solid and her life was changing for the better.

The house smelled as it always had, a cross between her sweet perfume, her delicious cooking and her fat cats. It was comforting. That said, I made sure I was out of the house for most of the day. I had an 11 p.m. curfew, which I was careful to observe, but most days I went to Leon's place in Hammersmith and smoked spliff. My system had become so clean it was like starting all over again. I was a cheap date and I was welcome there.

I had to have a face-to-face assessment for rehab. I went to an interview at offices in London, accompanied by Mum. As happy as she was that I was out, she wanted me in treatment as soon as possible.

'So, Miss Deaton,' the woman asked my mother, 'are you in a position to put any money towards Caspar's placement? It would really speed his admission up.' The fees were £1,000 a week.

'No, I'm sorry. There's no money.'

Mum was skint. It looked like my wait was going to be a long one. The woman went through a series of questions about my habit, punctuated by the repeated question about any extra money Mum might have access to. Mum was starting to look agitated.

'It'll be about six weeks before we can get Caspar an assisted place,' the woman told us.

Just as the meeting was coming to a close Mum piped up. 'Actually, we may be able to get up to £500 a week.'

I nearly fell off my chair. The woman was almost as surprised as I was. It seemed Jack had put the money up. He'd told Mum to hold out till the very last, in case there turned out to be another option. There wasn't. All these years later, the man my mum had chosen over me when I was just

241

a toddler was still around. Unlike Dad, he had become very successful in his antiques business. He and Mum had had an on/off relationship for most of my life. It was dysfunctional but they loved each other and, underneath the alcohol and anger, it turned out he had a kind heart. That's what Mum kept telling me. The man I had put a lot of energy into hating had turned out to be my guardian angel. I blamed Dad for most things, and I blamed Jack too. He was the original wedge that Mum had chosen to place between me and her. I believed the money was heavy with guilt. I believed I deserved it. I had just six days to wait.

Mum's house, two days later

Paul and I were smoking a joint in silence. Mum had hidden her hash after my arrest, but Paul had found it. It was bliss. I'd never felt so close to him. Mum wasn't due back for hours. The future was looking bright.

Two hours and three joints later I was dozing. In my half sleep I heard the doorbell go. It was a long buzz. Too long for a friend, too short for a salesman. Only bailiffs and police rang doorbells that long. We weren't expecting anyone. I heard Paul get up and look out of the window.

'Cas?' He was nervous.

'Yeah?' I murmured.

'It's the police!'

I was almost there. Almost back in the country, in a nice big house, getting myself clean and the fuckers were on me again. I thought they'd come to revoke my bail, that they'd changed their minds or someone else had surfaced and grassed us and I was going back inside. I wanted to run but there was no way out of Mum's place. I could get on to the next door neighbour's balcony, but that was it.

Paul went downstairs. I heard voices. Three people

coming back up. Their pace slow. There was no aggression in their footsteps. I had the feeling they weren't there to arrest me.

Paul came in first, followed by two young uniformed officers in crisp white shirts and black trousers, and the standard issue clip-on ties they all wore – in case someone tried to swing them around by it or throttle them. They had serious looks on their faces and they stood in silence for a long minute.

'I'm afraid we have some bad news.' I was trying not to panic. 'Your dad's in hospital.'

'I know. He's having his abscess treated.'

'I'm afraid your father is in intensive care. He tried to hang himself this morning.'

I held myself together. The police had been kind. He'd been gentle about how he told me. But I wasn't going to give them the satisfaction of seeing me cry. As soon as I heard the door shut behind them I broke down. My brother held me tight. I let myself go into his warm, safe hug and wept without shame.

19

A New World

This isn't an area of the hospital I've seen before. Dad has been on the main wards up till now. They've kept this part of the hospital hidden. I can't even find the signs for intensive care. The Tennants Super I had on the bus has done the trick. I've calmed down a bit. They haven't told me anything about how he is. They just said to come. This is it, through here. It's quiet. No one else around.

Two sets of doors, a bit like going into a prison. There's even a guard, a nurse. I can see her through the second door, sitting sentinel. The lights are low. I walk through the final door and up to the nurse. I'm nervous, like a kid.

'I'm Caspar Walsh. I've come to see my father, Frank.'

'Come through here, Mr Walsh. I have to go through some things with you before you can see your dad.'

We go into a small room and sit down.

'So, I'm going to go through what you will see when you go in, so that you're prepared. Your dad has a lot of wires attached to his body. They're basically keeping an eye on him, keeping his breathing and heartbeat regular. They'll warn us if he needs anything. He's asleep and probably won't wake up while you're in

there. You can touch him but nothing too vigorous. Holding his hand is OK, but no hugging I'm afraid. We restrict visits to twenty minutes. The nurses have to check on him regularly and there isn't much space for them to move around with a visitor in the room. You may get upset, that's fine, just come back over to me and talk to me if you need to. Do you have any questions?'

She's done this before, lots of times, but it still feels warm and personal. I'm ready to see him.

There were six other patients in the main part of the dimly lit ward, their beds illuminated by a soft yellow ceiling light. Each unconscious patient was surrounded by a mass of equipment keeping them alive. Everything else was in semi darkness. There were three other single rooms and Dad was in one of them. I walked up to it and looked through the wire mesh glass. The nurse was behind me waiting for me to build up the courage to enter. I looked at her for some encouragement. She smiled at me by way of separation and headed back to her station.

I walked into Dad's room and, sure enough, he had loads of wires attached to his body. The ECG monitoring his heart blipped a steady rhythm. He was asleep. He looked peaceful. I felt guilty I'd had the can of lager but I'd needed it. Out of all the shit I'd been through, this was without a doubt the most horrific situation I'd been in. I didn't know how I was supposed to act in there. Should I cry? Sit quietly and respectfully hold his hand like I understood what was going on? I didn't understand. Whatever I did in that room felt fake. I didn't know how to be myself.

I sat down and looked at him. I was so grateful I hadn't been in any way successful in my own suicide attempt. Looking at him like this was crippling me. I was shaking. This was what I would have put people through. It was the most selfish thing a person could do. What a fucking joke.

How self absorbed could a person get? A hot flush of anger moved through me and I felt like punching his gentle, sleeping face.

Twenty minutes passed too quickly. A nurse came in. She patiently waited for me to go, but I couldn't move. She checked the readings on his ECG, looked at me, smiled and left. What was the point of me being in there? I'd seen him, he was alive. Just. There was nothing to say. I wanted to leave. But my arse was glued to the chair for a further five minutes before I finally managed to get up.

As I rose I noticed a bandage around his neck. On the skin, just above it, was a dark blue line fading into a lighter blue, then into yellow; it was a bruise. I wanted to know what he'd done, how he'd tried to kill himself. The nurse told me he'd tried to hang himself in a broom cupboard down the corridor. He'd been under police guard. Dad had convinced the young copper to get them both a cup of tea. In the five minutes he was gone, Dad had slipped into the cleaning cupboard, tied a floor-polisher's cable around his neck and hooked it round the ceiling light. He was suspended for about thirty seconds before the light socket and false ceiling collapsed, dropping my half-naked father to the floor. By the time he hit the ground he was unconscious; it would have been humiliating to be found on the floor in one of those arse-exposing gowns.

I suddenly remembered a conversation I'd had with Dad in the hookers' flat. He had made it clear to me he couldn't do another prison sentence. 'If I get nicked again I'm going to top myself. I'm not doing any more time.'

It was a simple, clear sentence and I'd ignored it because the words had scared me. I hadn't wanted to believe them because I'd known we were going to get busted at some point. It was inevitable. I hadn't wanted to imagine what my life would be like without him.

But Dad was tough in mind and body. He could put himself through the most incredible stress and pressure and he would always spring back looking fitter than ever, like nothing that bad had happened to him. It seemed he could even survive his own attempts to kill himself either slowly through drugs or quickly through hanging. True to form he recovered fast from the suicide attempt and within a week was moved to HMP Wandsworth. The bruise around his neck was obvious. He began his next sentence carrying himself around the wing and yard, bruise on show, strutting like he'd been in a fight with someone who had tried to throttle him. It wasn't cool for fellow prisoners to know you'd attempted suicide.

The hospital visit was the last time I would see Dad for almost three years.

August 1988

It was my twenty-first birthday and I was going into treatment for drug addiction and alcoholism. My last morning in London was sunny and breezy; the best kind of weather. I snuck into Mum's bathroom and smoked the joint I'd prepared the night before. There was still enough of Mum's hash for another three big joints but there wasn't enough time to smoke them all. I'd do that later. I put the dope in my pocket, finished my smoke and went back upstairs. My godmother Anna was there. She was going to drive me down to rehab in her five series BMW.

I arrived stoned. Unable to find a place to smoke it, I'd eaten the last of the hash. It was starting to take effect. I sat down to my first meal. At the end of it someone came up to me with a card that had a lollipop stuck to it. To my amazement, every resident in the dining room turned to face me and sang 'Happy Birthday'. I hadn't celebrated my birthday properly for the last three years. The card had a silver key embossed on it and next to it in red the words '21 today – key to the door'. I hadn't heard that phrase before. The guy next to me opened his arms for a hug.

'Standard twenty-first birthday greeting, mate. Reckon it means more than one door for you, eh? Welcome to the next chapter.'

The place was beautiful. That evening I wandered around the grounds, staring at the trees, telling everyone how beautiful it was. I got some odd looks. The following day, after the hash high had worn off, I realised why. However beautiful the place was, the cold reality of why I was there hit me.

That was my first day clean: 17 August 1988.

I went to the nurse's station to be weighed and measured. I was six feet five inches and weighed eight and a half stone – five stone underweight for my height. But my appetite was back and I was eating like a horse. Miraculously, I gained three stones in the first month of being there.

The other residents were all in different stages of withdrawal from a whole range of drugs: uppers, downers, smack, coke, alcohol, speed, crack, methadone. It was like living in a circus of emotional misfits. People were randomly bursting into tears, jumping up and walking out of groups, trying to get it on with each other, arguing, even fighting. Some were thrown out for getting stoned or having illicit sex in the adjoining woods. I couldn't understand it. Why weren't they playing the game? I was keeping my head down. I had nowhere else to go except back to prison. I was in a big house in the country, surrounded by trees, getting three good meals a day and people were listening to me. They wanted to help. Seemed like a wise choice to me. I was ready. I'd had enough.

I got my introduction to the treatment programme

on day three. My initial reaction to the counsellors was that they could fuck right off with it all. There were a lot of references to 'god' in the literature. At that point in my life, my belief in God was stretched to the limit. After a few weeks, however, it became clear the literature was talking about a 'god' of my understanding. I could find that 'god' in a one-to-one counselling session, a therapy group, a support group, the countryside, whatever. It was up to me. That seemed reasonable.

The philosophy of the treatment programme was based on complete abstinence from all 'mood altering chemicals'. That wasn't something I had considered when I got there. Smack, crack, acid, speed, sure. I could well do without those kind of narcotic handicaps. But spliff and booze had been with me since the beginning and, as far as I was concerned, they were staying. They were close friends and were not the chemicals I would ever consider stopping taking. I was up for a semi-enlightening experience, not the full monty.

Part of the process was about getting down on paper what was going on inside, writing about the difficult stuff, sharing it with other people in recovery and finding a way to get support through it all. I was being given a route map to find my way round this new territory. Everyone in rehab had been lost. We were all handed an emotional guidebook to get us out of the wasteland.

I'd been off the smack for nearly two months and in treatment for four weeks. This was usually the time my depression would start to creep back in. True to form, I started to feel as though I was on the edge of it again. I was getting scared. I'd been a very vocal member of all our group therapy sessions. But one afternoon I tried to slip through the hour unnoticed. We got to the end of the session and I was asked how I was doing. I had been in a daze, spaced out, not listening to what others were saying. But it was like I had been slapped around the face by that question. I came back into the reality of the room and lost it.

I started to rock backwards and forwards and a roaring noise came out of me, followed by tears streaming through my closed eyes. It was the only way I could do it.

'I want this fucking thing out of me. I'm sick of it!' I screamed.

The 'thing' was my depression. It had hunted and infected me in one way or another since I was fifteen. At its core was my addiction. My addiction to do whatever was necessary to stay shut down and keep people out. It was my fear, my hate, all the toxic emotions inside that kept me where I was – stuck in an awful place and unable to move forward. It kept me stoned, drunk, scared, self absorbed and lacking the will to live. It was the part of me that told me it was a good idea to loop the curtain tie-back around my neck in that room in Wimbledon; it was the part of me that shut everyone out. It had been protecting me from my car wreck of a life. In some ways it kept me alive, at least in a physical sense. But I was dead inside. This 'thing' inside me had outgrown its usefulness. In this new place, where I was getting real emotional support, it was time to trust others and take some healthy risks.

The counsellor replied calmly. 'Well, you're in the right place for it, Caspar.'

I looked around the room and saw the looks of acknowledgement on my peers' faces. I thought I would have been told to shut up or get out. Instead I was given unconditional support. This was new territory and it felt safe to explore.

Each resident had their own one-to-one counsellor; mine was an old guy called Ben. He had been in recovery for over twenty years. An incredible man. Everything that came out of his mouth made sense. I went in to his office to speak to him about my depression, about my fear that it would come back now the smack was out of my system. I sat down. Early autumn sunshine was coming through his open window. It reminded me of the time before the drugs.

'Has it ever occurred to you, Caspar, that if you stopped taking drugs altogether, this depression of yours may leave you altogether? Maybe it's been your body's way of telling you to stop?'

It was irritatingly simple. His words crashed into me like cold water. I knew that what he had just said was true. On reflection, I'd always suspected my mental state was some kind of a warning to me to stop trying so hard to kill myself. All doubts about complete abstinence from drugs and alcohol left me for good in that office.

I left rehab early one morning and headed from the centre of the countryside back to the centre of London. The judge had wanted to keep an eye on me. He'd set a date for me to come back to London to check on my bail and to review my progress. The rehab centre didn't normally take people in who had to have their treatment programme broken up by court cases. The extra £500 a week from Jack towards my treatment fees helped me out on that front.

It was a shock to the system. I was only twenty-one, but my body was clear of drugs and alcohol for the first time in nine years. The experience reminded me why I'd done the drugs in the first place. I was scared, unable to sit still for more than a couple of minutes and felt completely exposed. I couldn't wait to get back to the sanctity of the countryside.

The court appearance went well. The judge was happy with my progress. I was released on extended bail to continue my treatment. I had seven months until my next appearance, seven months to get into recovery and to prove to the judge that I was a changed man.

Early evening, the taxi dropped me off outside rehab. I walked in through the main entrance, which looked through the sitting room doors and beyond. I could see a few familiar faces. As I'd entered they'd been talking, but then fell silent. They must be talking about me, I thought; slagging me off, no doubt. I nervously walked towards them. Everyone was sitting together, looking straight at me. They suddenly erupted into applause, they cheered me and came up to hug me. I had no idea what the fuss was about but I liked it.

There had been real concern, about whether I'd return. Leaving treatment in such a state of vulnerability was a tough thing to do. Up until that point I didn't know whether I was liked, much less accepted. That greeting did something powerful to me. It told me that I was, without a doubt, on the right track. These were people I could trust, people who cared about me, despite having only met them a few weeks before. It was a simple relationship. They didn't want anything material from me because I didn't have anything. All they wanted was what was best for me. I stepped through those doors and felt the applause. It was a clear sign that this was a place where I was meant to be.

The routine at rehab was set up to be a fast track into recovery from drugs and alcohol. There was hardly any time to stop and think about what was happening. We were up at 7 a.m. and in our first group by 9 a.m. Groups were always set up in a circle with two counsellors present, one experienced, one in training. There were two main groups and these in turn were broken down into smaller 'split groups'. The main groups would meet twice a week and the split groups would meet once a day. These smaller groups were where the nitty gritty of our stories came out and where we got feedback, identification and support from both the counsellors and our peers. Throughout the rest of the day there would be a mixture of lectures, videos and workshops on specific aspects of addiction. I was learning a lot about myself.

None of us knew what was going on in the outside world. All our books and radios were taken from us and there was no access to newspapers. We watched movies on Saturdays but these were confined to stories about addiction and alcoholism. Family visits were on Sundays. Dad had been moved to HMP Coldingley. Mum felt it was best to let me get on with my treatment and not to visit. I felt sad to watch people with their families but I was happy to go without the emotional fallout my newfound friends went through when their loved ones left.

These visits weren't just about having a nice stroll around the country house garden. Each individual's counsellors were in attendance, and there would be a family session at some point during the visit. It was the counsellor's job to help the family to understand their part in their loved one's addiction. The sessions could often get heated and some of my mates emerged more traumatised than ever.

After a particularly rough night's sleep I called an emergency 'mini group', something we could do at any time. It had to be made up of people from our main group and we could simply find a quiet room where the person who called it could let the others know how they were feeling. I had been struck by my first wave of guilt and I didn't know what to do with it. There were three people in the room with me, two men and a woman. I stood in front of them.

'So what's up, Caspar? What's bugging you, mate?' It was the same hippy who'd hugged me on my birthday.

'I don't deserve to be here.'

'How do you mean?'

'I'm only here to stay out of prison. I mean, I like it here,

I like the people, I like you. But the only reason I came here was to get out of prison.'

'And?' the woman asked. 'What's the problem with that?'

'Well, like I said, I don't deserve to be here. I'm a phony.'

'Doesn't matter how you got here, mate,' the hippy responded. 'Fact is you're here and I can see in your eyes that you want to be.'

I sat down, relieved.

'You'd have never just got up and walked out on the drugs, would you? No chance. You had to be physically removed from it and getting nicked made sure of that. The rest was up to you, and you came back. You went to London, you could've got stoned, drunk, disappeared but you didn't. You came back sober and straight and we all knew how bloody difficult that was, bang in the middle of your treatment. Not sure I could've done it.'

Out of all the experiences I had in rehab it was the welcome home and that mini group that have stayed with me to this day. I finally realised that I had a choice. Up until then my direction had been one track and drugs dominated. I had finally looked at the options: prison or recovery? Where I'd been for the past twenty-one years was known; what lay ahead of me was what mattered. I chose to move further into recovery, to take a completely unknown route that seemed at times very risky and scary. But I went by the example of the other people around me.

Each week we were driven from rehab to a support meeting. This was a way of getting us used to the support network we would have when we left treatment. The traditions of this fellowship state the need for confidentiality for personal safety and anonymity so I will simply call them 'the meetings'. There were people at the meetings who had six months, a year, even three years clean time. They looked together, had jobs, and seemed to be happy. I wanted what they had.

CRIMINAL

October 1988, Weymouth

My second-stage treatment centre was in Weymouth. The treatment became focused on getting us ready to live in the outside world, without the use of drugs.

Part of recovery concerns a concept I'd never really understood – service. Putting something back into the community was meant to be good for the addict, as well as others. I decided to sign up to take a meeting in the Verne prison on Portland, a desolate, windswept place. I was six months clean. I went alone without really thinking what I was doing.

The bus dropped me off at the base of a long, winding hill that wiped me out walking up it. I got to the prison gates and suddenly thought, 'Hang on a minute, what the fuck am I doing here?' I was standing outside a grim, two-hundred-year-old building in the pissing rain, voluntarily waiting to be let in. I should have gone in with another recovering addict, that's the guideline, but my mate couldn't make it at the last minute.

As I walked through the various doors and corridors, memories of my first prison visit aged twelve flooded back. The prison officer led me out into the main courtyard. The sea wind and salty rain came down at a sharp angle and stung my face. I started to feel braver, aware that I was doing something worthwhile. It wasn't a feeling I was familiar with but I liked it.

I was escorted into an old chapel. There were already three men in there, sitting silently, smoking roll ups. I sat down with them. I was very nervous and my hands were trembling. I steadied myself and shook hands with each of them, then started to lay out the bog standard meeting literature.

I went through the introduction, telling them what the meeting was about and what I was doing there. I told them that I would first read out the preamble to the why, what and how we got into recovery. Then there would be a reading from the meeting's main guidebook. Then everyone would get a chance to speak, without interruption or feedback. I would start this off to give them the steer on the things that were generally shared in the meetings: ourselves, our drug history, our rock-bottom point, how we got into drug and alcohol recovery and what we were doing with our lives now that was different from scratching around for drugs. The readings and what others had to say about their lives were also a launch point for the prisoners to identify and connect and, with any luck, feel a part of the meeting.

We started the meeting by sitting in silence for a few minutes to remember the still-suffering addict. I thought about Dad. The prison officer left us to it. I was alone with a group of men whose crimes I didn't want to know about. About ten minutes in, a big bald bloke walked in. He was the living, breathing cliché of a hard nut. He looked pissed off with me and, frankly, I was terrified. He sat at the back of them room, staring me out.

The readings finished and the meeting was opened up for general sharing. The bald nutter was the first in with a series of tricky, aggressive questions. I began to realise that he didn't want me there in the prison. He was trying to rubbish what I was doing and what the meeting was about. He started to piss me off. His intimidation was for the benefit of the other prisoners in the meeting. I did my best to steer his questions back to the readings and said that I was there voluntarily because I was in recovery and I wanted to help. He was having none of it and after another ten minutes he stood up, stared at me long enough for me to think he was going to bring a chair down on my head, then left, opening the door to the wind and rain. He slammed it hard behind him.

I was told later he was the 'daddy' of the prison, the bully in charge of the drugs that came in. The meeting was threatening his turf. I didn't go back to the Verne alone again. But I did go back.

The routine at the house in Weymouth was pretty much the same as in rehab. It was set up to be full of recovery-based activities: groups, one-to-ones and, a new concept to me, therapeutic duties. This basically meant keeping the house clean, inside and out. The focus was on encouraging us to create our own motivation. I started to put the same kind of energy into staying clean as I'd put into my using. It was paying off.

My main counsellor there was another inspirational man and he was in recovery, too. He was clear, sharp and funny and unflinchingly dedicated to helping the scrawny junky or hopeless alcoholic get back on their feet.

I had several more court appearances during the first year of recovery. My counsellor drove me to London for each court date. We got up at six in the morning and were back by dinner time. His support blew me away. Without him, I doubt I'd have been able to cope with the feelings of fear and anxiety that surfaced for me on those trips.

My final court date for sentencing finally came around. My guilty plea meant that I avoided cross examination by the prosecution. But if I got a judge on a bad day it was possible I'd get a custodial sentence. I was still looking at four years. I was getting into recovery and enjoying the benefits of staying off drugs but everything up to that point had been underpinned by a desire to stay out of prison. If I managed to avoid prison it was possible that, without that hanging over me, I'd just go back to the drugs. It scared me.

In the first seven months of being clean I'd created a recovery CV even Dad would have been impressed by. I'd been going to five meetings a week, was secretary of one, had taken the meeting in HMP the Verne and was about to start college. Most importantly I'd stayed off drugs and booze the whole time. A miracle. The judge would have been an idiot to have sent me down. He didn't. I got an eighteen-month suspended sentence. After that I'd be free. Dad got four-and-a-half years.

20

Live and Let Die

Dad sent me a letter from HMP Wandsworth soon after the conviction.

SO, DARLIN. IT SEEMS WE STILL HAVE LUCK WITH US, FOUR AND HALF YEARS WAS NOT WHAT I WAS EXPECTING, NOR I PRESUME ANYONE ELSE BUT THE MOST IMPORTANT THING IS THAT YOU DID NOT HAVE TO SUFFER THIS PLACE AND THAT HAS MADE ME SO HAPPY. GOD DID I WRACK MY BRAINS FOR SOME KIND OF MITIGATION FOR US. IN THE END I WROTE A WHOLE DISCOURSE ON THE KING OF THEBES AND BACCHUS, THE GOD OF WINE, AND MUCH MORE, I WILL EXPLAIN ONE DAY, YOU'LL LOVE IT. 'I CAN'T SEND THAT UP TO THE JUDGE,' SAID MY BARRISTER. 'OH YES YOU CAN,' I SAID, AND WHEN I SAW THE JUDGE SMILE BRIEFLY WHILST HE READ IT I KNEW SOMETHING HAD GONE RIGHT.

So that was what the look on the judge's face had been about. He'd been reading Dad's letter. I didn't know what the word discourse meant and I'd never heard of the King of Thebes or Bacchus but they seemed to have done the trick.

I had been assigned to the local probation office and went every month for the next year and a half. My probation officer was an ex navy seaman and became a solid mentor. Every four weeks I got a one-to-one session with him outside of my day-to-day drug treatment programme. He listened to me and supported me in my decision to go to college.

The moment I got clean I started to meet men I could trust, men who weren't going to try and rip me off, have sex with me or give me drugs. These men were inspirational mentors. They gave me the guidance I'd needed and had clearly been missing.

Not everyone stayed the distance with recovery. Some of the guys I was in there with struggled to stay clean. The longer any of us were off drugs the more our demons came to the surface and the clearer the reasons became why we'd started to take drugs in the first place.

I still had a good amount of 'fuck you' attitude left in me. It was this attitude that kept me going when people around me doubted I would make it through my first year in recovery. When I told my life story at the second stage in Weymouth, most of it was directed at the older, more bitter alcoholics who'd questioned my membership into recovery. Some of them couldn't deal with the fact that it wasn't necessary to have had a lifetime of drinking to qualify for recovery.

'How could someone so young have seen or done anything so bad?' they kept asking. By the end of my story I was getting the nods of respect I had known would come. There were very few people my age in recovery when I first got clean and very few who stayed clean. One of the key things that kept me clean when I was struggling was listening to people return to the meetings after a relapse back on to drugs or alcohol. No one came back into the meetings saying it had been great, suggesting we come and join the party. Every single person that returned said that within days of being back at it, sometimes hours, they were right where they had left off and that it was worse, much worse this time around. I only had to look into their sunken eyes and see the sweat glistening on their detoxing skin to see the horror they had just stepped out of. I knew exactly what that felt like.

There were two men I knew who didn't make it back into the meetings after their relapses, Kevin and Charley. Kevin OD'd on smack in his caravan in Portland. He'd put the same amount in the needle he had always done, forgetting his tolerance had dropped. Charley was found in a pool of blood after he'd cut his own throat in the house his mother had bought him. Another man narrowly missed death when he relapsed on vodka. Unable to walk straight he got on his 500cc Honda motorbike, and riding at 100 mph, wrapped the bike and himself around a lamppost on the Chesil Beach Road. He lost half a leg. He got back into recovery and every time I saw him hop on his crutches into our weekly group I was reminded what was waiting for me if I gave up the ghost. Death felt very close.

With drugs and alcohol out of my system, sex was on my mind almost all the time. In the top bathroom there was a stash of porn mags. It was the only place I could have a wank in peace. I was in the middle of my moment when I heard someone coming up the stairs. Sitting frozen, naked arse on the black plastic seat, trousers round my ankles. It was my mate Tom. I breathed out slowly, trying not to be heard.

'It's Ben, from rehab,' he said through the door.

'What about him?'

'Dead, mate. Died this morning. Heart attack. You OK?'

I had no idea what to say. 'Yeah. I'll be down in a bit.'

I felt a wave of sadness rush through me, then shame. Sitting on a toilet seat with my trousers resting on my trainers and a copy of *Club* magazine on my lap was not the way I wanted to receive such bad news. I looked at myself in the mirror and waited to see myself cry but nothing came. Not until his funeral the following week. It was to be the first of many.

By August 1990 I was in my second year of recovery in Weymouth. After eight months of stage two I went on to the third and final stage of the treatment process, which would last a further nine months. By this time I had rented a room of my own and I'd started college doing a year-long back to school course called 'Access to Jobs'. I was ready to take the exams I'd missed at Stoke. I studied English, Sociology, Art and Maths. There was also a work experience element and I knew I wanted to get into some part of the media. I went for it and put all my new-found energy into it.

Passing my exams at the end of the year and getting high grades was a shock. I'd been maturing into a pretty rubbish criminal before I got clean. I'd thought that if I couldn't get that right then there was little hope for me doing anything else right. I'd grown up believing I was stupid. Dad hadn't helped matters by losing it every time I'd fucked up a deal or bungled a burglary. Dad loved that I was going to college, but getting clean was my own brand of teenage rebellion, albeit delayed. He'd never stood me in front of a blackboard for a systematic teaching of his criminal ways but a lot of what I'd experienced in my life, up to the point I got clean, had something to do with crime, drugs or violence. I was going against everything Dad and life had taught me by choosing to get clean and go straight.

I got into writing, especially letters to old friends and family. I wrote to Mrs T. and told her about the journey I'd been on since I saw her that day on her doorstep. I wanted her to know I was all right and although I didn't hear back from her, I think she got the letter. Dad and I got into writing a lot to each other in the first two years of my recovery. They were a lifeline. They were full of advice about what to read, what to listen to and what to watch. Even though we had all the time in the world when he was out of prison, he was always too busy getting stoned to be able to have a proper conversation with me. When he was in prison he had all the time in the world and no distractions. So he focused on the letters, usually one a week, and we built our relationship through them. I searched hard between the lines for affection and for the Dad I wanted. His love for me usually emerged in the last lines as he said goodbye. It was enough to keep me going.

It was suggested to addicts in recovery that we wait a year before we got involved in what was called a 'special relationship', or what I called sex. I took things very literally; it helped. On my twenty-second birthday a girl I'd gone to school with came down to celebrate my new sexual freedom. We booked into a bed and breakfast and spent three days in bed. It was the best sex I'd ever had. But unknown to me at the time, it triggered a secondary addiction to women that was going to get me into a lot of trouble.

January 1991

In the beginning of my third year at Weymouth I started working at a community radio station at the local hospital. Initially I'd just collect the requests from patients, but I went on to become a DJ. I loved it. I indulged in my favourite music and got musicians to play live. I'd got into current affairs through studying sociology and had an idea that I wanted to become a radio journalist. I got myself talked into a general media course that was to last two years. I managed to get government funding for the first year and topped it up with casual labouring and garden work. At the end of my first year on the course I headed to London for the summer holidays, confident now that it held no demons for me.

I was in regular contact with Mum throughout those early years of recovery. It was difficult at times but whatever tensions there were between us our love for each other was getting the space it needed to breathe and slowly grow. When I was around three years clean she started to go to meetings and was finding her own way into recovery. I think my recovery was an inspiration to her.

I had been back in touch with Sam. She was really happy that I was off the drugs and out of trouble. She invited me to stay with her, her man and their kids at their house in Wimbledon. Her man clearly wasn't completely into this, but he did his best to welcome me. At the meetings in Weymouth I'd been looking for a mentor, a 'sponsor', but with no luck. Part of my mission in going to London was to find one there, as there was a lot more clean time in the city, a bigger pool of people in recovery. I found a sponsor and I also found a job as a runner for a video production company. I phoned my college tutor, another good man, and told him about the job offer. 'If you've got a job in the first year of study,' he said, 'then we've done ours. Go for it.'

I did as I was told. I moved back to London after three-and-a-half years in Weymouth. It was like a new city to me. I was off drugs and seeing it in a completely different light. The beauty of meetings was that wherever I was in the country I could find one. There were meetings every day in London and I immersed myself in my recovery.

March 1992, Wimbledon, London

After serving three of his four-and-a-half-year sentence, Dad was out. I discovered he was staying with a friend in Chelsea, just a few miles down the road from Sam's. I wasn't sure I wanted to see him. I knew he'd be stoned. That's what he did when he got out. The intensity of the transition from prison to freedom was too much to handle straight. He hadn't got involved in the recovery meetings while he was inside; that was never going to happen. He was off the smack but had told me he'd kept a consistent flow of hash, weed and prison hooch in his system.

When I saw the silhouette through the frosted glass of Sam's door I knew it was Dad. I felt a rush of blood to the head. I opened the door and we hugged long enough for it to feel uncomfortable. Then there was an awkward cup of tea with me, Dad, Sam and her man. As soon as we could, Dad and I headed out for a walk on Wimbledon Common. This was different to the last time we'd had this time together. I had grown up, cleaned up and changed. But Dad seemed to be in the same place. He looked fit and healthy but he was nervous about being out. He was putting on a cool front that was easy to see through.

He respected my recovery. 'But it's not for me, kid. I just can't see myself in one of those meetings, talking about my feelings. I wouldn't be able to keep a straight face.'

He was happy that I was clean but not impressed by my service work in prisons. What really got him going, though, was my work on the recovery phone helplines. This involved me answering calls from still-suffering addicts on the street who were looking for help. Mostly he didn't seem to like the picture he had of me as some kind of recovery crusader. Maybe it was the tough street junkies he took against. Having spent so much time inside he was disillusioned with the people he met in prison, never fully trusting or believing anyone inside could get clean. I knew different. Manning the phone line and taking the prison meetings were equally important and effective types of community-based service work, both aimed at helping the still-suffering addict.

'How is it . . . being out?' I asked, not sure I really wanted to know.

'I keep getting these fucking black clouds rolling over my head, kid. Every morning. I can't even get out of bed, it's so bad. By twelve they've usually lifted but every morning, like clockwork, they come back.'

Dad was having his own crisis. It had started when he was in prison. I wanted to tell him what the root of his problems was but I knew he wouldn't listen. Smack was back in his system and all his prison dreams had faded to black. When he was in trouble he always ran, either back to a seven-by-five prison cell or away from England altogether. He told me he was desperate to get away.

Soon after he got out, an eighteen-year-old girl called Annie appeared on the scene. She had been looking for Dad for a long time. She was a daughter from a fling he'd had. He had known about her but never talked about her to me. I suddenly had another half-sister. I spent a few evenings with her, a confusing experience because I fancied her. Fortunately the crush faded.

Annie and I were walking on Wimbledon Common one Saturday afternoon. She was distressed.

'What exactly did he say to you?' I asked her.

'He said that if I didn't give him £500 to go to India he might as well kill himself.' Annie had a wealthy, well-connected mum and could get her hands on that kind of money.

'Under no circumstances are you to give him the money or any money, whatever he says to you or however bad you feel,' I told her.

She agreed it was the best thing to do.

Two weeks later I was walking with Dad on the same patch of common. I wanted to find out what was up with him.

'Here's the thing, kid. All this is for nothing . . . it's all for shit.' He was stoned. I didn't respond. 'Nothing really exists. You only have to read Buddhist literature to know that. Everything is an illusion, there is no such thing as love, truth, honesty. There is no point to any of this.'

He had a fag in the corner of his mouth and he was waving his arms around.

'What about Sam?' I asked him. 'What about when you told me you were in love with her, more than any woman you'd ever known?' I was getting alarmed at the way the rant was escalating.

'It doesn't mean anything. There is no God and there is no one you can really trust. No one.'

There was no discussion to be had. He was too far gone. I didn't want to be around it any more. I didn't have the strength to deal with it, not at that stage of my recovery. I thought that being three years clean and going to meetings would have been enough to withstand his routine self-destruction. It wasn't. I had to cut contact with him. I did it by phone three weeks later, the most difficult conversation of my life.

'I can't be around you right now. I have to look out for my recovery. What you said on Wimbledon Common the other week, it's not what I believe. It's best I just get on with my recovery for now.'

There was a heavy silence on the phone.

'I understand, kid.' His voice was flat, matter of fact, like he'd given up.

'I'm sorry, Dad.'

'Don't be. You don't need to be. Really. Sounds like you're really starting to grow up. I'm happy for you. Good for you. I love you, Cas.'

Two weeks later I was in bed, trying to sleep. It was hot and I was agitated. There was a party going on next door and the music was way too loud. I was meant to be at work at 9 a.m. At about one in the morning I leaned out of my window and screamed at the top of my lungs into the darkness. *'Will you turn that fucking music down!'*

They did, for a few minutes. I got up to get a glass of water. I saw the phone blinking in the darkness. The music had been loud enough for long enough for me to miss three calls. I pressed play on the answer machine.

'Hey, kid, it's me. Pick up, will you? It's late. I want to talk. Pick up. Kid?'

Message two was just silence. Someone was there, listening, waiting. It was Dad again, I knew it. Eventually he hung up.

Message three went like this: 'Kid, hey, pick up. I want to . . . forget it. It's too late.'

It was three in the morning. I had a very bad feeling. I didn't want to call him back. I was afraid of what I might find out. I waited until the following evening, and called Annie's granddad. They'd become friends and spent time together. Dad didn't have a phone of his own.

'Hi. It's Caspar. Is Frank there?'

'Caspar. Ah . . . hello. Err . . . you haven't . . . you do know Frank's dead, don't you?'

He apologised for the bluntness with which he'd delivered the news, caught offguard. They had only just found Dad's body. As I stood there with the phone in my hand I felt like a cliché: a weight had lifted from my shoulders and I felt lighter, better. I was deeply relieved. It was over.

Then I panicked. I thought about how I *should* be reacting. I put the phone down and called a cab to take me to Battersea, where Dad had rented a room above a posh butcher's. He was living in one room, alone. That's where they found him. His old mucker George was already there when I arrived. We were surprised to see each other. He was amazed I'd heard the news so quickly. There was also a nervous young copper in the kitchen. Dad's death was being treated as suspicious.

'Where is he?' I asked with surprising authority.

'Upstairs.' George was white with shock.

'I want to see him,' I told the officer. He nodded. I turned around and headed upstairs. There were twenty wooden steps on that staircase. I counted them. Each footfall jarred an image into my head. Each image was about Dad. How he had been when I was a kid. How I imagined he would look in that room when I saw him. What my life would be like now he was gone. Images of past, present and future mixing in and out of each other, snapping and flashing in front of my eyes. They filled me with every emotion I'd ever felt. I wanted to laugh, cry, shout, punch something, sing, pass out. I kept walking and kept preparing myself for what I was going to see.

The door to his room was slightly open. I could see the white shirt and black trousers of another policeman, sitting on the bed. I knocked and another officer came to the door.

'I'm his son. Can I see him?'

'Err . . . I'm not sure. I mean, are you sure? It's a bit grim in here.'

'Yes. Can I come in?'

He opened the door. They were treating the room as a crime scene. I noticed the frame and the length of the door were splintered and the lock was bust. The room revealed itself to me in slow motion. First, the bed, with the policeman sitting on it, looking straight up at me in dumb silence. I expected them both to leave, to give me a moment alone with him. They weren't going anywhere. I could smell something sweet, sickly, pungent. It was the smell of my

271

father's death. I will never forget that smell. It was the last scent of his body as it cooled down and started to decompose. He had been dead in that locked room for twenty-seven hours.

The cheap bedside cabinet had various pill bottles on it, vitamins and narcotics, paper packets, syringes, cigarettes, matches, a lighter and an ashtray full to the brim with half-smoked roll ups. A single rectangle of black-lined silver foil and a crumpled silver foil pipe lay discarded next to the ashtray. In my peripheral vision, I could see Dad in the corner. Turning my head towards him was like turning my face into a hundred-mile-an-hour wind. My eyes dragged slowly past the window. Beyond the panes of dirty glass it was blue-black at garden level, getting lighter the higher my eyes looked.

I was playing for time. I could see the outlines of suburban gardens. London's city lights made the night sky glow orange. It reminded me of those nights I'd spent looking out of my bedroom window in Wimbledon five years earlier. I imagined that he'd stared out of his window and felt the same sense of desperation and loss I had felt. He had listened to the fear and desolation and followed it.

I noticed something tied to the window latch, a tight white line of plastic. My eyes followed it across the wall to the top of my dad's shiny hair and behind his neck. His golden locks looked freshly washed and brushed. He'd had a bath before he'd died. His head was slumped down, hair completely covering his face, chin on his chest. He was dressed in a blue sweatshirt, blue tracksuit bottoms, a paisley scarf around his neck, no shoes and a single green elastic band hanging loosely round his left wrist. He was sitting cross-legged on a rocking chair, his refined hands resting delicately on his thighs. The curved legs of the chair were prevented from rocking by books on the floor, books on philosophy. I continued to scan his body, to make sense of what I was seeing. I was being watched as well. The two policemen waited silently behind me, as though they feared I might do something crazy.

I sat down on the bed. It was ridiculously soft and would have done his back in. I looked at him for a moment. I still couldn't see his face. He looked as though he was asleep. Maybe I could wake him up, I thought. Maybe they'd made a mistake. I reached across and, very slowly, let my hand rest on his leg. He felt warm. He wasn't. It was just the soft cotton of the tracksuit bottoms.

'Stupid cunt,' I said, almost affectionately.

I slowly raised my hand to his chin. I gripped my fingers gently on his skin. It was cold and clammy. It had lost its elasticity. I respectfully lifted his head up. It was heavy and difficult. I did this with great respect. As I got his head fully raised, his hair fell away from his face. My heart ached like it had just been hit with a hammer. Dad was dead but I felt deeply connected to him at that moment. Like I understood what our pain had been about. Although he was right in front of me, I already missed him like crazy.

His eyes were shut. His face seemed to have been freeze-framed in a moment of confusion, as though he might have been changing his mind even as his eyes closed for the last time. He looked like he was having a bad dream that he was unable to wake up from. I noticed the white line again, running from the window lock to behind his head. Light reflected off it. It ran behind his head and came out at the side of his neck and continued under his paisley scarf. It was a piece of flat electrical flex, carefully hidden by the colourful, soft material of his favourite neckwear. White plastic was effective but cheap. He'd wanted to cover it with something more stylish. I let his head rest gently into his chest.

I looked at the door to try and take in the last thing he would have seen. A white, empty space. Very Zen. On the wall to his right was a picture of a World War Two bomber. Not his style of art at all. It had obviously been there when he moved in, three months before. Wherever he'd lived, even in his cells, he would put his life on the walls: pictures, poetry, wall hangings. He made even the shittiest place into as much of a home as he could. This tacky picture had stayed on the wall all this time. The rest of the walls were bare. It told me he'd given up long before Annie refused to give him the money to go to India; long before our agitated conversation on Wimbledon Common and the phone call that followed.

There were three letters on the tiny table beside him, along with four empty syringes placed neatly in a row. I couldn't touch anything until the police had done their thing and established no foul play. The door was locked from the inside, as was the window. George had broken it down. I could have told them it was suicide.

Dad had tied one end of the white electrical flex around his neck and the other end to the window lock behind him. He had loaded up the four syringes, each with a gram of smack, and begun to inject them into his muscles, one by one. If he had jacked the first into his veins he would have passed out before he'd got the second syringe in. Into the muscles meant he had time to get all four grams into his body before he passed out. The melted-down opiate coursed through his bloodstream over a period of ten minutes until finally, gram after gram, it reached his heart. After fifty-two years of beating, the smack finally forced it to stop. His head slumped forward and the flex tightened around his neck, which strangled the carotid arteries supplying oxygen to his brain. This wasn't a cry for help. He had had enough.

After the coroner's report had come through I got to see

the last three letters that he'd written. The first was to Barry, the posh butcher who had rented the room to Dad.

> DEAR BARRY.
> SORRY ABOUT BEING A NUISANCE. PUT ME IN THE FRIDGE, I MAY FETCH A FEW QUID. I'M SURE THE WIFE CAN WHIP UP AN EXCELLENT SAUCE.
> WELL YOU WERE RIGHT, EVERYONE'S FAVOURITE QUESTION OF LATE 'WHAT'S FRANK GOING TO DO?' PROPHETIC TOO, REMEMBER WHAT YOU SAID ABOUT HANGING FROM THE BALCONY! WHO GIVES A FUCK ANYWAY, EXCEPT PERHAPS ANNIE AND CAS. AND I'M DOING THEM A FAVOUR TOO. THANK YOU FOR EVERYTHING BARRY. YOU ARE, AS THEY SAY, A DIAMOND.
> LOVE FRANK
> PS PLEASE FIND THE DUKE OF KENT ENCLOSED.

He'd been thoughtful enough to pay the rent he owed. The second letter was for George.

> HELLO G.
> OR SHOULD THAT BE GOODBYE. FIVE MINUTES AGO I TOOK FOUR VIT C TABLETS AND SOME COD LIVER OIL PILLS, A LITTLE ECCENTRIC REALLY AND MADE ME LAUGH. OH WELL CAN'T THINK OF MUCH TO SAY. DO YOU KNOW THE STORY OF THE TWO FRIENDS WHO'VE BEEN IN BUSINESS FOR YEARS: THE ONE ON THE BED DYING SAYS TO THE OTHER, WHO'S LATE AS USUAL, 'WELL FUCK ME, YOU ALWAYS ARRIVE JUST AS I'M LEAVING.'
> WELL G I THINK THAT'S IT FOR ME. IF THERE'S ANYTHING GOOD GOING ON I'LL SEND A MESSAGE BACK. THE PAGER'S THE BEST BET I SUPPOSE.
> LOVE YOU,
> FRANK
> PS I LOVE ME TOO.

And the third was for me. I read mine last, repeatedly.

> HELLO CAS.
> WHAT TO SAY? WELL I LOVE YOU VERY MUCH AND I'M PROUD
> OF ALL YOU'VE ACCOMPLISHED IN THE LAST FEW YEARS, JUST
> KEEP AT IT, YOU'LL EVEN SURPRISE YOURSELF. SPEAKING OF
> SURPRISES I'M SURE WHAT I'M ABOUT TO DO WON'T BE THAT
> BIG A ONE FOR YOU. IT IS WHAT I WANT, WELL, MAYBE NOT
> ABSOLUTELY BUT AS USUAL I'VE LEFT IT ALL TOO LATE. I
> ALWAYS SEEM TO BE REPEATING MYSELF LATELY. I LOVE YOU
> VERY, VERY MUCH.
>> DAD
>>> PS AIN'T MUCH BUT THERE'S SOME NICE SUITCASES HERE
> IF YOU WANT.

He was right about what he said on his last message to me. It was too late. The party and its loud music had kept me from my last conversation with my father and I was grateful. If I'd have spoken to him that night I would have known what was up, that he was trying to say goodbye. If we had spoken I would have been compelled to stop him. It was important that he had no interruptions that night. He knew where he was going and he had to go there alone.

21

The Key to the Door

June 1992, Streatham Vale Crematorium, London

This is the day I bury my dad. Well, not so much bury as burn. There are twenty-two people here. Sam, her man, my brother, mother, sister, cousins and a selection of friends Dad met recently and some he's known all his life, including George. For the life he lived and the amount of people he knew this is a poor turn out. On the other hand, for the amount of people he pissed off, this is a good turn out.

I'm reading the speech I've written. It's going down well. People are listening. It's an emotional moment. I've decided not to go down the simple 'he was a wonderful man' route. I'm telling everyone how it was, how I saw it. I've worked that 'mad, bad and dangerous to know' line in. Bit of poetry. Dad would have liked that. And here's some more. Deep breath.

'Death, will you be my friend, my beginning, middle or my end?

'When I look back to those now all out of reach, I wonder who I will meet upon your beach.

'Death, will you be my beginning, middle or my end?'

Dad wrote that. Bit dramatic. Not bad, though. Fits the moment, I think.

Annie has done her speech. It was short and sweet. She was very nervous and upset and couldn't speak towards the end.

Another deep breath. Now's the time. 'Press the button and the coffin will roll along the platform,' I've been told. The curtains and doors will open and my father will disappear forever. But there are three buttons. This moment has to be flawless, no fuck ups. It's Dad's last performance before he exits stage left.

The first button. Shit. That's the chuffing reading light. Someone's giggling. The last button. That has to be it. Yes! Hang on a minute. The doors haven't fully opened. The coffin will never get through there.

It didn't. The front of it rolled into the half-open doors and stopped at an angle. The steel rollers beneath it kept spinning and Dad's cheap wooden box refused to go through. Standing up there in front of everyone, I was dying of embarrassment. I was also aware that I felt like I was being fucked around with, like Dad was having a laugh with us. There was muffled, knowing laughter coming from various parts of the congregation. Someone was getting the joke. I pressed the red button over and over and, finally, the doors opened fully.

We played Miles Davis at the funeral. 'So What' from the album *Kind of Blue*. The funeral director, the one who had given me the duff button instructions, asked if I would like it played on the crematorium organ. I politely refused, trying to hold back my laughter. We played it on a ghetto blaster. It could have been louder.

That track and the rest of the album would go with me all over the world on my personal stereo. I took my memory of Dad and his music with me wherever I went. He was always alive in my headphones. I took him to places I knew he would've loved: a windswept walk on the west coast in Ireland, a drive in the highlands of Scotland, a moped ride on a hot beach in Goa, an insect-roaring night on an island off Madagascar, a rain-battered tin hut in Canada and, finally, it was the main music for my first feature-length play for BBC Radio 4. This piece of music was a route to my memories of him. It gave me permission to grieve. He gave me Miles Davis when I was a child and I took that music, and him, with me to some of the most beautiful places on earth.

Two days later I collected his ashes. I was told we would get a portion of what is left. The unburned bits of the coffin and the larger bones are picked out and we are respectfully given a sample of our loved one. This, I later found out, is usually mixed in with the finer ashes of someone else's loved one from earlier burnings.

I went to Wimbledon Common with Leon, Mum, Paul, his girlfriend and Dad's ashes. I had been given permission to plant a tree for him, a silver birch. Wispy, skinny and elegant; an appropriate choice. I dug the hole while everyone watched in pensive silence. Before I put the tree in the ground I sprinkled some of his ashes into the freshly dug ground. Leon knelt down, licked his finger and dipped it into the dusty grey pile of Dad. He brought the ash to his lips and tasted it.

'All those chemicals in his body for all those years. I had to know what that tasted like,' Leon said, grinning.

I followed suit. Dad tasted musty and sour. Leon and I looked at each other and smiled.

I finished planting the silver birch and scattered the rest of the ashes in a circle of pine trees by a place called Caesar's Well. Mum said she and Dad had been there in the sixties. He'd ridden his Triumph motorbike around the trees while tripping on California Sunshine LSD. It was a fitting place to cast him to a warm July wind.

CRIMINAL

My dad's death was a slap in the face that woke me up from a sleep I hadn't known I was in. It woke up my joy of life, my fear of death and my rage at not being able to control either. I'd made a clear decision to stay off drugs and alcohol. It was obvious; if I got stoned my life turned to shit. What was less obvious was my growing dependence on sex and work. In an attempt to deal with the pain and confusion of losing Dad I explored these new addictions in a lot of detail. Sex and work addiction are on another level altogether. Sex is part of life, so is work: I have to put food in my belly and a roof over my head. They are both very tricky areas for an addict, for me, to engage with in a healthy way. It's easy for me to kid myself into thinking I'm connected and in a loving relationship when in actual fact I may just be avoiding a difficult feeling or situation by losing myself in the adrenaline and excitement of sex. Non stop work without healthy breaks and holidays can lead to sky-high stress levels and reduced mental health. Both sex and work addiction, if not kept in check, can quickly lead back to a relapse on drugs and alcohol. I carried on going to my meetings and explored more of my childhood trauma in one-to-one counselling. I went as far as I was prepared to go. Part of me still wanted to do what most twenty-somethings want to do: to go out into life, explore it, fuck up and hopefully come back alive and in one piece. All was still not well in my world.

Dad had been dead for three months and I was still working in TV. I was starting to hate it. I told someone I worked with about the emotional experience of walking up the stairs to see Dad's body. He was captivated by my story. He convinced me to make a short film out of it. I called in a lot of favours from people I'd met in the industry. I discovered I was good at producing and directing. Filming the reconstruction of my ascent of the staircase and the discovery of Dad's body with two very good actors really knocked it out of me emotionally and physically. The process took me three years from start to finish. Most of my energy, my anger, my sadness and my desperation were channelled into making it and for a time the distraction helped me to ease up on the addictive sexual behaviour I had been losing myself in. The production process was providing me with the adrenaline I was looking for. It was creative and therapeutic and worthwhile. A neatly boxed time capsule of my take on my life with Dad and the time shortly before and after his death. It even won an award.

Something started eating away at me after I had completed the editing of my short film. It was evident I needed to do more to deal with the pain of losing Dad and deal with the aftermath of my life with him. Encouraged by Leon, I left my work in TV to start training as a Shiatsu practitioner. I'd watched him change his career and study to become a practitioner himself. I liked the change I saw. To pay for my study I worked as a waiter in a hamburger restaurant on the Fulham Road, another place I used to go to with Dad when I was a kid. It was a hundred yards from The Goat in Boots pub and fifty yards from where we'd lived and dealt drugs together. I found the proximity to my past, and my relative sobriety, strangely comforting.

Studying Shiatsu was just about keeping me together but my recovery was starting to falter. I was going to fewer meetings. My behaviour was becoming more and more erratic. I was losing my temper regularly and I was looking for ways to earn money other than working as a waiter. This meant crime. This kind of thinking grew over a few years and I feigned surprise when I finally acknowledged that my life was once again falling apart around me. I kidded myself that if I was eating three meals a day and keeping my clothes and body clean then I must be all right. Truth was that without the anaesthetic of smack I was in more of a state emotionally than when I'd been using. Smack was the best thing to keep the negative feelings down.

By the time I was eight years clean, aged twenty-nine, I was what's known as a dry drunk. I was on a daily white-knuckle ride through life and regularly going off the rails: anonymous sexual encounters, pornography, fighting, lying and thieving from shops. The only thing I didn't do was drink or drugs. I was seriously pissing off my friends, family and work colleagues with my erratic behaviour. The long stream of women I was having affairs and one-night stands with started to kick back at me and give me an increasingly hard time. The worse my behaviour got the more I tried to shut down emotionally in order to cope with what would normally be a truck load of shame, regret and ultimately raging anger. I realised I'd shut down and refused to fully trust anyone from a very early age. No surprises there. I couldn't figure out how to deal with any of it. I had lost all contact with my mentors.

I was on my lunch break with an old friend, Tor. I had known her since I was sixteen and we had got clean around the same time. She invited me to stay at her place in Ireland while I figured out what I was going to do next. I completed my Shiatsu course and left England immediately. I was running. I took my troubles with me.

The beauty of Ireland blew me away and distracted me momentarily from my grief and anger. I met a girl who was ten years younger than me – physically. I'd been told in rehab that addicts stop maturing emotionally when we start using addictively. We gain a year of that lost growth each year we stay clean. By that philosophy, emotionally I was about fourteen when I went into treatment. Me and the nineteen year old were equals, a car crash of confused feelings and dysfunctional fucked-up lust. This highly destructive relationship reflected the wild Irish landscape and weather. I was in an emotional tail spin and came very close to drinking and getting stoned. I started to become a real liability and was slowly alienating myself by my bad behaviour, which also included a series of short-lived affairs and one-night stands. They were impossible to keep secret in such a small place. Some people were often so bored they'd make up damaging gossip about each other just to pass the time. There was no need to do that when I arrived. I walked straight into the overblown drama of it all and gave them plenty to talk about.

The girl played with me and my emotions in the way I had done countless times with other women in the last ten years. I realised for the first time how much it hurt. I felt empty and wasted, with nothing to hold on to. I continued running, this time from Ireland back to England under a self-imposed black cloud. I went to live in Bristol, a city close to the country. I wanted quick access to both.

I was cold and empty inside, thirty years old and at my all-time emotional rock bottom. I'd been clean for nine years. But sex as an emotional avoidance technique was no longer working. I needed a new addiction. I chose work. Shiatsu was off the cards. I couldn't offer support and guidance to anyone in the state I was in. I had to throw myself into something else. Off the back of my passion for writing and the inspiration from the live storytelling I'd heard in the pubs of Ireland, I set up a production company to promote myself and other writers. I quickly found a business partner and a new friend, Andrew, who was like a twin brother to me. Without him the business would never have got fully off the ground or been nearly as successful.

We made our own luck. We used our combined experiences and skills to wheel and deal our way into fundraising, advertising, marketing event management and editorial work. We surprised ourselves at how good we were at it. I was loving it. I couldn't walk down the street without bumping into someone connected to our work. It was an extra impetus to stay out of trouble – mostly. I was focusing my energy into one area again and it was working well at keeping me numb from the hard-core emotions I was keeping a lid on. I was starting to find my way in life and my self esteem was slowly rising.

The main drive of the production company was performing our work live, in front of an audience. I started to get an unexpected therapy from this. People liked what I wrote and performed. I got applause for each story. I was putting myself on the page and getting acceptance for the dark words I was weaving in my tiny bedsit in Redland.

A year after I got to Bristol my brother Paul told me about a personal development training programme for men that he was about to go on. The training was about looking at the core damage done to us when we were young and finding a way to heal it. It was about getting angry or sad or scared in a safe place with people you could trust. When I heard him describe it something inside me woke up. I felt a mixture of fear and excitement and I signed up.

What was unearthed and expressed that weekend, for the first time in my adult life, was my initial rage and sadness at the abuse by the porter. The rest would unfold over time. I also started to look at deeper wounds. When I'd first got into recovery, a tidal wave of traumatic feelings had begun to rise to the surface. The deeper stuff was too much to bear or talk about so I'd turned the abuse on to myself in the form of sex and work addiction in a vain attempt to control what was going on. On that men's weekend I finally gave myself permission, in a safe environment, to get really angry about what had happened to me.

I decided, at last, to get the police involved in what had happened to me in that basement flat and caravan. I wanted to deal with the porter's abuse through official channels. I made a statement and got into therapy. The abuse when I was twelve was one part of a layer of neglect and harm that I slowly began to acknowledge and accept had clearly been with me throughout my life. There was no prosecution of the porter because we couldn't find him. I didn't think we would. I needed to go through the process of my story being heard and noted down and acknowledged. It helped a great deal.

I heard the phrase a few years back that our parents wound us in exactly the right place. My father wasn't essentially a bad man. He was very screwed up and looking for some kind of an answer. He was lost. He looked for it in drugs, books, women, religion. He was lost and wounded. What little I know about his childhood makes that very clear to me. He loved me. He told me as often as he could. He did the best he could for me but got distracted time and time again from his best intentions by his demons and his addictions. This meant wounding me in ways he was only beginning to understand when he died. Leon said to me he thought it was partly down to this realisation that Dad killed himself. Who knows?

It's not easy to kill yourself. I have tried and failed. My second suicidal urge emerged when I was fourteen years clean from the drugs and alcohol. When I stopped the sexual acting out, the pornography, the work addiction and the aggression I was, true to form, left only with myself. There was a moment in my attic room in my second flat in Bristol when everything I had been running from and why became ice clear. The pain in my heart and my gut felt too intense to bear. A voice inside me tried to convince me of this.

'I can't handle this. This is why I used. This is too much.'

It was loud, aggressive and scared. I sat in front of my computer screen trying to write down what was happening to me, trying to drown out the suicidal urge with loud music and silent prayer.

Inside this desperation a smaller, stiller voice emerged and said, simply and clearly, 'Yes. *You can do this. You're not dead yet, not by a long shot.'*

I decided to sit with this pain. I thought I'd give it a couple of weeks before making any decisions. The anxiety in my belly was constant and my nerves were in shreds. I reacted to the slightest comment, sound or innuendo. I felt overwhelmed by shame. Shame about the pain I'd caused in those first fourteen years of recovery. Shame about the women I'd used to take me away from myself. Shame about all the people I'd offloaded unreasonable anger on to. I realised I'd been stuck in a very fucked-up loop. I acted out my pent-up emotions sexually or with anger or by working way too hard. Any one of these would keep me numb for a few days. The numbness would eventually wear off and I would start to feel bad about what I'd done, bad about myself and I would return to sex or anger or work to distract myself from my self-loathing long enough to forget. This went on for years.

The two weeks I'd given myself to look carefully at the darkest parts of myself turned into two months. Then two years. It was almost three years after starting this process of core emotional recovery that I began finally to level out. The constant anxiety in my belly and nervousness in my chest started to ease up. It was simple. I was angry and I was grieving. I was single and I was alone. It was exactly where I needed to be. It's human nature to withdraw from the flame that burns. It seemed like insanity to turn and face the stuff that had scorched me the most. Finally, inside the darkest part of myself, I started to see a small flicker of light.

Dad gave me something when he died. Like his suicide note said, he did me a favour. His death was a powerful gift. It woke me up to the importance of my life and what I could do with it. Suicide is no longer an option for me. I would never have asked for him to die, but he did and I've done something very important with this life-changing experience. I am living my own life now and fulfilling my dreams. It is incredible to be alive.

September 2006, Wales

There are four secure doors to go through before we get to the meeting point. This is where all the wings meet. There is a big, glass-fronted security room against one wall. Men get their food opposite. There are three floors above me. The walls are yellow and the floors a muddy green lino. There is a smell of disinfectant, institution dinners and an ancient reek of male body odour. As I arrive, all the inmates are on the move from their cells or from one education block to another. Education is a big deal here. It is a big deal in all prisons these days. The inmates do arts and crafts, GCSEs, cookery, building work and creative writing workshops.

The prisoners moving past me are a mix of every race under the sun. It's like walking down a city street, except each of these guys is wearing sky blue denim jeans and a blue and white striped shirt. Some look straight at me, some straight through me. Some fit an old stereotype of what I think a crook should look like. Some look like my bank manager.

This is unbelievable. I'm standing in the heart of the prison waiting to run a workshop and I'm here by choice. Nine months into our thriving business, Andrew and I were approached to work with young offenders and prisoners, helping them to write about their experiences. Out of these original workshops we created a platform for writing that has proved itself to be a powerful tool for rehabilitation and healing. This is what I'm doing here today and

CRIMINAL

I'm a little scared. This fear is always with me. It's healthy. A small group of men approach me. I'm introduced to each of them, six in all. They are polite, they seem intelligent and make good eye contact. We turn and head for the education block. Louise, the prison education officer, leads the way. I'm glad she's here. I talk to the men as we walk and start to make a connection. I don't want to know what they did to get in here. Knowing their crimes will compromise my position.

We sit down in a tiny classroom full of computers. There isn't enough space in here. The windows are small. I change the normal classroom set up where all the tables face the white board. I want us in a circle; it makes us equal. Given the circumstances, we get as comfortable as we can. I clear my throat and get ready to speak.

'OK. So you know my name. This is an introductory workshop to see who is into creating an original piece of writing so that your kids can have it on CD by Christmas, and who isn't. You're probably wondering why I'm here. I might be some middle-class busybody wanting to do a bit of prison work to stop me feeling guilty about my nice life on the outside and get a look at how tough you've all got it.'

A few of them smile and nod at each other.

'I'm here because my dad was in prison for nine years out of the last thirteen years of his life. I ended up inside as well. I'm here because I want to be and because I'm good at what I do. I can help you write and I know from personal experience that writing helps heal some of the nastier experiences in life.'

The six men visibly loosen up. A few of them even smile at me. The atmosphere in the tiny classroom has changed. I have their attention.

'One final thing before we start. I want to get something crystal clear with all of you.' I don't do this in a heavy way. I'm as relaxed as I can be about it. It's important to be relaxed about it. 'There'll be no violence, threats of violence or intimidation in my workshops. This is your only warning. It's important for us all to

feel safe here. If anyone steps over that line, and I'll be the judge of whether the line has been crossed, you will be asked to leave. I don't like having to say this but it's important. Does everyone agree to this?'

They do. On the wall there is a red alarm button no more than the length of my arm away. I always make sure the alarm is within easy reach. There has only been one incident in a workshop before and it's not going to happen again. I want to get on with the work and know that I'm safe. But there is one man here who makes me feel uncomfortable. He reminds me of Dad. He is bright and intense and very good at eye contact. His will probably be one of the best pieces of writing.

I get out my CDs, pens and paper and start to teach.

Afterword

Work and recovery

I still go regularly to my recovery meetings. I still have several powerful mentors in my life.

Andrew and I no longer work together but we are close friends. I suspect and hope that we will be in each other's lives for many years to come.

My work in prisons has continued. I thought for a while that it was just something I was doing to make a living, something to pass the time. I worked on two projects in 2006, which confirmed, much to my relief, that this was definitely not the case.

I had written an article for the *Observer* to promote my second Radio 4 play, written with a group of young offenders. A prison education officer, Louise, had read the article and got in touch with me about some work in prisons she wanted me to get involved in.

The first project was working in a sex offenders' prison. I made the decision to focus on the work in hand. I didn't want to know about what they had or hadn't done, and I wasn't thinking about what had happened to me as a twelve-year-old boy. I was interested in working with the part of these men that wanted to make a better life for themselves. I ran a radio drama workshop. We developed stories into scripts and recorded them. I then took them away to edit them into Radio 4-style mini dramas. We used the drama as a safe way of looking at their lives and their actions.

It seems pretty pointless to me to write these or any other prisoners off because of what they've done. Imprison them if they're guilty, sure. Some people need to be off the streets. Get them inside and shock them out of their criminal lives, if possible. But give them a chance to get some rehabilitation. I would want that for myself. It's what I got. Some people don't find a way out of their cycles of crime and violence, but some definitely do. Prisons can be breeding grounds for crime. They can also be springboards for rehabilitation.

The second of the workshops with Louise was working with dads and their sons, daughters, nieces, nephews and other family members on a project called 'Audiobook Dads'. I helped the men to write fairytales, myths and legends. The kids chose a hero or heroine who then became part of their favourite character in their story. I recorded the dads reading the stories and turned them into professional audio pieces with sound effects and music.

There is something very powerful about a child being able to listen to the voice of their father reading to them each night, over and over, even if that voice is only on CD. The project was a way for kids to keep in touch with their dads in prison; to create something together and to improve their understanding of the importance of writing as a way to connect.

I noticed that nearly all the stories the dads were writing with their children had 'goodies' and 'baddies' who were very black and white, no grey areas. The baddies would come to a nasty end, usually getting struck by lightning or burnt to a crisp by a space laser. In one-to-ones, I asked the dads if there was a way they thought the baddies might get punished for their 'evil doing' without wiping them off the face of the earth. It was at this point, after building trust, that I used the dads themselves as an example. I got a similar reaction from each of them. They smiled with the realisation that there was much more to them than bang up and hustling for a living on the wing.

'Now, I don't know why you're in here or whether you're guilty or not and to be honest I'm not interested,' I said to them. 'The thing is, someone thinks you are and you're in here and that's what you've got to work with. It doesn't mean you're a bad man and that you should be written off. What's going on now is just part of your life. There's more to you than this. I know it because I've seen it. You know it, too. Maybe there's a way you can bring out the honest, brighter parts of yourself in the story? Maybe your baddies could be punished for what they've done but not be wiped out. Give them a chance to learn from their mistakes.'

This approach clicked with all of them. They discovered a new way to look at consequences of actions and how to pass that on to their kids without a lecture, which kids rarely, if ever, listen to. And maybe, just maybe, in the process they could start breaking the life cycle of crime and punishment some of these guys' families have been in for generations. My work with prison dads and their families is about helping them find a way out of a life of crime into a life of freedom. I call these ongoing workshops 'Write to Freedom'.

I was sitting in a meeting with a career mentor in early 2007. She was looking at a five year plan for me. We talked about my life and its links to crime, about my prison work, about my time visiting my dad as a kid, my time in and out of cells and the young offender institution, about my voluntary work in prisons, my meetings, my mentoring, my Radio 4 prison plays and about my teaching. She fed all this back to me and it hit home. Prison is a part of my life. It keeps coming back to me and finding me in one form or another whether I like it or not. I realised so much of the positive work I do today has come out of the criminal nature of my upbringing. I have done something incredible in stopping the destructive pattern of my life, a pattern that's been in my family line for God knows how long and I now help others to do the same. It was all I could do to not cry in front of her. It was time to accept that I've got something important to bring to this work.

For the purposes of this book I have focused on the part of my dad's life that involved making a living through crime and the effect that had on me and our relationship. The life written about in these pages is a fraction of the story. I have focused on the criminal aspects of our life together because that's what this book is about. It's in the title. I hope I have conveyed some of my father's wider personality, beyond the drugs, crime and violence. He was a talented, passionate man who loved life. He was very popular and despite his often crazy behaviour was liked, respected and loved by a lot of people. He spent his life trying to find a way to be happy and not to have to constantly struggle to find money and security. He took shortcuts way too often and they invariably led to dead ends. His search for some kind of peace was through books, people, spirituality and philosophy. From my very first memory I was surrounded by all of this. If it hadn't been for this positive, inspiring influence, this very particular environment, this book simply wouldn't have been written; I wouldn't have become a writer at all, nor a teacher and Shiatsu practitioner and I wouldn't have the vision I now have of a life of hope and limitless possibility. He handed on the baton of inspiration, soul searching and determination to me. I am finally living the life he struggled so hard for. I honour his memory here and what he gave me. Thanks, Dad. No one said it was going to be easy. The struggle has been worth it and I don't regret a single second of it.

Family and friends

Both of Alex's parents died and we discovered new common ground. We rekindled and deepened our school friendship. We supported each other in our grief and in our healing. Alex became, amongst many other things, a Shiatsu practitioner and teacher. He is one of my closest, most trusted and loved friends. We have known each other since 1974.

I still hang out with Leon. He is a trusted and dear friend. He has a family and a good community-based business and is doing great work as a teacher.

There are five of us from primary school who are still in touch with each other. Four of us are Shiatsu practitioners and one of us is a homicide detective. The continuity and depth of these friendships, my new friendships and my family are all alchemical gold to me.

I've lost touch with Annie and Grainne's cousins.

My relationships with my mum, my brother and my sister Eliza, my nephews and nieces deepen by the day. Mum and Paul are both in recovery from drugs and alcohol.

Sam is still very much a part of my life and I see her most seasons of the year. She is still with her man, who I now get on well with. Their children are grown up and moving out into the world. Sam is a second mother to me and I owe her a great deal.

I met Emma in 2005 and didn't fall head over heels in love with her. 'If you walk into a room and lock eyes with the best-looking woman there, go weak at the knees and your stomach starts flipping, turn around and get the hell out,' a mentor once said to me. Wise words. The kind of connections that left me feeling weak at the knees usually ended up being empty and pointless. The locking on of eyes and the buzz that followed was about addiction and little else. This didn't happen with Emma. Thank God.

Before we met we both wrote down a list of the qualities we were looking for in a partner and put them away for safe keeping. Three months after we got together we talked about our lists and were amazed we had both written one. We compared notes. We ticked *all* of each other's boxes. I fell in love with Emma over the course of a year. I was thirty-eight years old and experiencing a truly healthy, loving relationship based on trust and honesty. I proposed to Emma in 2007 on a bright, crisp, winter's afternoon on the Mendips in Somerset. After a few moments of panic and surprise, through a snot-filled nose, she said yes.

Appendix:
Where to Get Help

Self-help groups

Adult Children of Alcoholics (ACoA)

– a non-profit group for the adult children of alcoholics to share experiences and information addressing the emotional disease of family alcoholism

Web: www.adultchildren.org
Email: info@adultchildren.org

Al-Anon

– Al-Anon family groups provide understanding, strength and hope to anyone whose life is, or has been, affected by someone else's drinking

Phone: 020 7403 088
Web: www.al-anonuk.org.uk

CRIMINAL

Alcoholics Anonymous (AA)

– for men and women who want to share their experiences of alcoholism in order to solve their common problem and help others to recover from alcoholism

Phone: 0845 769 7555
Web: www.alcoholics-anonymous.org.uk

Co-Dependents Anonymous – UK (CoDA)

– a fellowship of men and women whose common purpose is to develop healthy, loving relationships and overcome co-dependency issues

Web: www.coda-uk.org

Families Anonymous

– a self-help worldwide fellowship of families of drug users and those with behavioural problems

Phone: 0845 1200 660
Web: www.famanon.org.uk

The ManKind Project

– offers training to support men wishing to develop lives of integrity, accountability and connection to feeling. The trainings challenge men to develop their abilities as leaders, partners, fathers and elders

Phone: 0870 7879784
Web: www.uk.mkp.org
Email: centremanager@mkp.org.uk

Narcotics Anonymous (NA)

– a non-profit fellowship of men and women for whom drugs have become a problem. Recovering addicts meet regularly to help each other stay clean

Phone: 0845 3733366/020 7730 0009
Web: www.ukna.org

Sex Addicts Anonymous (SAA)

– for men and women who want to overcome sexual addiction and help others recover from sexual addiction or dependency

Phone: 020 8946 2436
Web: www.saa-recovery.org

Write to Freedom

– creative-writing workshops designed to meet individual client and participant needs. The aim of each project is to provide short- and long-term support for personal and professional development through creative writing

Web: www.casparwalsh.co.uk

Organisations

Action on Addiction

– offers research, advice and support to help addicts cope with the fear, confusion, guilt and uncertainty of living with a drug or alcohol problem

Phone: 0845 126 4130
Web: www.actiononaddiction.org.uk

Mind

– the leading mental health charity in England and Wales, working to create a better life for everyone with experience of mental distress

Phone: 0845 766 0163
Web: www.mind.org.uk

Samaritans

– provides confidential non-judgemental emotional support, 24 hours-a-day, for people who are experiencing feelings of distress or despair, including those that could lead to suicide

Phone: 08457 90 90 90
Web: www.samaritans.org

SANE

– has the objective to improve the quality of life for people affected by mental illness by raising awareness, undertaking research and providing help and information to those experiencing mental health problems and their families and carers

Phone: 020 7375 1002
Web: www.sane.org.uk
Email: info@sane.org.uk

Treatment centres and hospitals

The Priory Hospital

– a group of private residential psychiatric hospitals, most with an addiction unit attached, offering a comprehensive range of treatments to help people take control of their lives and achieve their maximum potential

Phone: 01372 860 400
Web: www.prioryhealthcare.com
Email: info@priorygroup.com

Clouds House

– residential treatment for all addictions, both private and health authority funded, working to disarm addiction through research, treatment, family support, education and training

Phone: 01747 830733
Web: www.clouds.org.uk
Email: admissions@clouds.org.uk

Broadway Lodge

– a non-profit-making organisation and registered charity providing residential treatment, counselling and support services for alcoholism, drug addiction, eating disorders, gambling and co-dependency both to individual sufferers and concerned others

Phone: 01934 815515
Web: www.broadwaylodge.co.uk
Email: mailbox@broadwaylodge.org.uk

Acknowledgements

My first thanks go to my special agent Broo Doherty, who approached me at a literary festival in Wales in 2006. She told me I had a book to write. My first reaction was, 'Not another story about my past, please.' My second reaction, three months later was, 'Why not?' Broo has guided me through times of real difficulty during the writing process with great understanding and warmth. Without her this book would not have been written.

I always wondered why writers thanked their editors so enthusiastically in their books. Now I know. Andrea Henry has been an inspiration to work with. An editor of real integrity and sharp-mindedness, someone I trust completely and have real faith in. Thank you for everything.

Thank you also to the rest of the team at Headline: Bernard Dive, Sally Sargeant, Jane Butcher, Sam Combes and Emily Furniss. You are a top team.

Thank you to the Arts Council of England for their initial financial support and their continued belief in me and my work.

I have changed almost all of the names in the book,

but you all know who you are – family and friends, alive today and passed away. Thanks to each of you for your part in my life, for your support, your love and your continued faith in me.

Thank you to my partner, Emma. You have been a core support to me throughout the writing of this book and beyond. You have seen me go through some very tough times and you have stuck by me continually, reminding me that I'm always on track. Thank you for your love, passion and all-seeing eyes. Bless you.

Big blessings to my much-loved, hugely respected warrior brothers, Alex Turner, Paul McNicholls, Chris Brackley, Paul Watson, Robin Botley, Hugh Newton, Hugh Piggot, Nick Ross, Mike Carrol, Collin Hope, Alex Stanhope, Mathew Burton, Nathan Roberts, Michael Boyle, Tony Wilkinson, and *all* the men from my men's community near and far. You are too many to mention here, but you know who you are.

To my dear and very close companions, Andrew Nava, CT, Justin Culver, Tor Cotton, Tex, Nathan and Lucy Ng, Clive Chamberlain, John Lonsdale, Heidi, Brendan Georgeson – and your families – thank you all for supporting me in the darkest of times and laughing with me whatever the weather.

All my fellow recovering addicts over the last twenty years, I'd be dead without you, plain and simple. All of The Mankind Project over the last eight years, thank you for your empathy, love and commitment to your recovery and individual paths. You are an inspiration to me: a torchlight in the dark times, a bright light in the easy times.

Trevor Felgate and all at Carlton House.

All at Clouds House, past and present.

Sara Davies for your years of no-messing support, inspiration and encouragement.

The Parsons crew.

Acknowledgements

The lecturers at Weymouth College media department.

Louise Richards – your contacting me in 2005 has led me to places and opened doors I have dreamed of for most of my life, bless you.

Doug Sawyer for your warm, gentle and deeply compassionate mentoring.

To all the prisoners that I've had the honour to work with past and present.

And, as they say on the radio, thank you to everyone who knows me. If I have left anyone out please forgive my slightly addled post-dope-smoking brain. My heart loves you – you know that.

The journey and adventure continues for us all.

Caspar Walsh, March 2008